Using Picture Storybooks to Teach Character Education

Susan Hall

ORYX PRESS
2000

The rare Arabian Oryx is believed to have inspired the myth of the unicorn. This desert antelope became virtually extinct in the early 1960s. At that time several groups of international conservationists arranged to have 9 animals sent to the Phoenix Zoo to be the nucleus of a captive breeding herd. Today the Oryx population is over 800, and nearly 400 have been returned to reserves in the Middle East.

© 2000 by The Oryx Press
4041 North Central at Indian School Road
Phoenix, Arizona 85012-3397

Published simultaneously in Canada
Printed and Bound in the United States of America

∞ The paper used in this publication meets the minimum requirements of American National Standard for Information Science—Permanence of Paper for Printed Library Materials, ANSI Z39.48, 1984.

Library of Congress Cataloging-in-Publication Data
Hall, Susan K., 1943–
   Using picture storybooks to teach character education / by Susan Hall.
      p. cm.
Includes bibliographical references (p.) and index.
   ISBN 1-57356-349-8 (alk. paper)
   1. Moral education (Elementary)—United States. 2. Picture books for children—Educational aspects—United States. 3. School children—United States—Books and reading—Bibliography. I. Title.
LC311 .H33 2000
370.11'4—dc21

                                                                00-009664

To Monica,
one Iowa principal who fosters principles of
character education, no matter what.

CONTENTS

PREFACE

The Role of Picture Storybooks in Teaching Character Education

The human community has a reservoir of moral wisdom in great stories, art, history, and biography. Character has a long history of being passed from elders to young through stories, which hold the key to life and the important lessons that keep a culture strong. It's impossible to conceive of a society that does not have and preserve a legacy of stories people need to explain, justify, and instruct.

We tell stories because a statement would be inadequate.[1] And story characters come alive in comparison to hypothetical moral dilemmas that are removed from the context of narrative. A situation dilemma assignment, designed for intellectual discussion, may engage students' minds but only marginally their emotions. There are no obvious heroes or villains.

In a story, character issues evolve in natural situations. All kinds of literature is rich in ethics. In fact, literature doesn't really work well without an ethical scale in the background. Science and history convey practical wisdom but don't stir our passions unless the human element of a story is present. Children are much more engaged when their reading draws out ethical and moral issues rather than just rote learning of names and dates.[2]

Consider the virtuous examples that can be observed from such personages as Eleanor Roosevelt (kindness), Jackie Robinson (courage), the Wright brothers (self-discipline), Harriet Tubman (helpfulness), Beethoven (fortitude), and Peter Rabbit (justice).

Research indicates children see themselves as starring players in a story. Reading fiction or nonfiction stories affords us the opportunity, as we can't in life, to become thoroughly involved in the inner lives of others, sharing not only adventures but values, too. Stories engage our sentiments and make us feel deeply about people. Use of literature makes perfect sense to help children foster the ability to imaginatively reach beyond the self.

Teachers have traditionally looked to literature as a way of instilling a sense of right and wrong. Literature is studied for its richness of language, its structure, as a reflection of the author's personality or social background, and for the nature of its character building lessons.[3] Use of children's literature, whether stories are read, retold, or acted out, is probably the most accessible approach teachers can use to share society's ethics.

Through the lives of book characters, real or fictional, children can come to sense what it means, for example, to be empathetic. Psychology says no other factor is more crucial to moral development than empathy. Empathy "unlocks our prison house of self-absorption."[4] When we see others from the inside, as we do in stories, "when we live with them, and hurt with them, and hope with them, we learn a new respect for people."[5]

Engagement in thought and discourse about values exhibited by characters in literature provide children with stimuli to develop their own code of ethics and provide a wealth of good examples that make sense out of life. As writer Kilpatrick observes, recommended stories are "animated by a sense of moral order."[6] Evil must be punished and virtue rewarded. Things must be set right. Efforts must pay off. Books can convey depth and normality, a sense of moral fixity in the midst of flux, a sense of satisfaction that an ordered life offers.[7]

As neutralizers in character discussions, books are a step removed from the child. They are not threatening and do not carry the sting of personal accusation when Peter Rabbit is discerning the wisdom of obedience or Huck Finn is learning issues about right and wrong. The fact that books can be used to help children solve their personal problems and become sensitive to societal concerns has become an accepted part of teaching.[8]

The picture book genre is the particular form of literature designed for children as a cultural and character-shaping tool of instruction. The stories children hear convey values widely held by society and are believed important for children to accept. Stories supply reinforcements to listeners or readers about how to recognize virtues in the practical world of shared ideals.

When a moral principle has the power to move us to action, it is often because it is backed up by mental images (as well as actual pictures). Stories buttressed with illustrations help children develop a picture in their minds of the way things should be, of how people can act when they're at their best.

Reality-based picture books such as biography, history, or science can be a source for finding out what we don't know about life but ought to know, especially when they exhibit positive character traits in action such as responsible environmental behavior or tolerance of diversity. So can purely imaginative picture storybooks teach us how to live when fictional characters struggle with character development. Whether in nonfiction or fiction, values don't have to be lit up in neon, but they do have to be there.[9] If other things are in place in the child's life, the emotional attachment to goodness that is possible through stories can grow into a commitment to emulate a life of goodness.

Picture books expand children's experience and heighten their awareness of life's moral dilemmas. Reading and listening to picture books can influence children's lives before problems occur and provide strategies for dealing with moral issues prior to and during encounters with them. In a picture book, children meet characters that have something to learn or to teach. Children can reflect on the moral actions of book characters and relate these behaviors to their own lives.[10] In the imaginative process students become vicarious participants in book characters' lives, sharing their challenges and wanting them to make the right choices as they think about what they would do in a similar situation.[11]

Child psychologist Lawrence Kohlberg advocates discussion of story situations to nudge students into a new way of thinking to arrive at concepts of right and wrong. But here caution is advised. Don't reduce the study of literature to a search for a moral lesson. Enjoy the narrative quality before plumbing for moral meaning. Avoid stories that preach first and tell a story only secondarily. Said Jacqueline Briggs Martin, 1999 author of the Caldecott-winning story *Snowflake Bentley*, "If stories are lessons, children won't take them into their hearts."

Select stories that enlighten, entertain, and move students, ones that offer the gift of transport. Choose stories that feature making difficult choices but not stories written around a particular message. Look for books that reinforce courage, responsibility, and perseverance rather than prepackaged opinions on divorce, euthanasia, etc. Avoid selecting books about moral controversies rather than virtues. Don't seek trendy issues in lieu of character-developing values.

A literature-based approach to character education can be implemented without extensive training in how to teach character. Individual classroom teachers can emphasize positive character traits through the sharing of quality children's books.

Sometimes an introduction is warranted before students read or listen to a story that illustrates the value(s) a teacher wishes to discuss. Perhaps an instructor might stimulate reflection by asking students to think about someone they admire or want to be like when they grow up. What words would describe this person? The list is posted. The story is shared, and discussion about the book's characters might relate to some of these character values students have indicated they admire.

As discussion proceeds, student attention is focused on the ethical dimension of the story and how it might apply to one's life. Sometimes students are encouraged to write letters to story characters which either applaud or take issue with the characters' behaviors.

PICTURE BOOK SUBJECTS

Resources selected for this guide are fiction stories, not concept books, nor nonfiction, and not, for the most part, that large territory of folklore, though a few retold folktales or "modern" folk stories did creep into the overall collection. Wordless picture books, when they exhibit character traits without text, were given serious consideration, and some have been included in the collection.

Picture books, as any creative art, reflect the fashion of their time. Recently, the market has been offering much in fictionalized history and biography, using real or imagined historical characters or events to illustrate a past era. Emily Arnold McCully's *The Ballot Box Battle* (Alfred A. Knopf, 1996) spotlights Elizabeth Cady Stanton's struggle for women's voting rights. Her *The Bobbin Girl* (Dial, 1996) reveals life for working girls in New England textile mills in the 1800s.

The Boy Who Loved to Draw (Houghton Mifflin, 1999) by Barbara Brenner, is the story of artist Benjamin West. Other artists featured include Edgar Degas, Vincent Van Gogh, Giotto, and Winslow Homer.

Today's picture books do not avoid culturally serious social issues. Terminal illness is the subject of Mavis Jukes's *I'll See You in My Dreams* (Alfred A. Knopf, 1993). Suicide is the topic of Sherry Garland's *I Never Knew Your Name* (Houghton Mifflin, 1994). Genocide is behind Jane Cutler's *The Cello of Mr. O* (Penguin Putnam, 1999).

Other stories illustrate the modern Asian refugee experience as in Pegi Deitz Shea's *The Whispering Cloth* (Boyds Mills Press, 1995) or Sherry Garland's *The Lotus Seed* (Harcourt Brace Jovanovich, 1993). Earlier refugee experiences are illustrated in Eve Bunting's *A Picnic in October* (Harcourt Brace, 1999).

The Jewish holocaust is addressed in Jo Hoestlandt's *Star of Fear, Star of Hope* (Walker & Co., 1995). Earlier Jewish persecution is the subject of David Wiesniewski's *Golem* (Clarion Books, 1996).

Race relations in Eve Bunting's *Smoky Night* (Harcourt Brace, 1994) and Elinor Batezat Sisulu's *The Day Gogo Went to Vote* (Little, Brown & Co., 1997) cover both national and international issues.

There are stories featuring America's stateside role during wars, including those that highlight social mistakes such the Japanese American internment during World War II, which Eve Bunting addresses in *So Far From the Sea* (Houghton Mifflin, 1998) and Yoshiko Uchida portrays in *The Bracelet* (Philomel Books, 1976).

The western migration experience is still being featured in recent picture books. *Lewis & Papa* (Chronicle Books, 1998) by Barbara Joosse, is a sensitive account of a Santa Fe Trail adventure.

Nowadays the element of genealogy often links past to present as in George Shannon's *This Is the Bird* (Houghton Mifflin, 1997) or Betsy Hearne's *Seven Brave Women* (Greenwillow, 1997).

There are stories about women in nontraditional positions of authority, such as Mary Anning, the nineteenth-century British archaeologist, and a young woman who accomplishes her yearning ambition to become a train engineer.

There are also stories about little-known or unacknowledged heroes and heroines such as photographer "Snowflake" Bentley and aviation pioneer Louis Blériot.

Of course, there are still plenty of picture books that express the ordinary truths in stunningly unique ways. Peter Collington's *A Small Miracle* (Alfred A. Knopf, 1997) is a wordless picture book for all ages that tells a tale of kindness and generosity, while turning the Christmas story on its head.

And there are still plenty of picture books exhibiting that genre's tradition of hilarious comedy with social overtones. For example, there is the "to-be-continued" tale by Mike Jolley of *Grunter: A Pig with an Attitude* (Millbrook Press, 1999). His farmyard cohabitants successfully deal with his obnoxious behavior. So do the characters in Diane Stanley's *Rumpelstiltskin's Daughter* (Morrow, 1997) and the similar *Duffy and the Devil* (Farrar, Straus & Giroux, 1973) by Harve and Margot Zemach successfully cope with an irritating personality. Along the way, these three humorous stories show children what being resourceful is all about.

Cinderella's Rat (Houghton Mifflin, 1997) by Susan Meddaugh is a marvelously inventive perspective from the rat's point of view before, during, and after the fairy godmother turns him into a coachman for Cinderella's ride to the palace ball. Students learn something about justice and being tolerant of things that they may not particularly like.

Mary Jane Auch's chicken in *Bantam of the Opera* (Holiday House, 1997) exhibits fortitude and perseverance in order to achieve a life's goal. Similarly, Duncan Edwards's swan in *Honk!* (Hyperion, 1998) holds on to her hope for stardom in spite of great odds.

Picture book authors, it seems, often favor telling stories that demonstrate perseverance and fortitude in the face of great odds. Other favorite virtues are respect for self, others, and environment and all kinds of personal courage and empathy for the feelings of others.

PICTURE BOOKS INCLUDED IN THIS GUIDE

Resources chosen for inclusion in this index were primarily selected from copyrights less than 10 years old except for suitable Caldecott award picture storybooks. The rationale for including only recent books and Caldecott winners is availability. If a school library lacks a title suggested in this guide, it could prove difficult to obtain older copyright books from publishers or even through interlibrary loan.

In order to obtain the drama necessary to illustrate development of good character traits, picture storybook fiction and occasional modern "folktales" were selected. Not included were nonfiction biography, history, poetry, and concept picture books. All titles were reviewed positively in the *Horn Book* magazine. To escape possible taint of "indoctrination," all books come from mainline trade publishers that are not especially affiliated with any religious group, organization, or particular cause.

POSITIVE CHARACTER TRAITS INCLUDED IN THIS BOOK

For the sake of simplicity and to enhance quick reference, the following list of traits that are included in the guide are purposely defined succinctly.

LIST OF POSITIVE CHARACTER VALUES

Bold traits are covered in the guide; traits in parentheses are not.

Cooperation
Association in an enterprise for mutual benefits and a common purpose.

Courage (*use for* Integrity)
Attitude of facing what is difficult, painful, or dangerous in a brave manner.

Courtesy (*use for* Civility, Compassion, Thoughtfulness)
A polite, civil, or considerate act or remark.

Diligence (*use for* Dedication, Integrity)
Being steadfast and careful in effort.

Discernment (*use for* Understanding)
Ability to comprehend, analyze, distinguish, judge, or interpret with keen insight.

Empathy (*use for* Compassion)
Ability to share another's emotions, thoughts, or feelings in order to better understand the person.

Forgiveness
To give up resentment against and stop being angry with someone in order to pardon or release one for an offense.

Fortitude (*use for* Dedication, Integrity)
Strength to bear patiently misfortune or difficulty with courage.

Generosity (*use for* Charity, Giving, Sharing)
Unselfish willingness to give or share.

Helpfulness (*use for* Caring, Civility, Compassion, Thoughtfulness)
To give one in need or trouble something beneficial to provide relief or assistance.

Honesty (*use for* Integrity, Trustworthiness, Truthfulness)
Free of deceit and untruth.

Hope
Desire accompanied by expectation.

Justice (*use for* Fairness, Integrity)
To uphold what is right, correct, honorable, and fair and to be free of prejudice, partiality, discrimination, and dishonesty.

Kindness (*use for* Caring, Charity, Civility, Compassion, Thoughtfulness)
Acting with goodwill toward another.

Loyalty (*use for* Dedication)
Faithful support and devotion.

Patience
Waiting or enduring without complaint.

Perseverance
Continued persistent effort.

Prudence (*use for* Self-reliance)
Exercising sound judgment and discretion in personal matters.

Resourcefulness (*use for* Self-reliance)
Ability to deal promptly and effectively with problems and difficulties.

Respect
Feelings of deference, regard, and honor.

Responsibility (*use for* Dependability, Trustworthiness)
Accountable and dependable.

Self-discipline (*use for* Integrity, Temperance)
Controlling one's conduct and desires.

Tolerance (*use for* Integrity)
Accepting that which one may not especially like.

The list is not intended to include of every virtue known to humankind. Rather, in the interest of avoiding redundancy, some terms, very similar in meaning to others, are excluded.

For example, between *kindness* and *caring* or *courtesy* and *civility* or *justice* and *fairness*, a choice was made and a "see" reference was inserted so that the teacher who looks under the term not included in the list, will be directed to the term that is.

Also, a conscious attempt has been made to select values that fit today's culture. There are some positive character traits such as "temperance," "silence," "thrift," or "humility," which are certainly valued but which may be part of another concept sufficiently more "universal" to merit community acceptance. One might be temperate, silent, thrifty, and humble if one has *self-discipline* or exhibits *respect* or even shows *tolerance*.

Core values close in meaning but still possessing some bit of difference in connotation or common usage are included under separate headings in the list. Consider *fortitude, diligence, perseverance,* and *patience*. The dictionary often uses the same language to define all four. Yet, common usage assigns slight but significant nuances in meaning between them. *Fortitude* carries the element of bearing up under stress. *Diligence* implies careful effort. *Perseverance* focuses on continued, persistent efforts. And "patience" refers to waiting without complaint.

The list includes both *kindness* and *helpfulness*, which might seem rather too similar. But the dictionary indicates an interesting concept for "helpfulness"—giving to one in need or trouble. "Kindness" is simply acting with general good will across a broad spectrum of human interaction.

On the other hand, *kindness* (which makes the list) does incorporate in its meaning "thoughtfulness" (which doesn't make the list) just as *courtesy* (in list) incorporates "civility" (not in list). Putting too fine a point on the distinctions between virtues doesn't seem to be, well, quite the point!

In a few instances, one word is arbitrarily chosen in lieu of another perfectly good term. In this guide, the concept that means *generosity* was selected over "giving" or "sharing" and *justice* was chosen over "fairness." The "see" references will guide the user. And, if the user absolutely prefers to discuss giving rather than generosity, or fairness rather than justice, the stories under the heading of justice will suffice as well for the concept of fairness and those under generosity will likely also apply to the concept of giving.

One word, which does not appear under a heading, or a "see" reference for that matter, is the term "love." And though it is, as the children's author Astrid Lindgren has said, the "main word for what we need," it is also actually the only virtue we need. If we understood the term completely, it would incorporate all commonly accepted virtues. Because we clearly do not sufficiently internalize all its nuances, we must separate its facets into discrete, manageable concepts that can be comprehended, piecemeal; hence, a list of 23 separate virtues.

Some words are simply too multifaceted to be "core" virtues—words like "integrity" and "friendship." Integrity includes at least *honesty, courage, fortitude, loyalty, justice, tolerance, prudence, self-discipline,* and *diligence.* "Friendship" also encompasses many core values such as *kindness, generosity, courage, cooperation, loyalty, patience, respect, forgiveness,* and *helpfulness,* to name a few. The concept of "friendship" is often a special topic of concern in school settings among staff and students. It is recognized for its contribution to successful social interaction among students and for later success among adults in their work and social environments.

Therefore, following the main section is an appendix (Appendix A) of those resources that especially exhibit a particular focus on some aspect of friendship.

Appendix B lists resources that represent picture books suitable for all ages. These books exhibit a depth of content appreciated, particularly, by older students. In the main section, these books are starred (*).

Appendix C: Curriculum Tie-Ins lists books that can be used in other aspects of the curriculum; for example, stories that will complement a lesson in history, or art, or social science.

INDEXES AND BIBLIOGRAPHY

Both author and title indexes are included to enable teachers to find books by particular authors and titles. The bibliography lists works cited and further studies in character education.

NOTES

[1] William Kilpatrick, Gregory Wolfe, and Suzanne M. Wolfe, *Bonds That Build Character: A Guide to Teaching Your Child Moral Values through Stories* (New York: Touchstone Rockefeller Center, 1994), 21.

[2] Esther Schaefer, Letter to the Editor, *Time* 155, no. 23 (14 June 1999): 21.

[3] Meriel Downey and A.V. Kelly, *Moral Education Theory and Practice* (London: Harper & Row, 1978).

[4] Kilpatrick, *Bonds That Build Character,* 39.

[5] Kilpatrick, *Bonds That Build Character,* 19.

[6] Kilpatrick, *Bonds That Build Character,* 49.

[7] Kilpatrick, *Bonds That Build Character,* 53.

[8] Lamme, Linda, and others. *Literature Based Moral Education: Children's Books and Activities for Teaching Values, Responsibility, and Good Judgement in the Elementary School* (Phoenix: Oryx Press, 1992), 14–15.

[9] Kilpatrick, *Bonds That Build Character,* 36.

[10] Lamme, *Literature Based Moral Education,* 14–15.

[11] Kilpatrick, *Bonds That Build Character,* 21.

INTRODUCTION
What Character Is

"**O**ur youth now love luxury. They have bad manners, contempt for authority, and show disrespect for their elders. They contradict their parents; they chatter before company; they gobble their food, and they terrorize their teachers."

So said Socrates in the fifth century BC.

Now, at a different time and place we recognize a similar cultural problem. Our own social capital is at an all-time low in the United States. Following an act of horrific school violence in Colorado, Pope John Paul said on April 21, 1999, "Americans must provide children with a moral vision." And, while the future of a country rests on its moral fiber and ethics, not on momentary events, it behooves educators to do whatever possible to help bring up people who possess positive character traits for social interaction.

Certain words occur in the lexicon of any discussion of character, such as "values," "morals," "ethics," "principles," and "virtues." The following simple succinct definitions from *Webster's Third International Dictionary* (1993) put some perspective on nuances of meaning, but it's also a given that such terms will be used interchangeably.

Ethics

A group of values or beliefs that govern behavior.

Ideals

A mental image of excellence or a perfect exemplar that one believes to be attainable.

Morals

Habits of conduct relating to right and wrong, good or bad.

Principles

Guiding rules or codes of good conduct by which one directs one's life or actions.

Values

Successful social concepts held in general high regard, which are derived from pragmatic usefulness over time.

Virtues

Traits that adhere to the highest standards of good in order to further the pursuit of the general welfare.

Analyst Daniel Yankelovich of the public opinion and social trends in the Kettering Foundation, says that failure to benefit from economic growth, alienation between leaders and citizens, and weakening of common core values are among the three most destructive trends causing Americans to be pessimistic, cynical, angry, and frustrated.[1]

Rushworth M. Kidder, *Christian Science Monitor* columnist and founder of the Institute for Global Ethics, asked leading thinkers around the world to identify what they consider the most pressing issues of the twenty-first century. Among the big ones capable of destroying the future if unaddressed, they all listed ethics. Right up there with nuclear catastrophe and environmental accidents was breakdown of moral values.[2] Kidder's Global Ethics institute has focused on asking the question: What moral values should compose a global code of ethics? Kidder believes there is an underlying moral presence shared by all humanity. There is a "set of precepts so fundamental that they dissolve borders, transcend races, and outlast cultural traditions."[3] These are the guidelines that enhance human interaction rather than detract from it, like generosity instead of greed or kindness instead of cruelty.

Regardless of politics or religious persuasion, there is one fact upon which there is general agreement. Our democratic form of government can't be sustained without an intelligent citizenry imbued with positive character traits. Charles S. White said, "A society's success or failure hinges on how we form or guide the development of intellect and character among the young."[4]

Arkansas Governor Mike Huckabee said, "I wish people could see how state government must spend so much money dealing with people's moral failings that it has little left to invest in human potential."[5] He said it costs when we fail to see that character really is the issue. Regardless of succession of technological revolutions, none has done away with the need for character in the individual.

Candidates during the 2000 presidential election touted the need for character education in America's schools. At least one of them, George W. Bush, declared in his television commercials that he advocated teaching character directly.

Television producer and founder of "People for the American Way," Norman Lear said, "Greed is the order of the day in a society preoccupied at all levels with the pursuit of bottom lines, a society which celebrates consumption, careerism, and winning."[6] People tend to focus more attention on their rights than on their responsibilities. They aren't prepared to recognize any moral authority outside themselves.

Democracies have a special need for a morally educated citizenry, because this style of government is by the people themselves. The citizenry must care about the rights of the populace and assume responsibility for its welfare. Nationally syndicated columnist William Murchison said that morality is the heart of culture.[7]

The great questions facing the human race are moral questions. How should I live my life? How can we live with each other and with nature? Morality itself is the acceptance of such habits as express the helpful relations of society and the individual.[8]

CHARACTER DEFINED

A host of definitions for character have been offered by various learned persons. Basically, character is composed of the attributes that distinguish the individual. The goal is to achieve "good" character. Albert Schweitzer said a person of character has ethics, which is the name he gave to our concern for good behavior.

Aristotle defined good character as a life of right conduct in relation to self and others. Madame Chiang Kai-Shek said that character develops through moral action and leads to self-fulfillment. She believed a person of character rejects any value hostile to human freedom and development. Development of character, she felt, was education of the head, heart, and hand. Today, this might be called knowing the good, loving the good, and doing the good, or the cognitive, emotional, and behavioral aspects of character development. Her perception of good character is in line with the thinking of many professors and directors of character education.

Esther Schaeffer, CEO of Character Education Partnership in Washington, DC, says persons of good character know, care, and act, on core ethical values such as justice, honesty, compassion, and responsibility.[9] Thomas Lickona, a developmental psychologist, states that we want students to be able to judge what is right, care deeply about what is right, and do what they believe to be right, even in the face of pressure from without and temptation from within.[10] Kevin Ryan, the founding director of the Center for Advancement of Ethics and Character at Boston University, believes that having character is summing up a situation, choosing the right thing, and then doing it.[11] Journalist Kenneth L. Woodward said that a person of good character is someone who, through repeated good acts, achieves an appropriate balance of life's virtues. He likened a life of good character to the life of a successful tennis professional. The person plays a consistently good game.[12]

George Kuh, professor of higher education at the Center for Postsecondary Research and Planning at Indiana University-Bloomington, feels youth need to meet society's most pressing problems equipped with both interpersonal and intellectual skills. Taken together, character is an "integrated constellation of personal attributes such as self-understanding, appreciation for human differences, and a refined, interlocking set of ethical, civic, humanitarian, and spiritual values."[13] Character, he says, is the internal compass that enables one to live with integrity in a complex world.

This moral compass metaphor was used in a 1989 survey of children's beliefs and values conducted by Robert Coles, a Harvard University child psychiatrist. He concluded that between grades four and 12 children fall into five categories of principles that guide their moral behavior. About 25 percent of students, usually older ones, are civic humanists. They base moral judgements on what is the common good, best for everyone. Another 20 percent are conventionalists. They do what is generally accepted in their community, following the advice of authority. Expressivists, (18 percent) do what satisfies their psychological needs and makes them happy. Theistic students (16 percent) adhere to religious scripture or advice from clergy. And utilitarians (10 percent) do what it takes to get ahead.[14]

Virtues are a framework for the provision of a moral citizenry.[15] As a composite of both good habits (or virtues) and bad habits (or vices), character is what one would do if he knew he would never be found out. What would one do under pressure of keeping a grade point average, winning a court case, or conducting laboratory research?

Most definitions of character say the prima facie evidence for the existence of good character is regularity across time. Character means recognizing the right thing to do and doing it for the sake of "rightness" rather than expediency, while at the same time eschewing moral rectitude. Character is the ultimate measure of an individual and the ultimate measure of a nation.

HISTORY OF CHARACTER EDUCATION

Plato said that if you ask what is the good of education, the answer is easy, that education makes good people and that good people act nobly. Aristotle said, "We become just by doing just acts." He believed virtue must be practiced, not merely known.

Modern school administrators recognize that teaching youth scholarship and leadership are not enough. Complete persons must also develop good character. Cognitive academic development contributes to enhancing children's knowledge and intellectual skills. Character development contributes to forming their attitudes and behaviors. Both ends are the major purposes of schooling.

In 1850 Herbert Spencer said, "Education has for its object the formation of character." Though that objective is not so often directly stated as a goal of education these days, it was once the sole reason to educate the masses in America.

In earliest colonial America, educators, usually also preachers, taught the young to read the Bible to help ensure an ethical citizenship. This commitment to mass public education set a landmark in world education. Maintaining appropriate civility and decorum and preparing students for public service meant students would learn for themselves moral precepts from the Bible, and from this knowledge, moral action would prevail. The first law mandating public schools was named "Ye Old Deluder Satan" act and focused learning almost entirely on values instruction.

Thomas Jefferson supported the idea that public education should instill moral principles. Ben Franklin's curriculum outline included the study of ethics. And, much later, other persons of leadership such as Harry Truman felt the fundamental purpose of education is to "instill a moral code in the rising generation."

The nineteenth-century McGuffey's *Readers* extolled values of honesty, hard work, and thrift. Among the first of modern American educators, Horace Mann felt values could be universal and nonsectarian, "recognized by all civilized people" and "sanctioned by all enlightened creeds."[16] Even after vocational learning had assumed school-day primacy, he still viewed morality as central to a school's purpose, saying that a community without a conscience would soon extinguish itself. He exhorted educators to cultivate morality in all children as soon as possible.

Writing in 1908, George Palmer, a philosophy professor, was adamant about the importance of teaching moral character. He said, "A teacher who fails to impress elementary righteousness on his pupils brutalizes every child in his charge."[17]

Gradually, with the advent of the common school in the 1800s, the goal of academic knowledge began to take precedence over character development. The emphasis shifted from good habits of conduct to good reasoning skills.

Regrettably, some of the methods that had been employed to teach character proved unsound. Nothing set back the teaching of character education more than the conclusions of two researchers, Hugh Hartshorne and Mark May, in their 1919 *Studies in the Nature of Character* at the Institute of Social and Religious Research. They found that students who participated in school clubs with elaborate codes of conduct didn't benefit from the experiences. There was little impact on their character, and that, indeed, they did not seem to exhibit any stable character traits. The researchers stated that the "prevailing ways of inculcating ideals probably do little good and may do some harm."

Schools began quietly to take on the public perception that values were variable and essentially private, and, indeed, may not be able to be taught at all. They retreated from directly trying to teach character education. This legacy of right and wrong being relative to time and place exists to this day. The assumption is that in a pluralistic society, no single set of values is common to all. No school wants the onus of being accused of "indoctrinating" students with "our" set of core values.

In recent years, the idea of indoctrinating has come to not sound quite so off-putting. Professor of social education at the University of Georgia, A.G. Larkins, says schools are morally obligated to indoctrinate values and be committed to basic values of our society but to neutrally help students think clearly about ethical choices rather than to dictate right choices.[18]

The fact that throughout history, every enduring society has been passionately committed to passing on to its young its cherished values, seems to have been forgotten. Christina Hoff Sommers, a Brady Fellow at the American Enterprise Institute, said, "Let us not be the first society in history that finds itself hamstrung in the vital task of passing along its moral tradition to the next generation."[19] Benjamin Stein wrote in 1991, "America has lost its ethical infrastructure in a sense like a postwar condition in need of a Marshall Plan to rebuild its ethical base."[20]

Now after a generation of dissension and confusion about how to return to teaching values, schools are again grappling with methods to address the character development of their young charges. The high cost of neglect has become unbearable. Character education has caught attention in Congress. The Department of Education allotted $5.2 million in 1998 to pursue character education instruction.

William Bennett, former U.S. Secretary of Education, acknowledges that even those who don't believe schools should inculcate a specific set of values are coming to believe schools have a responsibility to make students aware of the importance of discovering and developing their own set of values. Character education represents an effort to teach moral behavior in a time perceived to be morally rudderless.

WHAT IS CHARACTER EDUCATION?

Teaching positive character traits goes by a number of program names. It has been variously called "values education," "moral maturity instruction," "character development," "prosocial behavior education," "efficacy training," "civic development," and just about any other title that is hoped not to offend school patrons.

The intent is largely the same, to enhance positive student behavior. The overall goal of character education is to help kids function in society with recognizably accepted virtues that are a community's best values and ethical ideals. E.A. Wynne says an anthropologist might describe this effort as socializing the young into tribal morality.[21] To do so sustains the community. Not to do so is irresponsible.

Interestingly, award-winning teachers such as National Teacher of the Year recipients as well as teachers ending long careers often speak to the topic of character development. And so do former students.

Otto L. Schluter, writes about his learning experiences in a one-room rural school in the early 1900s. "Personally, I feel that aside from the school books, the pupils in the country school absorbed a good many human values, without which a higher education is of no avail."[22] Rae Ellen McKee, 1991 National Teacher of the Year, said, "I am still perpetuating the philosophy that schooling in America was designed as a way to nurture beings in becoming more human. There are a lot of qualities that can't be traded in a world market."

Correspondent Kimberly J. McCarin interviewed 20 award-winning teachers and said, in a 1995 New York Times article, that they all expressed strong support for teaching values and personally fostered character in their teaching styles.[23]

There have been morality codes throughout history. In 1926 the U.S. Department of Education listed character traits that define a "good American." They have self-control, gain and keep good health, are kind, play fair, are self-reliant, dutiful, true, cooperative, loyal, and engage in right conduct for the right reasons.

Earlier, Ben Franklin listed the virtues he advocated in his autobiography. He believed a person of good character had temperance, silence, order, resolution, frugality, industry, sincerity, justice, moderation, cleanliness, chastity, and humility.

The cardinal virtues considered ethical ideals for the ancient Greeks were prudence, justice, temperance, and fortitude.

Nowadays schools and communities work together establishing character education programs at specific grade levels or within particular curriculum areas.[24] Eventually, the process of character education must explore with students some kind of "core universal values," upon which there is general community acceptance. The number of these positive traits may vary. For one district, it might be the "Top 10," or 12 or three. Some schools have embraced from the "Character Counts!" model promoted by ethics educator Michael Josephson the "six pillars" of good character: trustworthiness, respect, responsibility, fairness, caring, and citizenship (TERRIFICC).

Schools that avow the task of character development say so in their mission and goal statements, underscoring clearly defined, consistently expressed character traits selected through consensus before instruction commences.

COMPETING THEORIES OF CHARACTER EDUCATION

Where disagreement usually occurs in character education is not the particular character traits emphasized but rather the efficacy of methods used to teach those values. Should character education be taught separately or woven into curriculum? Should a program be based upon a traditional approach of inculcation of specific values or a process of helping students recognize their own values?

Character in the Classroom

Character Taught within Curriculum

Schools might choose to integrate and coordinate character education within subject areas. One principal in a Gaithersburg, Virginia, middle school calls character education "our philosophical glue."[25] Some authorities say that buried in skills-and-knowledge curriculum, are necessarily lessons on responsibility, respect, cooperation, and diligence, which is the essence of good character.[26] Teachers, presumably, would be on the lookout for "teachable moments" to emphasize positive character traits.

Character Taught Separately

Character education can also be taught as its own discipline. Columnist Roger Rosenblatt goes so far as to say, "If this movement is going to make educational sense, much less to have any larger social benefits, it …[must be addressed] in separate contexts of study and not as riders to existing curriculums."[27]

Critics of Integration; Critics of Separation

Those advocating integrating values into established curriculum, maintain that emphasizing character in curricula is a powerful force shaping school environment. If it is separated as a course by itself, students might conclude matters of morality belong to the class of moral education and fail to generalize to practical real-life situations.

Some say separating character enhancement into a separate course of study is the "bag of virtues" method. One virtue a week is pulled out to emphasize. Critical of character education in general and teaching it as a separate course of study in particular, reporter Andrew Ferguson cynically notes that "character education is transmitted by familiar methods beloved of today's pedagogues." He lists posters, banners, t-shirts, ribbons, role playing, and word-of-the-week, all of which he refers to as "cheerful paraphernalia that makes the modern American classroom seem like a Maoist re-education camp run by Barney the dinosaur."[28]

Esther Schaeffer rebuts his criticism by replying that the paraphernalia are "colorful, visible aspects" of character education, which "may look simplistic, but the subtle and more thoughtful work of character education make all the difference."[29] Character education, she feels, is important enough to single out and address.

Long-term research conclusions do not yet exist regarding the most effective pedagogical practice: character education that is promoted naturally through curriculum as an integral part of the school-day experience, or character education taught directly and separately.

Cultural Tradition

Cultural tradition, practiced throughout most of America's educational history, maintained that specific time-honored positive values exist, such as respect and self-discipline, which have supported civilized life throughout history. These traits don't have to be reinvented like the wheel with each new generation. Character values must be firmly upheld, reasonable, and justified. The way positive traits are passed on is by being internalized by children through imitation or explicit instruction accompanied by reward and punishment.

Proponents of Cultural Tradition

Those espousing tradition and habit feel adults must help children, especially younger ones, to learn particular virtues, become committed to them, and habitually act ethically. Children must develop an attachment to positive traits before moving on to reasoning why they act virtuously. They observe positive behavior in adults, and they emulate it. Herbert Wray said, "Making decent kids requires constant repetition and amplification of basic moral messages."[30]

Taking a strong position is favor of the cultural tradition method of teaching character, Christina Hoff Sommers says we are all born into a moral environment as well as a natural environment. Civility, honesty, consideration, and respect are as necessary to survive as are clean air, safe food, and fresh water. And it is our duty to protect both environments.[31]

Criticism of Cultural Tradition

Critics of cultural tradition warn that conformity and control do not constitute evidence of good character. Educational philosopher John Dewey maintained required beliefs or attitudes can't be hammered in or plastered on. Don't mistake good behavior for good character. Developmental psychology educator Alphie Kohn said that respect, responsibility, and citizenship are slippery terms frequently used as euphemisms for uncritical deference to authority.[32] He believes that most of what passes for character education is behavioral manipulation and not an invitation to reflect on values.

Like columnist Andrew Ferguson, Kohn feels the more one receives extrinsic motivation such as stars, certificates, or other tokens of recognition for right behavior, the more likely emphasis will be aimed at earning the reward rather than engaging in right behavior for intrinsic satisfaction. What children learn is that the reason to be good is to get rewards. And, eventually, over time, they lose interest in whatever had to be done to get the reward.

And what about competing value judgements? Which virtue is better, tolerance or loyalty, kindness or honesty, prudence or generosity, justice or forgiveness? Kohn says children need opportunity to make sense of concepts and to reflect on how to proceed when two basic values seem to be in conflict. While cultural values do exist over time, they are new to each new generation of children. So, to an extent, each child does have to reinvent the wheel of character values.

Values Clarification

Values clarification doesn't attempt to inculcate specific positive values. Rather, through student discussion and problem solving, students will weigh conflicting values in order to arrive at judgements of right and wrong and, thus, develop their own values system. Problems that naturally arise in a classroom or designed social dilemmas constitute a laboratory for developing social responsibility. Students arrive at reasoned decisions about proper conduct in a social context.

Proponents of Values Clarification

Proponents of values reasoning as a method of teaching good character draw heavily on the 1960s research of Lawrence Kohlberg, who in turn depended on the earlier research of Louis Raths, Sidney Simon, and others. These pioneers claimed that values clarification is not new, going back at least as far as Socrates, who sought ways to help people think through value issues for themselves by asking good questions, being a good listener, and accepting the seeker's results.

Kohlberg said humans go through several sequential stages of moral reasoning. Behavior is earliest shaped by avoidance of punishment and moves through various levels, including concern for how society will think of them, and finally culminates in action that is in accordance with universal moral principles.

Kohlberg said moral preaching isn't effective, because kids can't comprehend moral concepts until they are mentally ready to do so. For moral development to take place, one stage of moral thinking must be replaced by the next higher one. A mismatch of stages between teacher and learner leads to a failed grasp of the moral concept being taught.

The teacher's role is not to be coercive in any way, but rather to supply plenty of simulation games, to remain morally neutral, and to ask "why" questions to tease out students' personal values. The student's goal is to identify and recognize his or her own values.

Criticism of Values Clarification

Some educators believe those moral beliefs need direct guidance. For example, Thomas Lickona says character development goals for elementary school students should include promotion of cooperation and mutual respect, capacity to engage in moral judgement by knowing what is right and taking action, and behaving with fairness and empathy.[33]

Critics have found fault with the values clarification process of teaching character education as it emerged in the 1960s and 1970s. Unfortunately, using these processes, parents and community were kept at arm's length. Only qualified professionals were thought capable of leading children through the clarifying process. Values clarification probably failed as much from its lack of parent input as its flawed pedagogy.

Moral dilemma discussion, critics say, exalts process over content. It depends on reasoning and does not focus on behavior. Reasoning alone, say educators like Kevin Ryan and Thomas Lickona, will not build character. Because teachers are to serve as facilitators and not take a moralizing stance, they appeared to students to be morally neutral. They did not feel able to criticize student reasoning, and were unsure what to do after students had clarified their values.

For example, students might decide cheating on a test is justifiable in order to maintain a grade point average that enables them to attend a more prestigious college. The moral reasoning approach to character education does not reckon with the human phenomenon of rationalization, which all too often reflects morally unacceptable behaviors. Thomas Lickona said the "shallow moral relativism loose in the land was brought into the schools."[34] Students see no reason, he says, to cultivate character traits like self-discipline in a society that prizes material comforts and pleasure.

Kevin Ryan says, "Character comes not from acquiring particular points of view or values but from developing a set of common ideals upon which to base one's life."[35]

Values clarification as Kohlberg envisioned it had become discredited by the 1980s. Though these days, supporters of values clarification say that Kohlberg did not hold all values equally defensible or that one person's values were as good as anyone else's.

Nevertheless, values clarification was creating a peculiar system of ethics that led to selfish individualism. Patrick McCarthy, executive vice president of the Thomas Jefferson Research Center, said that we can't have 250 million individual value systems operating in this country and survive as a nation. Harvard psychiatrist Robert Coles says youth are "awash on a sea of relativism" without any values or goals driving their beliefs.[36] Christina Hoff Sommers reminds us the Ten Commandments are not the "10 Highly Tentative Suggestions." And Thomas Jefferson did not amend his statement that all men have the right to life, liberty, and the pursuit of happiness with the aside, "at least in my opinion." These he declared to be a self-evident truths and not personal judgements.[37]

The Kohlberg brand of values clarification fell short of expectations, because, as critics pointed out, children need first to understand what are the basic values a society prizes. There is nothing to anchor their moral choices upon, if they have no such understandings. This theory makes the mistake of treating kids like grown-ups who only needed to clarify already sound values. First, however, they need help developing sound values. Values clarification "proves a flimsy and vulnerable way of cultivating sensitive consciences and responsible conduct."[38] And "values neutral curriculum fails to bridge the gap between talking about ethics and living ethically."[39] Ironically, this was the original criticism of the older traditional means of inculcating character values through exhortation.

Neither cultural tradition nor values clarification as teaching methods are necessarily the foe of the other. Character education depends on people who know what they are doing and who teach values at the right age for students to comprehend.[40]

Before students can make important and difficult ethical choices, they must first have a substantial commitment to positive values they can understand. So, traditional indoctrination might pedagogically be prior to critical thinking in the values clarification process. Huck Finn had to first understand and develop empathy in order to choose to act on this positive trait. Then he could make the ethical choice not to turn in his friend Jim as they ran off together in Mark Twain's *Adventures of Huckleberry Finn*.

Just as long-term research has not yet shown which is the more effective, character education integrated through curriculum or character education taught directly as a separate course, neither is there evidence that points to a preference for traditional inculcation of values or allowing students to establish their own values.

What Next in Character Education

Today's schools are sifting through the relics of previous character education theories. No one wants an exclusive return to the old style of cultural traditions with its heavy-handed moralism, bigotry, and class prejudice that served only the privileged few. This kind of character education had proven largely useless and had gone by the wayside before the 1950s. And values clarification faded in the 1980s because it didn't connect the process of arriving at values with directing values outcome.

We have "shards of competing moral traditions, none of them coherent," says Alasdair MacIntyre of the University of Notre Dame. What is emerging may actually be a combination of both older theories revamped by current research. Character education is less about imposing or instilling values than it is helping students accept as their personal project the development of their own character after developing a sound understanding of positive character traits. Character education entails an attitude within a school district toward enhancing student understanding of values considered important in social interaction followed by a concerted effort by all adults to turn out citizens who practice positive character values.

Today, people dislike the old associations the term "character education" brings to mind. But they want schools to teach character. New Mexico Senator Pete V. Domenici says, "The impetus for character education comes from parents. It is the second most important thing that parents want from public schools, and it is a goal that most parents think the schools fail to achieve."[41] Ethics may be less of a bandwagon phenomenon in schools and "more the perpetual companion, accompanying everything we do, infusing all that we are and hope to accomplish."[42]

ANSWERING THE CRITICS OF CHARACTER EDUCATION

To those who are skeptical that universal values exist, consider the life's work of C.S. Lewis. He set out to discover if there was a "common way" of life that was enduring in all societies, regardless of politics, religion, geographical location, or, even, across time. He concluded that human kindness was essential to a fully functioning society. He found that a special loyalty is reserved for parents and family and that a special relationship exists to future generations, especially our own children. A degree of honesty is required in order to function smoothly. Right and wrong can't be defined based on the wisdom of the moment. Generosity exists for the sick, poor, and less fortunate. There is an understanding of basic property rights. Some things are worse than death; i.e., treachery, murder, betrayal, and torture.

Which values will be taught?

Diversity of today's student population would seem to indicate it is too controversial to foist off any single set of values in such a highly pluralistic group. Yet, schools are never values-neutral enterprises. There are the inevitable student and faculty codes of conduct. There are the teachers' value systems that come into play in the classroom environment. There is the administrative moral climate of the school building. Why not address the issue of character development directly, planning deliberately and constructively as with the science curriculum or physical education program? Keep in the forefront through policy and procedure the selected character traits being promoted. Deliberately encourage the full flowering of each child's humanity.

People mistakenly believe there is confusion about what credo to pass along. Ethics education need not defer to any special-interest groups. Basic moral concepts are, indeed, universal. A former president of Harvard, Derek Bok, said that there are certain fundamental principles, which are not a matter of debate. All civilizations worthy of the name have discovered a standard of ethical ideals for optimum human interaction. A culture that invites thievery, disloyalty, slothfulness, or intolerance will be short-lived.

The list of positive character traits needn't be identical from school district to school district. If one community includes "trustworthiness" and another lists "honesty," the basic concept has been covered. During community brainstorming sessions, there may be overlap in virtues, and choices will be made. Consider, for example, these related concepts: sensitivity, thoughtfulness, compassion, sympathy, charity, civility, giving, sharing, kindness, caring, understanding, concern, consideration.

Educators shouldn't be preoccupied with developing a perfect list of "ultimate values." The perfect list isn't essential or realistic. In one community, "forbearance" and "humility" might make the cut. In another, "hope" and "tolerance" could be included. During the selection process, strike a balance with the maxim, "Choose what does the most good and least harm."

A body of principles can be defined that will do no violence to community standards, will offend no moral or intellectual sensibilities, and can be taught. Some attributes of character, like "responsibility" and "respect," are on most values lists. Some, like "honor," show up on only a few. Lists might not come with supporting arguments, but they are, nevertheless, the result of considerable discussion and study.

Neither must schools feel obligated to struggle with consensus on all moral issues. It's not necessary to agree on capital punishment, but students ought to be clear about the facets of honesty. Moral dilemmas arise in every generation, but we have achieved agreement on some questions long ago. Thievery, laziness, and cheating, for example, have not been valued at any time.

The first step is to secure community input. Town meetings are popular nowadays. Hammer out that "top 10" list of positive character traits at such meetings of parents, school personnel, and community members. It's possible to respect differences of opinion, even in the midst of competing mass-media images of the "good life." What will emerge will be shared values that neither infringe upon nor promote religious teachings.

Who is competent to teach values?

Critics say that if the job of teaching character is botched, there will be a reaction against schools, and what little support now exists will be further eroded. Moreover, public education cannot be trusted with moral issues. In its insistent secularity, it will wind up being anti-faith. Schools ought not to be getting involved in what has traditionally been the province of religion and family.

Clearly, there is confusion about who is to hand down whatever set of values we are willing to say we stand for. According to results of surveys conducted in the early 1990s, the American Association of School Administrators found 48 percent of respondents said that families want help from schools teaching or reinforcing positive values. Fifty-four percent of those thought schools should do a better job of providing this help. Similar percentages approving school involvement were confirmed in a Gallup poll of the same time.[43]

From a purely pragmatic view, character education should be taught, because the very qualities that schools consider important, such as diligence, honesty, respect, cooperation, courtesy, helpfulness, responsibility, self-discipline, are exactly the same traits employers look for when they hire or evaluate job performance. There are currently no state codes of education or standards that outlaw, forbid, or in any way discourage character education.

And, quite frankly, without some emphasis upon desirable character development, children can be intractable and tyrannous, as Annie Sullivan discovered about her young pupil Helen Keller. Children do need to be socialized before they can learn anything, moral or otherwise. No school district expects a child to work out the principles and methods of fractions or chemical elements by himself. Neither should a child be expected to work out right and wrong left to his own devices. There are a few self-taught artists, but fewer people of character are totally self-taught. Developing character is a social act that needs to be nurtured; it is part of the acculturation process.

It's time for communities to practice their values, be supportive of young people in the development of their values, and serve as role models and mentors. It's a matter of saving our children.

There is no time to add anything else to the school day curriculum.

Beleaguered educators say character education is just one more duty that takes time away from reading or mathematics, upon which teachers are evaluated. Ironically, it may be inattentiveness to student values that results in exhaustion trying to cope with poor student behavior. There is, frankly, wasted time and energy spent tending to moral conflicts and challenges in today's educational environment. Writer Daniel Heischman calls it one of the greatest casualties of our hectic lifestyle. Adults in the school facility often don't notice, are in too much of a hurry to sense, or are less receptive nowadays to learnable moments. A scarcity of available time for adults to reflect and to respond has a serious effect on their capacity to act out of moral concern or sensitivity.[44] Perhaps a school cannot afford not to teach character education.

When a moral and caring climate does exist in the classroom, not only can the teacher teach academics, but students actually feel better about themselves, work harder, and learn more. Professor George Kuh says an institution's social and psychological environments can be a major factor in character development. Background of students is essentially irrelevant to character development and so is the affluence of a school, he says. What are most significant are environment and human resources, not money.[45]

Teaching cannot be extracted from the building of character. Teachers might deny they teach values in their classroom but would admit to addressing issues of respect, responsibility, self-discipline, honesty, cooperation, and kindness. Whether selecting material, asking questions, setting standards, or managing a classroom, values are being subtly promoted. The school day offers numerous situations in which staff and students confront issues of right and wrong. What could be more basic education than to help children grapple with these issues in an ethical manner? Schools must stop being ambiguous on matters of moral values.

Again, facing reality, if positive character traits are not emphasized in school, then the job of helping parents pass along our culture's values is left to the popular media of our consumer society. Parents and teachers have a vested interest in the cultivation of human goodness, the creation of decent people. And, while home is the crucial determining factor in setting value standards for behavior expectations, schools refine concepts of right and wrong.

All the great intellectual authorities from Confucius to Aristotle to Dewey strongly advocate giving conscious attention to character formation. People do not naturally or spontaneously grow up to be morally excellent. They become so, if at all, only as the result of a lifelong personal and community effort.

Various educators have provided labels to this character development process. Edward DeRoche says schools should help parents provide children with a values roadmap that leads to "moral literacy."[46] Thomas Lickona calls knowledge of our heritage of values "ethical literacy." It is the duty of adults to share that understanding and to know which values are prescribed for in various life situations.[47] What is lurking behind the vaguely defined back-to-basics movement is more than a concern for reading, writing, and arithmetic, Kevin Ryan says. People sense our schools' uncertainty and abdication of moral authority.[48]

Perhaps in an inarticulate way, this is the real dissatisfaction the public is expressing when it refuses to support bond issues and tax levies.

Does character education really improve character?

Paralleling the current obsession with academic testing is an inability to measure development of character. If you can't measure it, you can't manage it. Character education cannot test for competency. It's true that efforts expended teaching character education cannot generally point to definitive success. We are, after all, works in progress our entire lives. Still, there does seem to be a noticeable difference in school environment when courtesy and responsibility replace hostility and lack of respect. Order, quiet, and punctuality are but three signs that a child's life is being socialized. A 1992 survey of 176 schools that adopted a values curriculum found 77 percent reported decrease in discipline problems, 68 percent boasted increase in attendance, 64 percent noted decrease in vandalism, and academic test scores went up among all of them.[49]

When children engage in active role-playing of positive behaviors, evidence seems to indicate, say teachers and principals, that their attitudes do change for the better.

Every year, say detractors, something new comes down the pike. Character education is just another fad to distract schools from the essential task of promoting academic learning.

But what choice is there in the face of the contemporary drift toward a dearth of moral conduct? To accept that each person's creed is as valid as any other's and that whatever works best for the individual is what determines right or wrong is no better than the moral philosophy of a sociopath.

Inability to arrive at reasonable moral judgements and to know the difference between right and wrong is apparently rampant. Education must teach discernment. To actually believe, as some students claim, that there is no blame for the Holocaust, that it is "no fault history," a natural cataclysm, inevitable and unavoidable is, says William Kilpatrick and others, an example of the new moral illiteracy.[50]

James Madison asked the citizens of his era if there was "virtue among us." He pronounced that if not then "we are in a wretched situation." He said no form of government could render secure a people's liberty or happiness without virtue in those people.

Theodore Roosevelt said that educating a man in mind and not in morals is educating a menace to society. Students with sound values are more adept at resolving conflict without resorting to physical violence.

Ernest Boyer, President of the Carnegie Foundation for Advancement of Teaching, noted that helping students develop sound values means they should be concerned about not just what works, but about what is right. To have a well-informed student population unconstrained by conscience is, conceivably, the most dangerous outcome of education possible. In fact, he argued, ignorance is better than unguided intelligence. The most dangerous people are those who have knowledge without a moral framework.[51]

Jonas Salk said nobility was doing the right thing for the right reason. He said it can be taught just as is arithmetic or biology.

Evidence of positive character traits may be observed in actions as simple as finishing work on time, or refusing to join in the wolf-pack mentality of harassing another student. It is not shoving another student out of line in order to get to the water fountain sooner. It is picking up litter in a main hall without being asked to do so. It is helping a person of any age, older or younger, who has dropped a pile of books. It is not defying safety rules. It is respecting self and others.

Character must permeate a school. To insure that virtues are modeled, taught, expected and honored, it requires awareness and action from the cafeteria to playground, from classroom to faculty lounge, from administration to school board and parent.

Teaching values is the domain of religion.

Meriel Downey argues there is no logical connection between morality and religion.[52] It's possible to believe in honesty and kindness on secular grounds, and, it's possible to believe in the rightness of treating my neighbor like myself without being a Baptist or Buddhist.

According to the "Lemon Test" in *Lemon vs. Kurtzman*, 1971, teaching values is not promoting religion when it neither advances nor inhibits religion and fosters no entanglement with religion.

Critics of character education, such as Nadine Strossen of the A.C.L.U., argues, "It's very hard to sort out subtle indoctrination or abuse."

But Christina Hoff Sommers counters that to become a member of society means taking instruction in doctrines, theories, beliefs, and principles. That is the definition of indoctrination, and it's justified. Moral education must have as its explicit aim the moral betterment of the student. We know gratuitous cruelty and political repression are wrong and that kindness and political freedom are right and good. "If that be indoctrination, so be it." How effective is education if the society a child enters appears to offer no disincentives for antisocial behavior? Teachers should not be accused of brainwashing when they insist on basic decency, honesty, and justice. To brainwash is to diminish someone's capacity for reasoned judgement. It's perversely misleading, says Hoff Sommers, to say that helping children develop habits of truthtelling or fair play threaten their ability to make reasoned choices.[53]

While there are universal values such as generosity, there are no universal principles of behavior standards. They aren't fixed forever. Character education can be saved from the label of indoctrination or brainwashing, Syracuse Professor of Sociology Gerald Grant says by recognizing that moral concepts are a process in development. Over time our concept of "justice," for example, has changed. Over time courts have elaborated or expanded moral concepts such as "equality" so that they are ever subject to revision as human thought evolves. Ideals are organic in nature, but this is no excuse to surrender values to meaningless relativism.[54]

It is fair to revise the list of character virtues from year to year. Values have been valued differently in history. "Loyalty" and "courage" are more highly prized when a nation becomes clannish during a war crisis and feels the need for these character traits. "Thrift" and "humility," not very much in vogue now, were much more important in pioneer days. Now, particularly, there seems to be a thirst for "responsibility" and "respect," as the need for these concepts takes precedence. Remember virtues as old as Aristotle (prudence, justice, fortitude, temperance) can be as compelling today. Stimulating and guiding this kind of reflection is a crucial aspect of school leadership.

IMPLEMENTING CHARACTER EDUCATION

The first best thing a school district can do to affirm positive character development in students is to purposely recruit teachers and administrators with good character and with a character education mission in mind. People committed to character development don't just appear. They are sought out, carefully selected, and intentionally socialized to this point of view. George Kuh says "Institutions that leave a distinctive imprint on their students' values are typically blessed with people who persuasively articulate the institution's mission and commitment to character development."[55] School employees will be engaging students in the acquisition of virtues. If they do not, themselves, possess respect, empathy, and honesty, they cannot help students understand these basic virtues. If their classroom conduct or administrative leadership style lacks a positive ethical approach, there is nothing positive for students to model. Schools are strengthened when teachers and administrators are mindful of the profound power values play in shaping lives.

Yet, one of the most significant current impediments to character education today is a lack of university training for the job. In a recent study, which asked teacher interns how well they felt higher education had prepared them to teach character, respondents were highly critical of their experiences. They felt they were expected to teach character without having been provided the methods to do so. In the end, they all felt the task was essential, but due to inadequate preparation, many would hesitate to actually undertake it in a classroom setting and weren't even sure what was expected of them.

These teachers wanted parents, foremost, to accept the responsibility of teaching character. But, they agreed, someone needed to teach morals, and if that person must be the teacher, then they must be given the authority and the skills to do so.[56]

Many schools profess mission statements upholding their support of character education, which they then don't act upon—not in administrative decisions, financial practices, or learning environment. Just as students take creative writing seriously if the English teacher is a published, practicing poet, so will students respect honesty if adults don't skid along the edges of untruth. The school must not signal, by its actions, contempt for its avowed support of character development. Schools with character act in ways consistent with their espoused mission.

Just as true now as it was at the beginning of this past century, "A school might well be called an ethical instrument and its daily sessions hours for the manufacture of character."[57]

Educating for virtue is about awakening students' minds and hearts to new possibilities, a sort of "gradual soul turning" or acquiring of integrity.[58] And, even when a supportive moral culture does not exist outside the school, it is still possible to create one within the school. The school's cumulative effect upon students has the power to change their operative values and their character.[59]

Character education doesn't require teachers to be trained as moral philosophers. However, to be fair to educators, vigorous, comprehensive staff development and adaptation of programming along with ongoing evaluation will enable teachers to take advantage of recent character education research. This research is beginning to indicate that children learn commitment to ethical values from identifying with significant others who live by these values, from experiencing reinforcement of positive values, by experiencing logical consequences from adults for behavior opposing these values, and by practicing behaviors that exemplify positive values.[60]

There are strategies found useful in improving a school's moral climate. Altering teacher/pupil ratio to reduce class size is one obvious prerequisite to creating more sensitive and responsible attention to student character development.

Frequent communication between school, parents, and community is always essential. No one ever complains that the school is asking for their input or is keeping families too informed about concerns, goals, and accomplishments.

Educators recall Thomas Jefferson's advocacy of social action in the form of community service to prepare children for responsible citizenship. Service education has become an essential avenue for helping students move out of self-absorption to cultivate the habit of serving others. Some schools utilize older students to assist younger ones in their skills acquisition. It humanizes older students and provides younger students with positive role models closer to their age.

Extracurricular activities that lift student confidence and engage students in meaningful service projects should be woven into school and community life. Every time a natural disaster strikes, like a flood or tornado, news reports interviewing school students helping to sandbag or clean up debris always show these students saying how good it makes them feel to help out. Character demands action. Action results from caring about others' pain and suffering. Character recognizes one's responsibility to serve. Developing character is grounded in moral actions.

A consistent component in all character education programs is service to reinforce the values learned. A ninth-grade Maryland student said serving "gives me a reason to come to school." An Iowa sixth grader helps lay a walking path in a school butterfly garden, built for the whole community to enjoy. High school students, who look for opportunities to exercise their new drivers' licenses, take meals-on-wheels to local elderly housebound residents during their lunch period. Esther Schaeffer advocates surrounding students in an environment that "exhibits, teaches, and encourages practice in the values our society needs."[61]

Avoid the pitfalls of character education that have resulted in past criticisms of such programs. Character education shouldn't "belong" to a few enthusiasts or zealots while the majority of school personnel and community view it with suspicion, derision, or hostility. And, to avoid the appearance of a lightweight, trendy program, it might be wise not to rely on kits, pricey workshops, and "pop-ed" approaches.[62] Fads don't serve real needs and only promote further criticism of our schools. Further, don't count on extrinsic rewards to cultivate virtues. While students' developmental stages must be kept in mind in selecting teaching material, techniques, and objectives, singling out some students to reward for good behavior traits defeats the objective of doing good for good's sake.

Today, with knowledge based on Kohlberg's cognitive moral development process, a strong commitment to teaching age-appropriate values has emerged. Asking a young child to escort a new classmate to lunch and to the playground teaches helpfulness and kindness. An older student asked to engage in the same action might practice some empathy and discernment regarding how it feels to be in an unfamiliar setting among strangers.

Character enhancement focuses on a common core of shared virtues as agreed upon by school and community. Values taught are objectively rational, universally accepted qualities that people of all civilized nations subscribe to. They transcend political persuasions, ethnic differences, socioeconomic statuses, and religious beliefs.

NOTES

[1] D. Yankelovich, "Three Destructive Trends," *Kettering Review*, Dayton, OH: Charles Kettering Foundation (Fall 1995): 7.

[2] Rushworth M. Kidder, "Universal Human Values: Finding an Ethical Common Ground," *Futurist* (July/August 1994): 10.

[3] "Universal Human Values," *Futurist*, 8

[4] "Fulfilling the Promise of Character Education in the Classroom, Part I," *Journal of Education.* 179, no. 2 (1997). Contributions by Charles S. White and others.

[5] Mike Huckabee, "Character Does Count," *World & I* (June 1998).

[6] Kristen J. Amundson, *Teaching Values and Ethics, Problems and Solutions* (Arlington, VA: American Association of School Administrators, 1991), 5.

[7] William Murchison, *Reclaiming Morality in America* (Nashville: Thomas Nelson, 1994), 122.

[8] George Herbert Palmer, *Ethical and Moral Instruction in Schools* (New York: Houghton Mifflin, 1908), 37.

[9] Esther R. Schaeffer, "Character Education Makes a Difference," *Principal* 78, no. 2 (November 1998): 31.

[10] Thomas Lickona and Kevin Ryan. *Character Education in Schools and Beyond* (Washington, DC: Council in Values & Philosophy, 1993).

[11] Kevin Ryan and Karen Bohlin, *Building Character in Schools: Practical Ways to Bring Moral Instruction to Life* (San Francisco: Jossey-Bass, 1999).

[12] Kenneth L. Woodward, "What is Virtue?" *Newsweek* (13 June 1994): 31.

[13] George D. Kuh, "Shaping Student Character," *Liberal Education* (Summer 1998): 18.

[14] Amundson, *Teaching Values and Ethics*, 9–10.

[15] Keith Tester, *Moral Culture*, (Thousand Oaks, CA: Sage Publications, 1997), 115.

[16] Amundson, *Teaching Values and Ethics*, 18.

[17] Palmer, *Ethical and Moral Instruction in Schools*, 37.

[18] A.G. Larkins, "Should we Teach Values? Which Ones? How?" *Social Studies and the Young Learner* (September/October 1997): 31.

[19] Christina Hoff Sommers, "Are We Living in a Moral Stone Age?" *Current Directions in Psychological Science* (June 1998): 34.

[20] Benjamin Stein, "Reviving Ethics," *Commercial Appeal* (10 March 1991): 34.

[21] E. A. Wynne and Kevin Ryan, *Reclaiming Our Schools* (New York: Merrill, 1993), 138.

[22] Otto Schluter, "Quail Trap School," *The Cedar County Historical Review* (Tipton, IA: Cedar County Historical Society, July 1967): 71.

[23] Amundson, *Teaching Values and Ethics*, 25.

[24] Kevin Ryan, *Questions and Answers on Moral Education* (Bloomington, IN: Phi Delta Kappa Educational Foundation, 1981).

[25] Andrew Ferguson, "Character Goes Back to School," *Time* 153, no. 20 (24 May 1999): 69.

[26] Tomothy Rusnak, ed., *An Integrated Approach to Character Education* (Thousand Oaks, CA: Corwin Press, 1998), 4.

[27] Roger Rosenblatt, "Teaching Johnny to Be Good," *New York Times Magazine* (30 April 1995): 36.

[28] Ferguson, "Character Goes Back to School," 68.

[29] Esther Schaefer, Letter to the Editor, *Time* 155, no. 23 (14 June 1999): 21.

[30] Herbert Wray, "The Moral Child," *U.S. News & World Report* (3 June 1996): 52.

[31] Hoff Sommers, "Are We Living in a Moral Stone Age?" 32.

[32] Alfie Kohn, "How Not to Teach Values: A Critical Look at Character Education," *Phi Delta Kappan* 78 (February 1997).

[33] Thomas Lickona, *Educating for Character: How Our Schools Can Teach Respect and Responsibility* (New York: Bantam, 1991).

[34] Thomas Lickona, "What is Good Character? And How Can We Develop It in Our Children?" (Bloomington, IN: Poyner Center for the Study of Ethics and American Institutions, Indiana University Foundation, May 1991): 13.

....

[35] Ryan, *Building Character in Schools*, 39.

[36] Amundson, *Teaching Values and Ethics*, 10.

[37] Hoff Sommers, "Are We Living in a Moral Stone Age?" 32.

[38] Waldo Beach, *Ethical Education in American Public Schools* (Washington, DC: National Education Association of the United States, 1992), 31.

[39] Rushworth M. Kidder, "Ethics is Not a Luxury: It's Essential to Our Survival," *Education Week* (3 April 1991): 9.

[40] Rosenblatt, "Teaching Johnny to Be Good," 36.

[41] Pete Domenici, Letter to the Editor, *Time* 153 no. 23 (14 June 1999): 21.

[42] Daniel Heischman, "Beyond the Bandwagon: The Place of Ethics in a School Community," *Baylor* (Spring 1996): 4.

[43] Amundson, *Teaching Values and Ethics*, 23.

[44] Heischman, "Beyond the Bandwagon," 4.

[45] Kuh, "Shaping Student Character," 22–23.

[46] Edward F. DeRoche and Mary M. Williams, *Educating Hearts and Minds: A Comprehensive Character Education Framework* (Thousand Oaks, CA: Corwin Press, 1998): 24.

[47] Thomas Lickona, *Educating for Character: How Our Schools Can Teach Respect and Responsibility* (New York: Bantam, 1991), 3.

[48] Ryan, *Questions and Answers on Moral Education*, 29.

[49] Kathleen Townsend, "Why Johnny Can't Tell Right from Wrong: The Important Lesson Our Schools Don't Teach," *Washington Monthly* (December 1992): 30.

[50] William Kilpatrick, Gregory Wolfe, and Suzanne M. Wolfe, *Bonds That Build Character: A Guide to Teaching Your Child Moral Values through Stories* (New York: Touchstone Rockefeller Center, 1994): 19.

[51] Amundson, *Teaching Values and Ethics*, 13.

[52] Meriel Downey and A.V. Kelly, *Moral Education Theory and Practice* (London: Harper & Row, 1978).

[53] Hoff Sommers, "Are We Living in a Moral Stone Age?" 33.

[54] Gerald Grant, "Bringing the 'Moral' Back In," *NEA Today* (January 1989): 59.

[55] Kuh, "Shaping Student Character," 23.

[56] Charles S. White. *Journal of Education*, 179, no. 2 (1997): 35–36.

[57] Palmer, *Ethical and Moral Instruction in Schools*, 29.

[58] Ryan, *Building Character in Schools*, 140.

[59] Thomas Lickona, *What is Good Character? And How Can We Develop It in Our Children?* (Bloomington, IN: Poyner Center for the Study of Ethics & American Institutions, Indiana University Foundation, May 1991), 13.

[60] DeRoche, *Educating Hearts & Minds*.

[61] Schaeffer, "Character Education Makes a Difference," 32.

[62] Rusnak, *An Integrated Approach to Character Education*, 13.

POSITIVE CHARACTER TRAITS USED IN PICTURE STORYBOOKS

CARING. *SEE* KINDNESS, HELPFULNESS

CHARITY. *SEE* KINDNESS, GENEROSITY

CIVILITY. *SEE* KINDNESS, HELPFULNESS, COURTESY

COMPASSION, *SEE* COURTESY, EMPATHY, HELPFULNESS, KINDNESS

COOPERATION

Association in an enterprise for mutual benefits and a common purpose.

Anholt, Laurence. *Degas and the Little Dancer: A Story about Edgar Degas.* Hauppauge, NY: Barron's Educational Series, 1996.

Because Marie helps her poor parents by modeling for an ill-tempered artist, she becomes a famous ballerina, but not in the way she had dreamed.

Cooperation: Just as Marie enters dancing school with plans to be a famous ballet performer, her father becomes ill. To continue paying for her lessons she agrees to pose for the famous painter. He has a model for his sculpture; she continues studying ballet, a cooperative venture with mutual benefits.

Other character traits shown: *Discernment, Empathy, Helpfulness*

Atwell, Debby. *River.* Boston: Houghton Mifflin, 1999.

A river gradually becomes depleted as more and more people use its resources to build cities, transport goods, and handle sewage.

Cooperation: When animals no longer come to the river to drink and when the fish disappear, the people "remembered how it had been," and how "they wanted to share." By cooperating to tear down or change some of the ecologically harmful warehouses and factories, they return the landscape to its healthy condition. The river rests, and time passes.

Other character traits shown: *Responsibility*

Cooper, Helen. *Pumpkin Soup.* New York: Farrar, Straus & Giroux, 1998.

Cat and Squirrel come to blows with Duck, arguing about who will perform what duty in preparing their pumpkin soup, and nearly lose Duck's friendship when he decides to leave them.

Cooperation: Each animal is responsible for a part of the task of making soup. But when Duck upsets the routine by usurping Squirrel's job of stirring the soup, their careful cooperative effort falls apart. Squirrel refuses to share his job. Duck ends up leaving, taking with him knowledge about seasoning the soup. The other two don't know how to add the right amount of salt, so the soup is spoiled. They are all grateful when Duck, who finds he really can't manage without Cat and Squirrel, returns. Duck shares his knowledge of how to measure the salt, and suddenly, the other two don't mind Duck's messiness when he stirs. Once again they are cooperating and making the best soup they've ever tasted. They discover their friendship is more important than adhering to a rigid cooking plan.

Other character traits shown: *Forgiveness, Generosity*

Cox, Judy. *Rabbit Pirates: A Tale of the Spinach Main.* Illus. by Emily Arnold McCully. New York: Browndeer Press (Harcourt Brace), 1999.

Two old rabbit friends disagree about many things but join forces to deal with a tricky fox who threatens them and their business.

Cooperation: When it seems that gentler means prove to no avail, the two set upon one final task in their restaurant kitchen to rid themselves of their determined enemy, the fox. Together they use their culinary talents to prepare an irresistible pastry. One bite is all Monsieur Reynard needs to flee and never come back. Maybe it's the pastry, or maybe it's the hot peppers, garlic, and onion in the pastry.

Other character traits shown: *Loyalty*

Doyle, Malachy. *Jody's Beans.* Illus. by Judith Allibone. Cambridge, MA: Candlewick Press, 1999.

From spring to fall, with the help of her grandfather, Jody learns to plant, care for, harvest, prepare, and eat some runner beans.

Cooperation: Grandfather provides direction and shows Jody the skills it takes to prepare the soil and plant the beans. When the seeds emerge, a phone call from Grandfather explains about thinning the beans. On his next visit they put up a teepee of poles for the young plants to climb. They finish their cooperative venture in late summer by picking handfuls of the long thin ripe beans and preparing them for cooking. Just before fall turns to winter they pick the final large beans that will provide the seed for next spring.

Other character traits shown: *Diligence, Patience*

Ernst, Lisa Campbell. *Sam Johnson and the Blue Ribbon Quilt.* New York: Lothrop, Lee & Shepard (William Morrow), 1983.

While mending the awning over the pig pen, Sam discovers that he enjoys sewing the various patches together but meets with scorn and ridicule when he asks his wife if he could join her quilting club.

Cooperation: Though both the men's quilting club and the women's quilting club have entries to submit at the fair, a gust of wind sweeps up both quilts. "Each landed with a light splat in a giant mud puddle." They see how beautiful each quilt would have been. Too bad neither will win. All their work appears to be ruined until Sam thinks of a way for them to cooperate on one super quilt. They cut out the unsoiled sections of each quilt and piece them together. "As the sun set, the last stitches were being put in to complete their amazing design." Instead of two quilting clubs, the winning quilt went to the "just plain Rosedale Quilting Club."

Other character traits shown: *Diligence*

Fleming, Candace. *A Big Cheese for the White House: The True Tale of a Tremendous Cheddar.* Illus. by S. D. Schindler. New York: DK Ink, 1999.

In 1801, in Cheshire, Massachusetts, Elder John Leland organizes his fellow townspeople to make a big cheese for President Jefferson, who up until that time had been forced to eat inferior cheeses.

Cooperation: It takes the cooperation of all the community members, the farmers, who each donate the milk of one of their cows, the communal apple press to squeeze the curds, the village blacksmith to make the cheese hoop, the villagers taking turns to monitor the aging process of the cheese, and the transportation arrangements to bring the giant cheese to the White House.

Other character traits shown: *Courtesy, Resourcefulness*

Gibbons, Faye. *Mountain Wedding.* Illus. by Ted Rand. New York: Morrow Junior Books, 1996.

The children from two rival mountain families about to be joined in a wedding change their minds about each other only after they face the rescue of their household goods.

Cooperation: Seeing their families' goods in peril, the children begin picking up things falling off the runaway wagon without regard to whose family they belong to. As soon as they cooperate to save their belongings, their attitude toward each other changes. Finally, by the time the mules had stopped at the creek, "we were all mixed and mingled into one big dirty group." Looking at each other, "all of us began to laugh." Working together for a common end has broken the barrier of "them" and "us."

Other character traits shown: *Helpfulness*

Hoberman, Mary Ann. *The Seven Silly Eaters.* Illus. by Marla Frazee. New York: Browndeer Press (Harcourt Brace), 1997.

Seven fussy eaters find a way to surprise their mother.

Cooperation: For years, poor Mrs. Peters has been catering to each of her seven children's food preferences. To thank her, each child is going to make for her the food he likes best for her birthday. But, because they are not experienced cooks, their attempts turn out badly. They dump the results into one pan and hide the mess in the stove, which they have forgotten is hot. Surprisingly, a wonderful cake comes out of their unwitting cooperation. Ever after, they work together combining their food choices to make their special cake together.

Manson, Christopher. *Two Travelers.* New York: Henry Holt, 1990.

The emperor's messenger Isaac must accompany a gift elephant from Baghdad to France, and during the difficult journey, an unexpected friendship develops between man and beast.

Cooperation: Both elephant and Isaac are unsure how they feel about each other. Isaac fears the elephant's monster size. The elephant doesn't like Isaac's strange smell or his funny hat. Isaac worries that he will be stepped on; the elephant worries that he might be beaten with sticks or not given clean straw and water. Soon both are doing small things for the other to make the long trip bearable. To ease the elephant's concern, Isaac shows how safe is the raft upon which they must cross the river. And he covers the elephant's ears during the cold part of the journey. The elephant shows his growing regard for Isaac by shading him with his big ears during the hot part of the journey and lifting him with his trunk to save him from going overboard during a storm at sea. By cooperating they conclude the long journey safely.

Other character traits shown: *Helpfulness, Kindness*

McCully, Emily Arnold. *The Bobbin Girl.* New York: Dial Books for Young Readers (Penguin), 1996.

A 10-year-old bobbin girl working in a textile mill in Lowell, Massachusetts, in the 1830s must make a difficult decision.

Cooperation: Realizing it was unfair for an injured worker to be fired and for the owners to reduce their salaries, the young women employed at a cotton mill must decide to stand together to achieve their rights. Many are afraid they, too, will be dismissed, and they desperately need their wages. When one girl beckons the others to "turn out," some are afraid. But, the bobbin girl shouts, "I am going to turn out, whether anyone else does or not!" A line of girls follows her out. By cooperating, they have gained the attention of the mill owners. Though they lose their jobs, they have refused to become factory slaves and have paved the way to basic rights for future workers. "The next time, or the time after, we will win."

Other character traits shown: *Courage, Justice, Perseverance, Prudence*

Mitchell, Barbara. *Red Bird.* Illus. by Todd Doney. New York: Lothrop, Lee & Shepard, 1996.

Katie, also known as Red Bird, joins her family and other Indians at the annual powwow in southern Delaware, where they celebrate their Nanticoke heritage with music, dancing, and special foods.

Cooperation: The powwow serves to unite all people. "Red feet and white feet, black feet and yellow feet step to the beat of the heart." They join together once a year to dance "the dance of all peoples" to renew the bonds of friendship with Indian and non-Indian friends. And, though they go back to a life in today's world, "the heartbeat of The People stays with her all year long."

Other character traits shown: *Loyalty, Respect*

Nolen, Jerdine. *Raising Dragons.* Illus. by Elise Primavera. New York: Silver Whistle (Harcourt Brace), 1998.

A farmer's young daughter shares numerous adventures with the dragon that she raises from infancy.

Cooperation: The dragon took a lot of care, but at night they go flying together. "Up until then I had been afraid of the dark." Now, "Hank showed me my world from on high...and it was just grand!" The dragon helps with field plowing and seeding. Together the girl and dragon tend the crops. The excess corn they grow is sold because "Hank was making popcorn" with his fiery breath. This is an association for mutual benefits.

Other character traits shown: *Diligence, Kindness, Loyalty, Responsibility*

Rathmann, Peggy. *Officer Buckle and Gloria.* New York: G.P. Putnam's Sons, 1995. (Cladecott—1996)

The children at Napville Elementary School always ignore Officer Buckle's safety tips, until a police dog named Gloria accompanies him when he gives his safety speeches.

Cooperation: Officer Buckle discovers his tips are not as successfully received by his audience without Gloria, who pantomimes his advice while he talks. And Gloria really has nothing to demonstrate without Officer Buckle's narration. They need each other to make a successful presentation.

Other character traits shown: *Discernment*

Reiser, Lynn. *Best Friends Think Alike.* New York: Greenwillow (William Morrow), 1997.

Two best friends have a brief disagreement, but then decide that playing together is better than having your own way alone.

Cooperation: Both friends want to be the wild horse that knows tricks and each wants the other to be the rider with the ruffles and ribbons and the big hat and tall boots. They agree the horse will neigh and stamp its feet and the rider will hold the reins and yell "giddyup." They agree the horse will gallop and the rider will wave. Each thought the other would be the rider. They argue. So, they will each be the horse by themselves. But they realize they each won't have a rider. They declare they will each be the horse and the rider and play the game "all by myself." But when they start to play alone, they realize the game is not as much fun. "I wanted to play with you!" they both say. They think of a new game. They will each be the horse, and they will each be the rider "together."

Other character traits shown: *Resourcefulness*

Scheffler, Ursel. *Stop Your Crowing, Kasimir!* Illus. by Silke Brix-Henker. Minneapolis: Carolrhoda, 1988.

Katy's neighbors appeal to the authorities to silence her extremely loud rooster, but the final result is very different from what they had in mind.

Cooperation: When city neighbors move next door to Katy's small country home, they call it, "Just like a picture book!" They look forward to quiet and fresh country air. But trouble erupts when Katy's new rooster loudly crows. The neighbors are "outraged." Suddenly her old house is an "eyesore in our lovely area." And, when Katy moves manure from her barn to her plot of land, they complain, "Such an awful stink!" The neighbors, with a court summons, finally succeed in removing Katy. But they find that the new neighbor, a noisy night club, is far worse than simple Katy and her animals. By failing to cooperate, they have made their situation worse.

Other character traits shown: *Justice, Tolerance*

Siekkinen, Raija. *Mister King.* Illus. by Hannu Taina. Trans. by Tim Steffa. Minneapolis: Carolrhoda, 1987.

A lonely king searches his seaside kingdom for subjects.

Cooperation: A king has no subjects and a cat has no home. By joining forces the king is no longer lonely and cheerfully notices the beauty around him. The cat, of course, while pointing out things for the king to notice, is pleased to be served with food when he's hungry and a soft bed when he sleeps.

Other character traits shown: *Generosity*

COURAGE

Use for INTEGRITY
Attitude of facing what is difficult, painful, or dangerous in a brave manner.

Aardema, Verna. *Borreguita and the Coyote: A Tale from Ayutla, Mexico.* Illus. by Petra Mathers. New York: Alfred A. Knopf, 1991.

A little lamb uses her clever wiles to keep a coyote from eating her up.

Courage: Though no match in size or fierceness, Lamb does not hesitate to face Coyote's grave threats against her life. She does not shirk from encounters and refuses to be forced from her environment. And, finally when unavoidable, she resorts to a natural skill to stop her enemy.

Other character traits shown: *Prudence, Resourcefulness*

Aardema, Verna. *The Lonely Lioness and the Ostrich Chicks.* Illus. by Yumi Heo. New York: Alfred A. Knopf, 1996.

In this Masai tale, a mongoose helps an ostrich get her chicks back from the lonely lioness who has stolen them.

Courage: Small stature does not deter the brave mongoose from taking on the lioness. He risks his personal safety by angering the lioness, taunting her sense of pride by calling her a fool. He knows this will provoke an attack, yet he does not hesitate to act.

Other character traits shown: *Helpfulness, Honesty, Justice, Perseverance, Prudence, Self-discipline*

Atkins, Jeannine. *Mary Anning and the Sea Dragon.* Illus. by Michael Dooling. New York: Farrar, Straus & Giroux, 1999.

An account of the finding of the first entire skeleton of an ichthyosaur, an extinct sea reptile, by a 12-year-old English girl who went on to become a paleontologist.

Courage: Mary's family does not respect her digging. But Lord Henley understands her interest in fossils. His encouragement and her need to finish her task enable her to continue. Eventually, she does extract a rare specimen. Her Aunt Ruth remarks,

"Now will you settle down to a normal life?" Mary courageously replies, "I have work to do." She pursues her own way in life despite society's expectations.

Other character traits shown: *Diligence, Perseverance*

Auch, Mary Jane. *Bantam of the Opera.* New York: Holiday House, 1997.

Luigi the rooster wins fame and fortune when the star of the Cosmopolitan Opera Company and his understudy both come down with chicken pox on the same night.

Courage: Luigi must battle prejudice among his barnyard family, jealousy of a fellow performer, and the ridicule of a skeptical audience. His desire to sing is not well received. But he ignores threats, taunts, dangers, and hostility as he courageously pursues his heart's desire. Despite interference, he sings beautifully when he has his chance, and, thus, earns the applaud of the audience.

Other character traits shown: *Fortitude, Helpfulness, Hope, Perseverance*

Bunting, Eve. *Summer Wheels.* Illus. by Thomas B. Allen. New York: Harcourt Brace Jovanovich, 1992.

The Bicycle Man fixes up old bicycles and offers both his friendship and the use of the bikes to the neighborhood kids.

Courage: Lawrence and his friend Brady don't relish dealing with the mean boy who signs his name "Abraham Lincoln" when he checks out a bike. But Lawrence must confront him about the bicycle he has checked out and failed to return. Lawrence confronts him and convinces him to return it according to the bike shop's rules. Unbelievably, the Bicycle Man lets this irresponsible tough boy check out another bike. And, predictably, the boy doesn't return that one either. "The Man's our friend," they say. "This punk shouldn't be able to put one over on him." When they track the boy down he's in the middle of a group of big kids, who are admiring him as he rides it down stone steps. It's even worse confronting him among all his admirers. Lawrence tells him, "You have to bring it back." One of the biggest guys tells him, "He don't have to do anything he don't want to do." Yet Lawrence stands his ground, and the boy does follow Lawrence back to the bike garage.

Other character traits shown: *Empathy, Forgiveness, Generosity, Justice, Kindness, Respect, Responsibility, Tolerance*

Bunting, Eve. *Train to Somewhere.* Illus. by Ronald Himler. New York: Clarion Books (Houghton Mifflin), 1996.

In the late 1800s, Marianne travels westward on the Orphan Train with other children who hope to be placed with caring families.

Courage: Marianne knows, because she is not pretty, that it may be difficult for her to be placed with new parents. She also knows that her younger friend's plan to keep them from being split up by claiming they are sisters is not realistic. She must help little Nora face the separation and go on to a good life without her. And, at each stop she expects to find her mother, who had promised to send for her. Marianne is the last child to be placed. At the last stop, only one old couple is waiting. They aren't what Marianne wanted. She isn't the boy they wanted. Courageously, they each avoid hurting the feelings of the other. They will make the best of things and accept with loving grace the reality of their situation.

Other character traits shown: *Empathy, Hope, Kindness, Patience, Prudence, Respect*

Carter, Dorothy. *Wilhe'mina Miles: After the Stork Night.* New York: Frances Foster Books (Farrar, Straus & Giroux), 1999.

Because her father is out of town working, eight-year-old Wilhe'mina must go for help when the stork visits her mother to bring her a new brother.
Courage: Wilhe'mina is scared of the dark and toad frogs that might bite her. But the thing she fears most is the makeshift rattletrap bridge that must be crossed. "One misstep and you'd be wading in the water, tangled with the water moccasins." But Mama "was shaking and wringing her hands." So, Wilhe'mina knew she had to go get Mis' Hattie. She fears the trip. Nevertheless, with courage she does what must be done. "That night I was trembly and scared of losing my footing, so I got down on my hands and knees and crawled over that stream gurgling below."

Other character traits shown: *Responsibility*

Charles, Donald. *Chancay and the Secret of Fire: A Peruvian Folktale.* New York: A Whitebird Book (G.P. Putnam's Sons), 1992.

In Peru, as a reward for releasing the beautiful fish he has caught, Chancay is granted his wish of finding a way to relieve his people from the cold and darkness.
Courage: Without regard to personal physical safety, Chancay follows the directives of the fish by struggling to lift a basin laden with stones above his head on the top of the highest mountain peak during a freezing rain and wind storm. He battles stinging spiders, a field of snakes, crouching pumas, and an angry sun just so he can bring fire to his people.

Other character traits shown: *Diligence, Fortitude, Kindness, Patience, Perseverance, Prudence*

*Cutler, Jane. *The Cello of Mr. O.* Illus. by Greg Couch. New York: Dutton Children's Books (Penguin Putnam), 1999.

When a concert cellist plays in the square for his neighbors in a war-besieged city, his priceless instrument is destroyed by a mortar shell, but he finds the courage to return the next day to perform with a harmonica.
Courage: Though the children in the apartment tease the strange "thinking man" because he seems unfriendly, they soon grow to respect his courage as he plays out

in the street, at great personal risk, every afternoon. When his cello is destroyed, he returns the next day with a harmonica, playing to "feed" the hungry people.

Other character traits shown: *Fortitude, Generosity, Hope, Perseverance, Resourcefulness*

Daly, Niki. *Bravo Zan Angelo! A Commedia Dell'arte Tale with Story and Pictures.* New York: Farrar, Straus & Giroux, 1998.

In Renaissance Venice, Angelo, longing to be as famous a clown as his grandfather, decides to do something special with his small part in his grandfather's act during Carnival.

Courage: Angelo is told there is no place in his grandfather's theater for a little boy. Bravely, Angelo confronts his crusty old grandfather to ask for a part in the cast. He asks for one of the parts, and then another and another until he has asked to play each of the positions. His grandfather tells him each time why he is not suitable to play the part. Finally, to silence the child, he tells him he can be "the little red rooster who crows in the last act." Angelo knows there is no such part. But he courageously forges ahead to make the best of this concession that he can. Angelo overcomes all obstacles (such as finding a costume in a hurry) and makes himself the hit of the show.

Other character traits shown: *Courtesy, Helpfulness, Hope, Kindness, Perseverance, Resourcefulness*

Davol, Marguerite W. *The Paper Dragon.* Illus. by Robert Sabuda. Atheneum Books for Young Readers (Simon & Schuster), 1997.

The power of the artist's vision and the ever-sustaining nature of love are brought together when a humble artist agrees to confront the terrifying dragon that threatens to destroy his village.

Courage: Someone must face the dragon. Who would be brave enough and clever enough to do the job? The villagers convince Mi Fei the painter of heroic deeds of the past to try. He is afraid for his life, but "the worried faces of the villagers filled his mind." Mi Fei must perform three tasks before the dragon returns to its ageless slumber. If he fails, he will be devoured. Mi Fei turns for inspiration to his scrolls, learning from the past to find answers for the present. He succeeds with the first two tasks, but cannot find inspiration from the past to solve the final request, to tell the dragon the strongest thing in the world. So, knowing he will probably die, he paints one last time "what he cherished most," the people of his village, young and old, men, women, and children. Then he writes on the scroll a poem about love. When he reads his poem to the dragon, he is astonished to see the creature shrink. In a whisper rather than a roar, the dragon tells him, "You have found the way for me to sleep once more. Truly, the strongest thing in the world is love."

Other character traits shown: *Discernment, Fortitude, Responsibility*

Edwards, Pamela Duncan. *The Worrywarts.* Illus. by Henry Cole. New York: HarperCollins, 1999.

Wombat, Weasel, and Woodchuck won't be wimps when they wander the world using wise means of outwitting not-so-wicked rascals.

Courage: The three worry about such troubles as a swarm of wasps, a big wave, a wallowing walrus, and a whole slew of other improbables. But this doesn't stop them from their determination to wander the world, or at least down the pathway and through the woods. Weasel will take water wings, so he will stay afloat if a wave whooshes over him. Woodchuck will wear woolly underwear to prepare for a cold whirlwind. Wombat will wear a helmet if an owl should swoop down and whisk him away. "We won't be worrywarts."

Other character traits shown: *Prudence, Resourcefulness*

Fowler, Susi Gregg. *Beautiful.* Illus. by Jim Fowler. New York: Greenwillow (William Morrow), 1998.

A young gardener and Uncle George collaborate on a garden, so that when a very sick Uncle George comes home from the doctor he is greeted with beautiful flowers.

Courage: Though he misses the way Uncle George used to be, the boy focuses on what time is left between them. He had hoped Uncle George would see and admire what a great garden he has made. But he must settle for bringing a bit of the garden to Uncle George. He faces the reality of the situation with quiet acceptance. And, just before the end, the garden flowers obligingly bloom. The boy clips a bouquet and brings them to Uncle George, because he "knew he couldn't come outside."

Other character traits shown: *Helpfulness, Honesty, Tolerance*

Galbraith, Kathryn O. *Laura Charlotte.* Illus. by Floyd Cooper. New York: Philomel Books (Putnam & Grist), 1990.

A mother describes her love for a toy elephant she was given as a child, a gift she has now passed on to her daughter.

Courage: Though afraid of the dark, the child's mother (as a child) realizes she had left her precious toy outside during a game of hide and seek with her cousin. She does not wish to go out there under the "shaggy and dark" tree to get it. But then she thinks, "was Charlotte afraid without me?" It takes courage to run "under the arms of the willow" to find her beloved toy. But she puts aside her personal fears so that the toy will not spend the night on the "wet summer grass." And, when she discovers its ear chewed off, she bravely sits beside her grandmother watching while a new ear is sewed on.

*Garland, Sherry. *I Never Knew Your Name.* Illus. by Sheldon Greenberg. New York: Ticknor & Fields (Houghton Mifflin), 1994.

A small boy laments the lonely life of a teenage suicide whose neighbors didn't even know his name.

Courage: The younger boy wishes he had exhibited courage to reach out to the apparently friendless older boy, whom he had watched secretly and had admired. He kept finding excuses to avoid making the acquaintance, because he feared rejection. He missed a chance to invite the boy to go fishing with him. He considered going up on the roof to feed pigeons with the boy but again didn't follow through, because he told himself the boy probably wanted to be alone. Now, he rues the inhibitions that prevented him from so many missed opportunities.

Other character traits shown: *Respect*

Gerrard, Roy. *The Roman Twins.* New York: Farrar, Straus & Giroux, 1998.

Maximus and his twin sister Vanilla, slaves to the cruel and greedy Slobbus Pompius, risk their lives to save a horse and end up helping to save the city of Rome from the Goths.

Courage: When the children hear that the chariot horse Slobbus bought to impress his neighbors is about to be chopped up for meat because it would "snort and misbehave" with its owner, the "daring twosome creep in and steal away with Polydox, while nasty Slobbus sleeps." Then, because they do not wish to be a financial burden on the poor family that hid them, they enter the annual chariot race in hopes of winning the Emperor's Gold Cup. Slobbus demands revenge against them for stealing his horse. But before the Emperor can "punish the plucky children who had triumphed in the race," a threat to the safety of the city turns attention to a vulnerable bridge. To prevent invaders from burning the city, the bridge must be brought down. The children bravely volunteer to cut the ropes that hold it up. Their action results in a grateful Emperor.

Other character traits shown: *Justice, Loyalty*

Hazen, Barbara Shook. *Wally, the Worry-Warthog.* Illus. by Janet Stevens. New York: Clarion Books (Houghton Mifflin), 1990.

Wally worries about everything but discovers that the terrifying Wilberforce has as many fears as he does.

Courage: Wally and Wilberforce spend a lot of time worrying about many frightful things. When they admit their terror to each other, they band together to face what they might discover under the bridge. Courageously they confront their fears and find that worrying was worse than reality.

Other character traits shown: *Empathy, Honesty*

Hest, Amy. *The Purple Coat.* Illus. by Amy Schwartz. New York: Four Winds Press, 1986.

Despite her mother's reminder that "navy blue is what you always get," Gabby begs her tailor grandfather to make her a beautiful purple coat.

Courage: Gabby doesn't want to anger her mother, but she very much wants a different coat this time. She pursues her dream courageously without throwing a tantrum. She reminds her grandfather that, "Once in a while it's good to try something new, … You said so yourself." Later, she reminds her mother of the same fact. And, when her mother learns of the switch from navy to purple, Gabby bravely hopes to assuage her mother's objections by pointing out that the coat will be reversible: purple on one side and navy blue on the other. How could her mother, who has already admired the beautiful purple swatch, object to such logic?

Other character traits shown: *Empathy, Prudence, Tolerance*

*Hoestlandt, Jo. *Star of Fear, Star of Hope.* Illus by Johanna Kang, Trans. by Mark Polizzotti. New York: Walker & Co., 1995.

Nine-year-old Helen is confused by the disappearance of her Jewish friend during the German occupation of Paris.

Courage: Helen has invited her Jewish friend Lydia to spend an overnight on her 9th birthday. During the evening while Helen's parents are at work, the girls are disturbed by strangers pounding on the door to be let inside. Later, they tell Helen's parents. Her father goes out to investigate and returns with a woman, who says their neighbor was going to help her but is gone. She says she can't go home or the police will find her and take her away. "It's already started. They're arresting everyone like me." Suddenly, Lydia asks to go home. Helen's mother turns to her father, "What do you think?" They courageously agree to become involved. Helen's father takes Lydia home. Her mother allows the strange woman to sleep over in Helen's bed for the night. In the morning police pound on their apartment door, looking for the next door neighbor. As a policeman glances around their apartment, he sees the woman still in Helen's little bed, pretending to be asleep. From the doorway, he can only see her hair spread out over the pillow. "These kids could sleep through an air raid!" the policeman comments before he leaves. Later, Helen and her mother try, and fail, to find Lydia, while her father quietly takes the strange woman "somewhere safe."

Other character traits shown: *Discernment, Forgiveness, Hope*

Howard, Elizabeth Fitzgerald. *Virgie Goes to School with Us Boys.* Illus. by E. B. Lewis. New York: Simon & Schuster, 2000.

In the post-Civil War South, a young African American girl is determined to prove that she can go to school just like her older brothers.

Courage: Her brothers try to discourage their sister. School is too far, over seven miles. School requires the students to stay from Monday through Friday. School will be too hard for her. Not many girls go to the school. When Virgie finally receives permission to go to school, she not only keeps up with her brothers, she doesn't cry when she falls down on slippery stream rocks, and she doesn't show fear when they go through the dark woods. She even helps by suggesting they sing. "The walk went faster then. Seemed not so dark." Virgie's courage overcame all obstacles to her learning to read.

Other character traits shown: *Generosity, Perseverance*

Hutchins, Hazel. *Believing Sophie.* Illus. by Dorothy Donohue. Morton Grove, IL: Albert Whitman, 1995.

When a little girl is unjustly accused of shoplifting, she bravely tries to prove her innocence.

Courage: Sophie is taken to a back room to wait for the store owner. "She felt very small. And very strange. And she didn't know how she was going to make anyone, let alone Mr. Luca himself, understand that she had paid for the cough drops, only not just now." After she tells him what happened, she is relieved to be sent home, but sad, too, because she isn't sure he really believed her story. Then she remembers that she had put the receipt for the cough drops in her sock. She rushes back to show him. Her "heart was pounding" again. But she stands up for herself, and everyone in the store now knows the truth.

Other character traits shown: *Honesty, Resourcefulness*

James, J. Alison. *The Drums of Noto Hanto.* Illus. by Tsukushi. New York: DK Ink, 1999.

The people in a small village in ancient Japan manage to drive off the forces of a powerful warlord using only their ingenuity.

Courage: Though the villagers recognize they can never win in a battle fighting the invading samurai, neither do they want them to take their rice crop for taxes and steal the best of their fish and vegetables. They agree to make a stand by using trickery. "Four huge ships rounded the cliff into the bay. Their sides were stuck with oars. On their decks a thousand swords flashed red." The villagers are awestruck. Still, someone takes courage and lights the first of the planned bonfires. Even when the "rain of arrows came," the villagers remain firm in their commitment and carry out their scheme to make the invaders believe they are much stronger than they really are.

Other character traits shown: *Resourcefulness*

James, Simon. *Leon and Bob.* Cambridge, MA: Candlewick Press, 1997.

Leon and his imaginary friend Bob do everything together until a new boy moves in next door.

Courage: When the new boy moves in, Leon decides to visit him, but his imaginary friend Bob must come along. Half way up the steps to the new boy's apartment, Leon realizes he is alone. He can go ahead and ring the bell or he can go back home. "Bob" is not there to help him. Leon courageously rings the bell and even asks the new boy if he would like to go to the park.

Other character traits shown: *Kindness*

Jones, Rebecca C. *Down at the Bottom of the Deep Dark Sea.* Illus. by Virginia Wright-Frierson. New York: Bradbury Press (Macmillan), 1991.

Andrew hates water and intends to stay away from the ocean while at the beach, but he changes his mind when he needs water for the sand city he is building. *Courage*: He is very afraid of what might be lurking down at the ocean bottom. But he can't continue building his sand city unless he has wet sand. Perhaps if he hurries, the water won't drag him away. He returns many times to fill his bucket with wet sand. The water catches his toes and his heels, but he bravely continues. In fact, he becomes so focused on his sand city that he overcomes his aversion to the water. He courageously faces his fear in order to persist with an important project.

Other character traits shown: *Fortitude*

Joosse, Barbara. *Lewis & Papa: Adventure on the Santa Fe Trail.* Illus. by Jon Van Zyle. San Francisco: Chronicle Books, 1998.

While accompanying his father on the wagon train along the Santa Fe Trail, Lewis discovers what it is to be a man.
Courage: Lewis is glad to go with Papa but will miss his mother and sister. He finds that Papa, too, misses them. The sound of coyotes howling makes him shiver, but Papa knows what to say to comfort them both. A stampeding herd of buffalo that nearly flattens the wagon train causes Lewis to "make himself small under the wagon" and to admit he was afraid. Papa admits he, too, was afraid. When it becomes necessary to shoot Big Red, their ox, to prevent his suffering, Lewis "pushed his tears inside." And, this time, he even has enough strength to comfort Papa's loss.

Other character traits shown: *Fortitude, Honesty, Responsibility*

Jukes, Mavis. *I'll See You in My Dreams.* Illus. by Stacey Schuett. New York: Alfred A. Knopf, 1993.

A girl preparing to visit her seriously ill uncle in the hospital imagines being a skywriter and flying over his bed with a message of love.
Courage: Her mother tries to prepare her for unpleasant and frightening aspects of sickness at the hospital. There is a woman who walks the halls asking over and over where she should sit. And there are two disabled men on the ward who look at the ceiling and only say "A-a-a-h!" Then, perhaps her uncle might not wake up or even know she's there. Maybe she would prefer just to sit outside the room on a bench

while Mother and Aunt Hannah go inside. But the girl is firm. She will go inside. The "A-a-a-h" men won't frighten her. "She might even say hello to them, might ask the nurse their names." If the woman asking where to sit should speak to her, "she would suggest that she sit on a bench with her aunt and her mother." She would walk alone into the room where her uncle was sleeping. He might not know she was standing there, but she would. And she would know what to say to him. She would tell him the message she would have made if she were a sky-writer: "I love you. I'll see you in my dreams."

Other character traits shown: *Respect*

Keller, Holly. *Brave Horace*. New York: Greenwillow (William Morrow), 1998.

In the days before his friend George's monster movie party, Horace prepares for the frightening events he expects will occur.

Courage: Horace tries to buck up his courage by acting out all the fierce behaviors he can imagine in order to ward off his fears of the unknown possibilities awaiting him at the party. Finally, at the party, things are going very well until George's older brother Marvin turns out the lights and says no one can have cupcakes unless they first touch the "monster brains and livers" in the box he's holding. Horace tries to find the door and bumps into Fred, who is also trying to get out. Big brother Marvin accuses the party-goers of being a "bunch of scaredy cats." But when Horace sees his friend Fred is about to cry, he volunteers first to stick his hand into the gruesome box. The lights come on. In the box is green Jell-o. "Some monster!" But Fred knows the value of Horace's courage. "You were brave," he declares.

Lorbiecki, Marybeth. *Sister Anne's Hands*. Illus. by K. Wendy Popp. New York: Dial Books for Young Readers (Penguin), 1998.

Seven-year-old Anna has her first encounter with racism in the 1960s when an African-American nun comes to teach at her parochial school.

Courage: After an unpleasant classroom incident in which a racist poem is written on a paper airplane that sails past Sister's head, she tells the class, "I'll need some quiet time to think about this, if you know what I mean." The next day, students face an eye-opening wall of pictures, which show black people experiencing various kinds of suffering as a result of white fear and prejudice. The Sister's courage has a profound life-changing impact on her students and enables Anna to exhibit her own courage by acknowledging the magnificence of diversity.

Other character traits shown: *Forgiveness, Respect, Tolerance*

McCully, Emily Arnold. *The Ballot Box Battle*. New York: Alfred A. Knopf, 1996.

Elizabeth Cady Stanton, a famous nineteenth-century leader in the struggle for women's rights, inspires Cordelia to overcome all obstacles to carry on the fight for equality.

Courage: Cordelia can't understand Mrs. Stanton's determination to seek women's suffrage, but she can relate to her brother's taunts about "No votes for pea-brained females!" And she remembers his dismissive attitude about her horse-riding skills. "Oh, well, you are not a true horseman until you jump a four-foot fence," he says. Perhaps she cannot be as brave as Mrs. Stanton, but she and the old horse will find out together whether they can jump the fence and show her brother she is a "true" horseman.

Other character traits shown: *Diligence, Discernment, Fortitude, Hope*

McCully, Emily Arnold. *The Bobbin Girl.* New York: Dial Books for Young Readers (Penguin), 1996.

A 10-year-old bobbin girl working in a textile mill in Lowell, Massachusetts in the 1830s must make a difficult decision.

Courage: The girl's wages help her family survive financially. It is the same with the other employees. But worker rights are suffering. Wages have been cut, and girls are dismissed for no better reason than a work-related injury. It will take courage to stand up to the mill owners. The bobbin girl decides to "turn-out" even though she could lose her job.

Other character traits shown: *Cooperation, Justice, Perseverance, Prudence*

McCully, Emily Arnold. *Mirette on the High Wire.* New York: G.P. Putnam's Sons, 1992. (Caldecott–1993)

Mirette learns tightrope walking from Monsieur Bellini, a guest at her mother's boardinghouse, not knowing that he is a celebrated tightrope artist who has withdrawn from performing because of fear.

Courage: When Mirette learns that the man who has been giving her tightrope walking lessons has done some magnificent feats on the high wire, she asks him to teach her those things, too. He admits he cannot. "Once you have fear on the wire, it never leaves." She begs him to make it leave. He feels terrible about disappointing her. So, he faces his problem and sets up a high wire between two high buildings for a public performance. At the final moment, he cannot continue across the wire. Mirette knows what to do. She climbs out a roof window at the other end of the strung wire. She stretches out her hands to Bellini, and they begin to walk toward each other. Their mutual courage enables them to become performing partners.

Other character traits shown: *Helpfulness, Perseverance*

*Schur, Maxine Rose. *The Peddler's Gift.* Illus. by Kimberly Bulcken Root. New York: Dial Books for Young Readers (Penguin), 1999.

A young boy in rural Russia at the turn of the twentieth century learns that appearances are often deceiving after he steals a dreidel.

Courage: During display of the sales goods, a dreidel falls under a chair. The boy knows he should return it, but old Shnook won't miss it. He never notices anything. "I'll just borrow it, and the next time he comes to town, I'll find a way to slip it back to him." But thinking about the consequences of his action, he knows he has done wrong and must return the toy top. Through the stormy night he searches for the peddler. He will confess his sin and give back the dreidel and ask to be forgiven. He trembles with fear. When he faces the peddler, he courageously admits he stole the toy and says he is sorry.

Other character traits shown: *Forgiveness, Honesty, Kindness, Respect, Responsibility*

Singer, Marilyn. *The Painted Fan.* Illus. by Wenhai Ma. New York: Morrow Junior Books, 1994.

When a brave young maiden subdues a demon using a fan that had been given to her by her mother, she brings about the downfall of the tyrannical Lord Shang and reunites the imperial houses of Li and Chen.

Courage: Though assisted by the magical powers of the fan, the girl first shows bravery when she must choose whether to bring a forbidden object with her into her arranged marriage with the feared Lord Shang. She knows it is dangerous. If he discovers it, she will be killed. "But my mother risked death to keep the fan safe, and I will do the same." Later, when Lord Shang discovers her friendship with a common man, she again shows personal courage when she pleads for his life and willingly takes on the task of retrieving a valuable pearl from a demon's cave.

Ward, Lynd. *The Biggest Bear.* Boston: Houghton Mifflin, 1952. (Caldecott–1953)

Johnny wanted a bearskin on his barn like the other farms had, but what he got was a bear cub that ate huge quantities of food wherever it could be found.

Courage: The time comes when the family can no longer afford the pet bear. The bear is harming neighborhood relations when it raids food supplies. Johnny's father first asks him to take the bear back to the woods. Johnny will miss his friend, but he bravely obeys. The bear keeps coming back home. Finally, there is only one thing left to do. Johnny courageously "said he would do it." He takes the bear and a gun into the woods. An accident of fate preserves the bear's life at the last minute, but Johnny had the courage to do what was necessary.

Other character traits shown: *Responsibility*

Yorinks, Arthur. *Hey, Al.* Illus. by Richard Egielski. New York: Farrar, Straus & Giroux, 1986. (Caldecott–1987).

Al, a janitor, and Eddie, his faithful dog, live together in a crowded single room where they are dissatisfied with their lot until a mysterious bird offers them a change of fortune that soon makes them long for their old life.

Courage: Al and Eddie agree they need a change. And, at first, life on the island the bird takes them to seems like paradise. But, when they begin to change into birds and lose their own identities, the cloying life of ease turns to horror. Desperately, they wish they were back mopping floors in their old life. Courageously, they break the bonds of the island and flap furiously toward home.

Other character traits shown: *Discernment*

COURTESY

Use for CIVILITY, COMPASSION, THOUGHTFULNESS
A polite, helpful, civil, or considerate act or remark.

Bunting, Eve. *Smoky Night.* Illus. by David Diaz. New York: Harcourt Brace, 1994. (Caldecott–1995)

> When the Los Angeles riots break out in the streets of their neighborhood, a young boy and his mother learn the value of getting along with others no matter their background or nationality.

Courtesy: When their building is set on fire, families congregate in the street. A woman comes to lead them to a shelter. A firefighter comes to the shelter with two cats he has found. One belongs to the boy. The other belongs to Mrs. Kim, a neighborhood business owner. A woman puts down a bowl of milk and both cats drink from the same dish together. This reminds the adults that they should share things as well. The boy's mother invites Mrs. Kim to "come over and share a dish of milk" together. Mrs. Kim accepts the invitation. And the boy notices that Mrs. Kim's mean orange cat is purring! Courteous beginnings will lead to better relationships in the neighborhood.

Other character traits shown: *Discernment, Forgiveness*

Christelow, Eileen. *The Five-Dog Night.* New York: Clarion Books (Houghton Mifflin), 1993.

> Cantankerous Ezra constantly rebuffs his nosy neighbor, Old Betty, when she tries to give him advice on how to survive cold winter nights, until she finally discovers that his five dogs are his private source for warmth.

Courtesy: Old Betty worries for Ezra, whom she believes is not properly concerned about the realities of winter. In her experience, it takes extra blankets to keep warm at night. So, because he apparently is careless about taking precautions, she brings him a blanket. He is not appreciative, but she persists in her courteous acts toward one who must be crazy. She brings a thermos of hot chocolate; she brings cookies and makes tea. She checks on him regularly. And one day it is the grumpy Ezra who finds himself following her example and becoming concerned about her welfare.

Other character traits shown: *Generosity, Helpfulness, Kindness, Perseverance, Respect*

*Crimi, Carolyn. *Don't Need Friends.* Illus. by Lynn Munsinger. New York: Doubleday Books for Young Readers (Random House), 1999.

After his best friend moves away, Rat rudely rebuffs the efforts of the other residents of the junkyard to be friendly, until he and a grouchy old dog decide that they need each other.

Courtesy: After Possum moves away, Rat refuses to acknowledge the courteous overtures of Mouse, or Pigeon, who invites him to share the poppy seed muffin he offers, or Raccoon, who asks him to a party. But, later, when the grouchy dog doesn't trade insults with him as they customarily do in their peculiar relationship, Rat misses their exchanges and begins to worry something might be wrong with Dog. He discovers Dog is sick. Soon he is dragging a huge sandwich toward Dog's barrel to share with him. And then he crawls inside the barrel to share the cold winter night. And, finally, they are scrounging food together. The world is suddenly a better place. Good enough even to share a few French fries with the smaller animals.

Other character traits shown: *Generosity, Helpfulness*

Daly, Niki. *Bravo Zan Angelo! A Commedia Dell'arte Tale with Story and Pictures.* New York: Farrar, Straus & Giroux, 1998.

In Renaissance Venice, Angelo, longing to be as famous a clown as his grandfather, decides to do something special with his small part in his grandfather's act during Carnival.

Courtesy: Though "up to my ears in sewing" for a masked ball, Signora Rocco sees how disappointed Angelo looks when she tells him not to bother her for a costume. She pauses and tells him, "I think I see a rooster's tail in the red coat you're wearing!" Then she bunches up the fabric and ties his coattails with a red rag to stand out like "the proudest plumes a rooster could wish for." She also fastens a bit of frill around Angelo's neck before sending him off.

Other character traits shown: *Courage, Helpfulness, Hope, Kindness, Perseverance, Resourcefulness*

Duncan, Alice Faye. *Miss Viola and Uncle Ed Lee.* Illus. by Catherine Stock. New York: Atheneum Books for Young Readers (Simon & Schuster), 1999.

A young boy helps his two neighbors, one as neat as a pin and the other as junky as a packrat, become friends.

Courtesy: Mr. Ed Lee wants Miss Viola as a friend enough to clean up his yard so that she will feel comfortable paying him a visit. He's in a fresh bow tie and sets up a table and chairs. Then he provides a deck of playing cards and lemonade. "As only a good friend would, he poured lemonade for Miss Viola." These acts of courtesy set up a pleasant afternoon in the shade to enjoy a game of Hearts.

Other character traits shown: *Helpfulness, Honesty, Kindness, Respect, Tolerance*

Fleming, Candace. *A Big Cheese for the White House: The True Tale of a Tremendous Cheddar.* Illus. by S. D. Schindler. New York: DK Ink, 1999.

In 1801 in Cheshire, Massachusetts, Elder John Leland organizes his fellow townspeople to make a big cheese for President Jefferson, who up until that time had been forced to eat inferior cheeses.

Courtesy: It begins as an act of courtesy to the President in order to bring to his and the world's attention the town of Cheshire. The community will donate a gift of a "whopping big cheddar."

Other character traits shown: *Cooperation, Resourcefulness*

Jackson, Isaac. *Somebody's New Pajamas.* Illus. by David Soman. New York: Dial Books for Young Readers (Penguin), 1996.

When two boys from different backgrounds become friends and sleep over at each other's homes, they exchange ideas about sleepwear as well as about family life.

Courtesy: When Robert notices that Jerome has not brought along a pair of pajamas for their overnight, he assumes Jerome has forgotten them and courteously offers to loan him a pair of his own pajamas to wear to bed. Jerome is ashamed to admit that he doesn't own any pajamas and pretends that he forgot to bring them. When next they share a sleepover, it is Jerome who shares his family's customs with the houseguest.

Other character traits shown: *Honesty, Loyalty, Respect*

Little, Mimi Otley. *Yoshiko and the Foreigner.* New York: Frances Foster Books (Farrar, Straus & Giroux), 1996.

Though well-brought-up Japanese girls didn't talk to foreigners, there are exceptions, and when a young American Air Force officer mispronounces the language, Yoshiko's heart softens in a way that will change her life forever.

Courtesy: Others laugh at the young man's mistakes. He wishes to go see the Emperor's palace. But when he asks for help, the words come out wrong. First he says he is a dancing girl and is looking for a doctor. Then he says he's a boiled pepper. Finally, Yoshiko takes pity and asks him in English how she can help him. Their friendship is immediate. She explains that her father used to have fish in his garden pond. The young man brings her two goldfish he has raised himself to donate to the pond. When she explains about honoring ancestors at a home shrine with a bowl of wine and rice, he gives Yoshiko a package of the finest rice and wine he could find even though he knew he would not be welcome in her family's home. He has shown Yoshiko with these acts of courtesy that he cares for her and her heritage.

Other character traits shown: *Respect, Tolerance*

Naylor, Phyllis Reynolds. *Sweet Strawberries.* Illus. by Rosalind Charney Kaye. New York: Atheneum Books for Young Readers (Simon & Schuster), 1999.

A wife and her grumpy husband go to market.

Courtesy: The husband, who "wasn't the worst man in the world" nor is he "the nicest, either," lacks basic courtesy in his relations with society. His forbearing wife tries to help him be more understanding of life's little irritations. When she expresses her hopes that the market will have fresh strawberries, he accuses her of complaining. She replies that, "It was only a thought." When a child herds her flock of geese across the road, making him wait, he accuses her of being too impatient, always in a hurry. The wife says, "She is just a young girl." When the gate keeper is found asleep just as the pushy husband wants to go through, he accuses the boy of being lazy. The wife replies, "My dear, he is just a young lad." The husband shouts at a farmer with a wagonload of children, because the "selfish oaf" pulled into his favorite parking place. The wife says, "My dear, that farmer has . . . children needing shade." The greedy husband accuses a shopkeeper of cheating him out of a full sack of flour. "He is as stingy as they come." The wife's explanation that the merchant is old and his eyesight poor and the sack is almost full does not satisfy the husband. He thunders through life rudely until his gentle wife changes him and a latent ability to meet life courteously suddenly awakens in the husband.

Other character traits shown: *Forgiveness, Self-discipline, Tolerance*

Pomerantz, Charlotte. *You're Not My Best Friend Anymore.* Illus. by David Soman. New York: Dial Books for Young Readers (Penguin), 1998.

Molly and Ben are best friends and share everything until they have a fight.

Courtesy: Though the two are angry and don't wish to be together, there is the matter of their shared birthday celebration, a long-standing tradition. Molly acknowledges that "for the sake of the grown-ups" they "should have one party" according to custom. "After all, they buy all the birthday stuff." Out of courtesy, the two will maintain the custom everyone expects. And adhering to tradition finally brings an end to their stand-off.

Other character traits shown: *Forgiveness, Generosity*

Yorinks, Arthur. *The Flying Latke.* Illus. by William Steig with photos by Paul Colin and Arthur Yorinks. New York: Simon & Schuster, 1999.

A family argument on the first night of Chanukah results in a food fight and a flying latke that is mistaken for a flying saucer.

Courtesy: Basic courtesy is lacking in this family get-together. Inadvertently a pickle being shaken in the face of someone during an argument ends up flying in his face. That precipitates a salad bowl being dumped on the perpetrator's head. Then, it seems everyone engages in throwing their meal at one another.

Other character traits shown: *Forgiveness, Self-discipline, Tolerance*

DEDICATION. *SEE* DILIGENCE, LOYALTY

DEPENDABILITY. *SEE* RESPONSIBILITY

DILIGENCE

Use for DEDICATION, INTEGRITY
Being steadfast and careful in effort.

Atkins, Jeannine. *Mary Anning and the Sea Dragon.* Illus. by Michael Dooling. New York: Farrar, Straus & Giroux, 1999.

An account of the finding of the first entire skeleton of an ichthyosaur, an extinct sea reptile, by a 12-year-old English girl who went on to become a paleontologist.

Diligence: From the moment Mary unearths a row of teeth until the fossil is out of the ground, she steadfastly works at her task. "In one day she usually exposed an area half the size of her hand." It takes almost a full year to remove the fossil from the surrounding stone. Others try to help, but they don't have the patience. Her brother's fingers are "too rough to feel the slight impressions in the stone." So Mary works alone, "alert to changes in the stone's hardness, listening when her hammer hit the chisel. A faint sound told her to alter the chisel's angle or she risked cracking the part of the rock that she was trying to save."

Other character traits shown: *Courage, Fortitude, Perseverance*

Bogart, Jo Ellen. *Jeremiah Learns to Read.* Illus. by Laura Fernandez and Rick Jacobsen. New York: Orchard Books, 1997.

Elderly Jeremiah decides that it's finally time to learn to read.

Diligence: Jeremiah attends school with children in order to achieve his goal. He works hard first learning the letters and the sounds they make. He studies his lessons carefully and practices his writing every day. After a while, Jeremiah is putting words together and writing his own stories. Finally, he feels confident to bring home a book of poetry to read to his wife. "He read a poem about the soft petals and sweet smell of roses. He read a poem about the crashing waves at the seashore. He read a poem about love." His wife is inspired by his diligence to learn to read, too.

Other character traits shown: *Generosity, Respect*

Brenner, Barbara. *The Boy Who Loved to Draw: Benjamin West.* Illus. by Olivier Dunrea. Boston: Houghton Mifflin, 1999.

The Pennsylvania artist who begins drawing as a boy eventually becomes well known on both sides of the Atlantic.

Diligence: From the moment, as a child, he draws his baby niece, Benjamin West continues to perfect his artistry. He is never "without a pen and notebook." Other boys spend their spare time fishing or pitching horseshoes. Benjamin draws pictures, "anything his eye lit on—squirrel or cow, house or tree." Those around him soon recognize his potential. The local Lenape Indians provide him with his first paint. Then, he needs brushes. Using his fingers as suggested by brother Joseph and a quill pen as suggested by brother Samuel, or a butter paddle as suggested by sister Mary, all prove inadequate. A traveler from Philadelphia advises a "hair pencil." Benjamin West faithfully pursues this advice, much to his cat's detriment, until he finally graduates to professional level working tools.

Other character traits shown: *Helpfulness, Perseverance, Resourcefulness*

Burningham, John. *Whaddayamean.* New York: Crown, 1999.

When God sees what a mess has been made of the world, He gets two children to convince everyone to help make it the lovely place it was meant to be.

Diligence: Though the children fear, "Grownups won't listen to us," they do God's bidding and seek out the men with money, the people who said they spoke for God, the men who had the guns and the bombs, and the general population who took no notice of what was happening to the world. They carefully do God's bidding.

Other character traits shown: *Justice, Responsibility*

Charles, Donald. *Chancay and the Secret of Fire: A Peruvian Folktale.* New York: A Whitebird Book (G.P. Putnam's Sons), 1992.

In Peru, as a reward for releasing the beautiful fish he has caught, Chancay is granted his wish of finding a way to relieve his people from the cold and darkness.

Diligence: Time and again, Chancay's efforts fail in their outcome. He feels he has been sent on fool's errands, but he continues with careful effort to fulfill each of the directives he receives from the fish. None of his privations thwart his dedication to his task.

Other character traits shown: *Courage, Fortitude, Kindness, Patience, Perseverance, Prudence*

dePaola, Tomie. *The Legend of the Indian Paintbrush.* New York: G.P. Putnam's Sons, 1988.

Little Gopher follows his destiny, as revealed in a Dream-Vision, of becoming an artist for his people and eventually is able to bring the colors of the sunset down to earth.

Diligence: As expected of him, the boy paints the deeds of the warriors and the visions of the shaman. But what he really wants to paint is the setting sun with colors as bright as those in the sky. He "never gave up trying." Still, every morning when he awakes he faithfully takes out his brushes and his pots of paints and "created the stories of the People with the tools he had." Eventually, he is rewarded by being told in a night dream that because he has been "true to your gift," he "will find the colors you are seeking" to finally paint the subject of his choice.

Other character traits shown: *Hope, Loyalty, Patience, Perseverance, Responsibility, Self-discipline*

Doyle, Malachy. *Jody's Beans.* Illus. by Judith Allibone. Cambridge, MA: Candlewick Press, 1999.

From spring to fall with the help of her grandfather, Jody learns to plant, care for, harvest, prepare, and eat some runner beans.

Diligence: Jody is careful to water the beans as she waits for them to grow. She follows her grandfather's directions when it's time to thin the plants, when they make a teepee for them to climb, and later still when they pick them and prepare them to cook. She looks after the beans right into the fall when they harvest the seed beans that will grow next year.

Other character traits shown: *Cooperation, Patience*

Ernst, Lisa Campbell. *Sam Johnson and the Blue Ribbon Quilt.* New York: Lothrop, Lee & Shepard (William Morrow), 1983.

While mending the awning over the pig pen, Sam discovers that he enjoys sewing the various patches together but meets with scorn and ridicule when he asks his wife if he can join her quilting club.

Diligence: When he is rejected by the women's quilting club, Sam does not give up his desire to sew blocks of fabric together. He gathers the local men together and asks them, "Are you ready to show you can do more with your hands than plow a field?" He inspires them to enter the quilting contest themselves. The men meet diligently to work on their design. Their efforts turn out to be a beautiful flying geese pattern. They have proven that quilting is not "too delicate a job for men."

Other character traits shown: *Cooperation*

Feiffer, Jules. *I Lost My Bear.* New York: Morrow Junior Books, 1998.

When she cannot find her favorite stuffed toy, a young girl asks her mother, father, and older sister for help.

Diligence: The girl carefully follows the advice of her family. When her mother tells her to play detective to remember where last she played with the bear, she looks under her bed and in the bookcase, on the couch and under the chairs. When she still can't find her bear, she asks her father to help her. His less than helpful advice is for her to find it for herself for that "will be a lesson to you to remember where you put things." Next, she asks her sister, who, remembering a past transgression, screams at her not to play with her nail polish, before telling her to throw one of her other stuffed animals, because "sometimes it lands in the same place." But which stuffed animal? What if she loses another one? Her sister finally supplies one of hers to do the job. But throwing doesn't help. She tries many times. Not until bedtime does the missing bear show up. When the covers are pulled back, there is the bear. "Aren't I the best detective?" she surmises.

Other character traits shown: *Prudence, Self-discipline*

Gill, Janet. *Basket Weaver and Catches Many Mice.* Illus. by Yangsook Choi. New York: Alfred A. Knopf, 1999.

A little gray cat saves the day when Basket Weaver is ordered into a competition to make the perfect basket for the Emperor's newborn daughter.

Diligence: Basket Weaver's choices are not attractive. Though he would hate leaving his home to live at the palace if he wins the contest, he knows that to try to run away would result in punishment "10 times worse." And to be subjected to living in the underground mines if he loses the contest is too awful to think about. So, he toils to make the best basket he can make, only to find that he has just one marsh bird feather to decorate the basket. Still, he continues and awaits the critical eye of the Emperor.

Other character traits shown: *Generosity, Honesty, Loyalty, Responsibility*

Guarnieri, Paolo. *A Boy Named Giotto.* Illus. by Bimba Landmann. Trans. by Jonathan Galassi. New York: Farrar, Straus & Giroux, 1998.

Eight-year-old Giotto, the shepherd boy, confesses his dream of becoming an artist to the painter Cimabue, who teaches him how to make marvelous pigments from minerals, flowers, and eggs and takes him on as a pupil.

Diligence: Giotto is not very careful about looking after sheep, but he is completely engaged in his artistic efforts. While the sheep fend for themselves, he draws on any medium at hand, on "light-colored stones with a piece of charcoal, on dark stones with a piece of chalk, in the sand with a stick." By chance, he meets a famous artist, who shares with him secrets of making pigments. When, once again, he is herding sheep, he uses these marvelous colors on a large rock. Soon Giotto is taken as an apprentice and studies fresco painting with Cimabue, a pre-Renaissance master.

Other character traits shown: *Helpfulness, Patience*

Hopkinson, Deborah. *Sweet Clara and the Freedom Quilt.* Illus. by James Ransome. New York: Alfred A. Knopf, 1993.

A young slave stitches a quilt with a map pattern, which guides her and other slaves to freedom in the North.

Diligence: Clara squirrels away scraps and visits people in the Quarters, asking questions about the local topography. Then, she uses her quilting skills to carefully set the right fabric colors together to represent fields and streams and joins them with the careful stitching necessary to serve as a traveling guide. Sometimes months would go by without getting any pieces sewn into the quilt. Sometimes she must wait for the right kind of cloth. She listens and continues to put what she learns into the quilt.

Other character traits shown: *Helpfulness, Resourcefulness*

Hughes, Monica. *A Handful of Seeds.* Illus. by Luis Garay. New York: Orchard Books, 1993.

Forced into the barrio by her grandmother's death, Concepcion takes with her a legacy of chili, corn, and bean seeds and finds that they hold the key to her survival.

Diligence: Though the barrio is a difficult environment, Concepcion carefully tends her young garden. One evening when the police chase some young thieves through her garden, all her efforts are wrecked. She replants. The local barrio children help her this time. They work hard and have produce to sell so that they don't have to steal from shop owners.

Other character traits shown: *Fortitude, Generosity, Helpfulness, Perseverance, Resourcefulness*

Lasky, Kathryn. *Marven of the Great North Woods.* Illus. by Kevin Hawkes. New York: Harcourt Brace, 1997.

When his Jewish parents send him to a Minnesota logging camp to escape the influenza epidemic of 1918, 10-year-old Marven finds a special friend.

Diligence: Marven is apprehensive about leaving home and going into a harsh new environment. He is assigned two jobs at the lumberjack camp. He must keep track of wages owed the jacks, and he must make sure they all get up in the morning. The bookkeeping system is confusing and disorganized. Marven recalls that his mother always begins a task with a list. Soon he has an alphabetized system with the correct number of cord chits accounted to each lumberjack. He is just as careful in his task of getting up the late snoozers each morning. Marven becomes a valuable member of the camp.

Other character traits shown: *Empathy, Kindness*

*London, Jonathan. *Hip Cat.* Illus. by Woodleigh Hubbard. San Francisco: Chronicle Books, 1993.

A hip saxophone-playing cat goes to the big city to seek fame and fortune but finds that the top dogs own the cool clubs and sometimes you have to work in the Doggie Diner to make ends meet while learning to do what you love to do well.

Diligence: This is a blueprint for artists trying to make a name for themselves. Hip Cat finds if "cats wanted to make it they couldn't fake it." He can't make a living by working the bars that are unable to pay well, and the bars owned by the top dogs won't hire him. So, Hip Cat strengthens his skills playing out in the open for free. Diligently he plays all day, all night, for no pay. "But he kept up the fight." To earn money, he plays at tourist traps for donations and becomes a short-order cook. Finally, he feels ready to return to the nightclub circuit. Briefly, he goes back to his first bar. He has matured and blows everybody away with his horn. Pretty soon word gets around. Even top dogs pay top dollar to good musicians. The Hip Cat is playing at all the clubs. He is a success.

Other character traits shown: *Perseverance*

Martin, Jacqueline Briggs. *Snowflake Bentley*. Illus. by Mary Azarian. Boston: Houghton Mifflin, 1998. (Caldecott–1999)

A self-taught scientist photographs thousands of individual snowflakes in order to provide the world with a view of their unique formations.

Diligence: When early efforts fail to show more than the shadow of a snowflake, the scientist tries an experiment with smaller lens openings but longer exposure time. He carefully cuts away dark parts of the negative around the crystals to enhance clarity. He works in storms and in the cold every winter in order to collect the most comprehensive study of snowflake shapes the scientific world has known. Some winters he makes only a few dozen good pictures; some winters he makes hundreds. He loves the beauty of nature so much he would tie a grasshopper to a flower so as not to injure it in order to find it in the morning and photograph it dew-covered. His snowflake collection became a source of study for other scientists.

Other character traits shown: *Fortitude, Perseverance, Responsibility*

McCully, Emily Arnold. *The Ballot Box Battle*. New York: Alfred A. Knopf, 1996.

Elizabeth Cady Stanton, a famous nineteenth-century leader in the struggle for women's rights, inspires Cordelia to overcome all obstacles to carry on the fight for equality.

Diligence: Just as Mrs. Stanton is diligent about studying Greek and managing a horse as well as any boy could, in order to earn her father's respect, Cordelia is determined to learn horse-riding skills and the respect of those who do not believe girls can achieve the same accomplishments as boys. In her day, Elizabeth Cady's father never recognizes his daughter is as good as any boy. Nevertheless, she never stops fighting throughout her long life for equal rights. She paves the way for younger women to continue the work. Cordelia, too, takes her first steps when she and her horse show the local boys she can be a real horseman by jumping a four-foot fence.

Other character traits shown: *Courage, Discernment, Fortitude, Hope*

Moss, Marissa. *True Heart*. Illus. by C.F. Payne. New York: Silver Whistle (Harcourt Brace), 1999.

At the turn of the twentieth century, a young woman who works for a railroad accomplishes her yearning ambition to become an engineer when a male engineer is injured and can't drive his train.

Diligence: Though she longs to be the engineer, "while I'm waiting, I may as well grunt with you" Bee tells her friends as they load pipe, machinery, bolts of cloth, and dry goods onto train cars. "They saw I was good, and they needed my muscles." She also pays attention to the work the engineer does, asking lots of questions and sometimes coupling cars on the side tracks or driving all the way to the next station. With diligence she learns the skills and bides her time without complaint.

Other character traits shown: *Hope, Perseverance*

Nolen, Jerdine. *Raising Dragons.* Illus. by Elise Primavera. New York: Silver Whistle (Harcourt Brace), 1998.

A farmer's young daughter shares numerous adventures with the dragon that she raises from infancy.

Diligence: Even without parental involvement or support, a little girl follows through with the care of a dragon hatchling. She feeds him. "He did have a healthy appetite!" As he grows, she looks after his needs, finally taking him to the special island where dragons live. "I knew he had found the perfect place to be."

Other character traits shown: *Cooperation, Kindness, Loyalty, Responsibility*

Pilkey, Dav. *The Paperboy.* New York: Orchard Books, 1996.

The paperboy and his dog enjoy the quiet of the early morning as they go about their rounds.

Diligence: It is very early, but the paperboy leaves his comfortable bed and carefully tends to his task. He dresses warmly. Then, he puts rubber bands around each paper and puts each in his bag. He continues on his rounds until all are delivered. Only then does he return home to finish his night's sleep.

Other character traits shown: *Responsibility*

Robbins, Ruth. *Baboushka and the Three Kings.* Illus. by Nicolas Sidjakov. Adapted from a Russian folktale. Boston: Houghton Mifflin, 1960. (Caldecott–1961)

When three kings ask an old woman to join them in their search for the Christ Child, she declines because her day's work is not finished. In vain, she tries to follow them the next day.

Diligence: The woman's supper is lonely. She has time to think about the three kings' mission and decides, after all, that she does want to join them and bring gifts to the Christ Child. Legend says she diligently searches for the three kings every year and, meanwhile, passes out her gifts, intended to honor the Child, to all children she meets along the way.

Other character traits shown: *Generosity*

Rylant, Cynthia. *Mr. Griggs' Work.* Illus. by Julie Downing. New York: Orchard Books (Franklin Watts), 1989.

Mr. Griggs so loves his work at the post office that he thinks of it all the time, and everything reminds him of it.

Diligence: On the day that Mr. Griggs gets sick, he feels very bad that "someone else was taking care of his post office. Someone else was sorting through Mr. Griggs' letters, someone else was putting pennies and nickels in Mr. Griggs' drawer, someone else was taping up the corners of one of Mr. Griggs' ragged parcels." On the day that Mr. Griggs returns to work, he "ran his fingers over his old letter scale, he sniffed at his stamp drawer, he lined up his meters and punchers, and he glanced lovingly at all the brass mailboxes lining the walls." In all the world, no postman is as diligent as Mr. Griggs.

Other character traits shown: *Responsibility*

*Stewart, Sarah. *The Gardener.* Illus. by David Small. New York: Farrar, Straus & Giroux, 1997.

A series of letters relates what happens when Lydia Grace goes to live with her Uncle Jim in the city but takes her love for gardening with her.

Diligence: The gray dingy cityscape that Lydia Grace enters is slowly transformed. There are window boxes that can be put to use! She receives gifts of bulbs, seeds, and young sprouts from the family back home and finds a whole roof to work with. Lydia Grace never stops in her efforts to create gardening beauty and in coaxing a smile from Uncle Jim.

Other character traits shown: *Discernment, Generosity, Patience*

Yacowitz, Caryn. *Pumpkin Fiesta.* Illus. by Joe Cepeda. New York: HarperCollins, 1998.

Hoping to win a prize for the best pumpkin at the fiesta, Foolish Fernando tries to copy Old Juana's successful gardening techniques, but without really watching to see how much effort and love she puts into her work.

Diligence: Fernando fails to notice the real reasons Juana's pumpkins thrive. She prepares the soil and plants only three seeds per mound. She carefully waters each plant. She diligently removes insect pests. Fernando attributes her success to unrelated matters, such as the clothes she wears, the sound of her voice, and the presence of her mule. He is not diligent about the things the plants really require.

Other character traits shown: *Forgiveness, Helpfulness, Honesty*

DISCERNMENT

Use for UNDERSTANDING
Ability to comprehend, analyze, distinguish, judge, or interpret with keen insight.

Anholt, Laurence. *Degas and the Little Dancer: A Story about Edgar Degas.* Hauppauge, NY: Barron's Educational Series, 1996.

Because Marie helps her poor parents by modeling for an ill-tempered artist, she becomes a famous ballerina, but not in the way she had dreamed.

Discernment: Mr. Degas has a reputation for being bad tempered, always muttering and cursing at his models. Marie is forced into his company when she must pose for him to earn money for her dance lessons. She begins to understand his fear of losing his eyesight. An artist's eyes are as precious as a dancer's legs, she decides. Could his anger be the result of his failing eyesight? He must work in clay now, because he can no longer see the details of painting on canvas. In sympathy for him, she unties her hair ribbon and gives it to him as a sign that she feels his sense of loss.

Other character traits shown: *Cooperation, Empathy, Forgiveness*

Arnold, Katya. *Duck, Duck, Goose?* New York: Holiday House, 1997.

Based on a story by Vladimir Grigorievich Suteev, a goose who envies the attributes of other birds learns to appreciate her own qualities.

Discernment: The goose thinks that being a goose is too common. After trading all her body parts with other birds that she admires, she discovers her new self has no defenses against the fox. "Goose tried to fly, but Crow's wings were too small. She tried to run, but Peacock's tail got caught in a bush. She tried to swim, but she could not." Her fellow geese rush to her assistance. They peck and bite and pinch Fox from all sides until he lets Goose go. "Now I know what I need to do," she says. Before long she has traded back all her original parts. It is true she now "looked like every other goose. Only she was smarter, kinder, and happier."

Other character traits shown: *Prudence*

Arnold, Marsha Diane. *The Chicken Salad Club.* Illus. by Julie Downing. New York: Dial Books for Young Readers (Penguin), 1998.

Nathaniel's great-grandfather, who is 100 years old, loves to tell stories from his past but seeks someone to join him with a new batch of stories.

Discernment: A planned meeting for "The Century Club" is a failure. No one shows up. Nathaniel tries another plan. He puts an ad in the "Confidentials" section of the newspaper. He asks for a 100-year-old "fiery, fit" storyteller to share with same. He interviews the applicant and brings his grandfather. "Greatpaw, I've been thinking, maybe you don't need lots of storytellers to share stories with you. Maybe just one would do." And she did do just fine.

Other character traits shown: *Helpfulness, Resourcefulness*

Babbitt, Natalie. *Bub or the Very Best Thing.* New York: Michael di Capua Books (HarperCollins), 1994.

Nobody except the little prince himself knows what is the very best thing for the prince.

Discernment: The queen and king ask all those they come in contact with what is the best thing for his highness, the prince. They receive a variety of answers. But it is the cook's little daughter who discerns what is the very best thing. She asks the child. He tells her, "Bub." The prince's parents still aren't sure, because they don't know what it means. But the cook's daughter believes she does and tells her mother, "The Prince was right, Mama. Love is the very best thing."

Other character traits shown: *Helpfulness*

Bunting, Eve. *On Call Back Mountain.* Illus. by Barry Moser. Blue Sky Press (Scholastic), 1997.

Two brothers encounter a lone wolf on the spot where each summer night they had signaled their friend the fire watchman.

Discernment: Bosco the old long-legged fire watchman is sometimes known as the lone wolf, living all summer up on the mountain by himself. After he dies there is sadness. One night when the brothers are looking up at the mountain where Bosco used to signal them, they notice on a ledge a lone wolf, the first since the forest fire of several years ago. "That wolf had the longest, skinniest legs." Then they remind themselves, "Remember what Bosco said? Any creature that loves the wilderness will always come back?" The boys understand that maybe Bosco himself has somehow come back to them in this special way.

Other character traits shown: *Respect*

Bunting, Eve. *Smoky Night.* Illus. by David Diaz. New York: Harcourt Brace, 1994. (Caldecott–1995).

When the Los Angeles riots break out in the streets of their neighborhood, a young boy and his mother learn the value of getting along with others no matter their background or nationality.

Discernment: Until the fire that drove everyone into the street, there was ethnic separation in the neighborhood. Two frightened cats, who had a history of fighting, suddenly drank milk out of the same dish together. The boy's mother is amazed. "I thought those two didn't like each other." The boy explains, "They probably didn't know each other before; now they do." This bit of wisdom momentarily causes everyone to quietly think about their own attitudes. They will begin to get acquainted.

Other character traits shown: *Courtesy, Forgiveness*

Conrad, Pam. *The Rooster's Gift.* Illus. by Eric Beddows. New York: Laura Geringer Book (HarperCollins), 1996.

Rooster thinks his Gift is making the sun rise, until one morning when the sun rises without him.

Discernment: Rooster and Smallest Hen realize that on the day the sun comes up before Rooster calls it, that he is not responsible for making the sun rise. Anybody could call it, even Smallest Hen. But when she tries, the sound is not the same. What they discern is that even though both know when the sun is about to rise, Smallest Hen "can't announce it quite the same." Rooster realizes that the way he does it is really the Gift. "Not quite like pulling the sun out of the night, but a Gift nonetheless."

Other character traits shown: *Loyalty*

Davol, Marguerite W. *The Paper Dragon.* Illus. by Robert Sabuda. Atheneum Books for Young Readers (Simon & Schuster), 1997.

The power of the artist's vision and the ever-sustaining nature of love are brought together when a humble artist agrees to confront the terrifying dragon that threatens to destroy his village.

Discernment: Mi Fei unrolls one scroll after another in search for a clue to solving the dragon's three tasks. To make "fire wrapped in paper" he finds a celebration of light, the Festival of the First Full Moon, which he had painted on one of the paper scrolls. He cuts the paper, folding and fashioning it into a lantern into which he places a lit candle. Then he must "bring wind captured by paper." Again, he refers to the scrolls and finds a hero's rescue of a beautiful princess lost in the hot desert. This time he cuts the paper and folds and fashions it into a fan. Mi Fei's understanding of the history in his art enables him to know how to accomplish the dragon's tasks.

Other character traits shown: *Courage, Fortitude, Responsibility*

*Frasier, Debra. Out of the Ocean. New York: Harcourt Brace, 1998.

A young girl and her mother walk along the beach and marvel at the treasures cast up by the sea and the wonders of the world around them.

Discernment: Before she understands the nature of the ocean's true gifts, the girl has a limited comprehension of its treasures. She misunderstands what her mother means when she tells her, "You can ask the ocean to bring you something." She narrowly focuses on the fresh surprises each day that wash up on the beach, things like floating glass balls, pelican feathers, and abandoned rubber rafts. Eventually, as she watches and listens to her mother, she realizes the ocean's gifts are the regular grandeur of nature's dependability. It is easy to take for granted the magnificence of the rising sun each morning or the cloudbursts of rain, or the sweep of the tides. The girl comes to feel the importance of remembering to look.

Other character traits shown: *Empathy, Respect*

George, Jean Craighead. *Snow Bear.* Illus by Wendell Minor. New York: Hyperion Books for Children, 1999.

Bessie and a polar bear cub named Snow Bear play on the ice, while her older brother and Snow Bear's mother watch to make sure everyone is safe.

Discernment: A mother bear and a child's older brother watch as cub and child play together. They decide there is no danger in this association and do not interfere. They also assess each other's danger level and decide that each is more concerned about their young one's safety than in threatening harm and so choose not to move against each other. But, when a male polar bear erupts on the scene, the mother bear immedidcately slides down the ice to resuce her cub, and big brother raises his gun. The young ones both see the enormous male bear and decide to "run back the way they came." The male adult polar bear smells big brother's gun. he decides to slide back quickly into the water, knowing about the danger of guns. One day the Eskimo child will have learned the wisdom of the Arctic, and Snow Bear will grow so big no male bear will hurt him.

Other character traits shown: *Empathy, Patience, Prudence, Respect*

Goode, Diane. *Mama's Perfect Present.* New York: Dutton Children's Books (Penguin Putnam), 1996.

Led by the intrepid Zaza, their dachshund, two children troop all over Paris looking for the perfect gift for their mama, oblivious to the havoc Zaza causes along the way.

Discernment: Flowers would make a nice gift, but they "make some people's eyes water." Especially after Zaza knocks down beautiful expensive arrangements. Mama loves red. A sensational new dress would be a nice gift. But that "dress was too sensational. Mama doesn't like to show off." Especially after Zaza gets tangled in all the lush fabric. Maybe Mama would like a "sweet little songbird. Mama loves music." But "those birds were very noisy. They might disturb the neighbors." Especially after Zaza opened the cage doors. At the shoe store they consider, and reject, buying Mama shoes. Mama might fall down in such high heeled shoes as happens to a shop customer when Zaza is present. It is getting late, and they haven't yet found the perfect present for Mama. As they watch a man painting, they get an idea. Soon they have purchased some paint and paper. "I think this is just what we need. I knew we would find something." Soon they are in a Neo-Impressionist Georges Seurat-like park painting the perfect picture for Mama's birthday gift.

Other character traits shown: *Perseverance, Prudence*

*Gregory, Valiska. *Through the Mickle Woods.* Illus. by Barry Moser. Boston: Little, Brown & Co., 1992.

After his wife's death, a grieving king journeys to an old bear's cave in the mickle (thick) woods, where he hears three stories that help him go on living.

Discernment: When the king finally allows himself to remember his wife, he can share with others the terrible loss and thereby lessen his own burden. At last he can

hear the morning bells, "how merrily they ring."
Other character traits shown: *Empathy, Forgiveness, Generosity, Helpfulness, Hope, Kindness, Perseverance*

*Hoestlandt, Jo. *Star of Fear, Star of Hope.* Illus. by Johanna Kang. Trans. by Mark Polizzotti. New York: Walker & Co., 1995.

Nine-year-old Helen is confused by the disappearance of her Jewish friend during the German occupation of Paris.

Discernment: Helen lives an ordinary life, which is one day brushed by what her mother calls "the wickedness of some and the weakness of others." Her friend Lydia comes to her birthday party. During the evening, strangers come knocking on the door seeking sanctuary. When Lydia sees the star on their coats, very much like the one she must wear, she discerns danger for herself and her family. At once she senses she must return home. Helen's father obliges and takes her. Helen is hurt that her friend wants to leave. The family never sees Lydia again. Later, Helen sees a long line of people outside her bedroom window, all wearing the yellow star and all being marched away. Through the long years she has feared for the friend she treated shabbily when she was too young to discern the mortal danger Jews faced during that period of history.
Other character traits shown: *Courage, Forgiveness, Hope*

*Littlesugar, Amy. *Jonkonnu: A Story from the Sketchbook of Winslow Homer.* Illus. by Ian Schoenherr. New York: Philomel Books, 1997.

A young southern girl tells of the time Winslow Homer came to town to paint pictures and defied the town by portraying the lives of the poor Black people who lived down the red clay road.

Discernment: Cilla has none of her elders' prejudice, and she is curious about what can be down the red clay road that holds the famous painter's attention. After secretly following him for many days and watching him at work, she discerns that Mr. Homer is interested in the Black holiday called Jonkonnu. Maybe, she reasons, the Blacks are still lonesome for Jamaica and the music of the islands. Maybe they told Mr. Homer how they weren't allowed to march in the Fourth of July parade. Maybe dressing up for their old freedom holiday from slavery days "filled them with hopin' and wishin'." Cilla comes to understand that an artist "lights up the darkness" with his fresh perspective of everyday life.
Other character traits shown: *Respect*

McCully, Emily Arnold. *The Ballot Box Battle.* New York: Alfred A. Knopf, 1996.

Elizabeth Cady Stanton, a famous nineteenth-century leader in the struggle for women's rights, inspires Cordelia to overcome all obstacles to carry on the fight for equality.

Discernment: Mrs. Stanton's civil disobedience embarrasses Cordelia, who cannot understand why she wants to vote. "All that was done by men." But when Mrs. Stanton goes to the polling site and invites Cordelia to follow on Jule, Mrs. Stanton's horse, she cannot refuse. The woman's rude treatment by the polling officials shames Cordelia. Then, her brother yells at her to "Go on home where you belong." He chants, "No votes for pea-brained females!" Cordelia begins to sense what has kept Mrs. Stanton fighting all these years. "Something inside Cordelia snapped." She discerns that she must prove herself the equal of any boy and begins, finally, to understand a little of Mrs. Stanton's determination to fight for equality.

Other character traits shown: *Courage, Diligence, Fortitude, Hope*

Perkins, Lynn Rae. *Clouds for Dinner.* Greenwillow (William Morrow), 1997.

It takes a visit to her aunt's house to make Janet appreciate her parents and their unusual way of looking at everything.

Discernment: Janet is irritated that sometimes her family would eat apples and bits of cheese or muffins and call it dinner. And her parents are forever saying things like, "Look at those gorgeous pink clouds." But Janet knows they're only pink because the sun is on them. Or her father might offer her a bite of melon and say, "Taste this. It's like eating a cloud." Their house is on a hill with 87 steps to climb, because up there was a "view." If Janet complains, her parents say, "Keeps us young." Janet would like her family to live a sensible life like her aunt and uncle. When she is invited to visit the aunt and uncle, she is happy to go. It's nice to do regular things like bathing the dogs, playing basketball with her cousins, watching a soccer game, sitting down together for a big, noisy meal. But when she awakens early it is dark outside except for a wedge of pink at the edge of the sky. The pink light turns slowly to apricot, turquoise, lavender. Janet wants to tell someone about it. She tries to tell her aunt at breakfast, but her aunt doesn't understand. Later, she tells her mother, who immediately understands. "Wow, what a lucky thing to see. I wish I'd been there." Janet says she wishes her mother had been there, too. She has discerned how special her own family is and appreciates their qualities.

Other character traits shown: *Respect*

Rathmann, Peggy. *Officer Buckle and Gloria.* New York: G.P. Putnam's Sons, 1995. (Caldecott–1996)

The children at Napville Elementary School always ignore Officer Buckle's safety tips, until a police dog named Gloria accompanies him when he gives his safety speeches.

Discernment: Officer Buckle is pleased that his audience is responding better to his safety tips now that Gloria goes with him to the programs. He gets a note saying, "You and Gloria make a good team." It is signed, "Your friend, Claire." But when he finally sees a videotape of himself and Gloria, he understands that behind his back she has been pantomiming his tips and garnering audience appreciation. At first he is angry and refuses to make any more presentations. "Nobody looks at me, anyway!" But when Gloria goes by herself, she sits onstage looking lonely. "Then she fell asleep. So did the audience." Officer Buckle gets another note from his friend Claire. It said, "Gloria missed you yesterday!" Officer Buckle finally discerns his best safety tip yet—"Always stick with your buddy!"

Other character traits shown: *Cooperation*

Say, Allen. *Allison.* Boston: Walter Lorraine Books (Houghton Mifflin), 1997.

When Allison realizes that she looks more like her favorite doll than like her parents, she comes to terms with this unwelcome discovery with the help of a stray cat.

Discernment: Allison is devastated to discern that she looks like her doll, but not her own parents. She studies the other children at Day Care and their parents. They seem to belong together. Didn't Allison's real mother and father want her? She is angry. But when a stray cat comes to her, wanting a home, Allison makes a connection between her history and the needs of this animal. He, too, doesn't have a mommy or daddy. If he chews her toys she won't get angry. He wants a home. He helps Allison come to terms with her adoption. She had been selected when she needed a home just like she is selecting this cat that needs a home. Home is being in a family surrounded with love.

Other character traits shown: *Empathy, Generosity, Tolerance*

Say, Allen. *Emma's Rug.* Boston: Walter Lorraine Books (Houghton Mifflin), 1996.

A young artist finds that her creativity comes from within when the rug that she had always relied upon for inspiration is destroyed.

Discernment: No one can figure out why Emma always stares at her throw rug. When they ask Emma where she gets her ideas to draw, she replies that she just copies them. Soon she wins prizes for her drawings. But all that comes to an end when her mother washes the rug. Emma is horrified. It's clean, but there are no longer any pictures in it. She rips off all her drawings and paintings from her walls and throws away her crayons, paints, and awards. "All afternoon Emma sat in her empty room." Then from the corner of her eye she thinks she sees something move. Soon, Emma is seeing wonderful things to draw again. She realizes that she doesn't need the rug for her imagination to capture visions. These marvelous visions that she "copies" are with her always wherever she looks. "She saw the eyes watching her and then the faces of creatures all around. She knew them from before. She had thought she would never see them again."

*Say, Allen. *Grandfather's Journey.* Boston: Houghton Mifflin, 1993. (Caldecott–1994)

A Japanese American man recounts his grandfather's journey to America, which he later also undertakes and experiences the same feelings of being torn by a love for two different countries.

Discernment: The man, like his grandfather, lives his youth in Japan and then travels to America. He discerns that "the moment I am in one country, I am homesick for the other." And, now, as an adult, "I think I know my grandfather now."

Other character traits shown: *Empathy*

*Stewart, Sarah. *The Gardener.* Illus. by David Small. New York: Farrar, Straus & Giroux, 1997.

A series of letters relates what happens when Lydia Grace goes to live with her Uncle Jim in the city but takes her love for gardening with her.

Discernment: The dingy gray city is soon brightened with Lydia Grace's flower seeds and bulbs. The window boxes bloom. So does the roof above her apartment. Her infectious gardening spreads to others. But she is having trouble getting Uncle Jim to smile. When she plans a grand surprise Fourth of July party for him on the beautiful roof, he responds with his own talents. A few days later he closes the bakery early and sends her to the roof. He appears with the most amazing cake she ever saw covered in frosting decorated flowers. Lydia Grace observes, "I truly believe that cake equals one thousand smiles." She understands that Uncle Jim's "smile" is in his actions.

Other character traits shown: *Diligence, Generosity, Patience*

Yorinks, Arthur. *Hey, Al.* Illus. by Richard Egielski. New York: Farrar, Straus & Giroux, 1986. (Caldecott–1987)

Al, a janitor, and Eddie, his faithful dog, live together in a crowded single room where they are dissatisfied with their lot until a mysterious bird offers them a change of fortune that soon makes them long for their old life.

Discernment: At first the good life on the island the bird takes them to makes them think, "a guy could live like this forever." As memories of their old life slowly fade, they think this is ecstasy. "But ripe fruit soon spoils." They begin to find themselves turning into birds. They must act quickly if they are to retain their own identities. "We've got to get out of here." Suddenly the old life back in their humble apartment doesn't seem so bad. "I'd rather mop floors!" They discern that "Paradise lost is sometimes Heaven found."

Other character traits shown: *Courage*

EMPATHY

Use for COMPASSION

Ability to share in another's emotions, thoughts, or feelings in order to better understand the person.

Ackerman, Karen. *Song and Dance Man.* Illus. by Stephen Gammell. New York: Alfred A. Knopf, 1988. (Caldecott–1989)

Grandpa demonstrates for his visiting grandchildren some of the songs, dances, and jokes he performed when he was a vaudeville entertainer.

Empathy: The children are an appreciative audience. They clap wildly and howl with laughter. They can see how much Grandpa enjoys his own act. Reverently he refolds his costume and rewraps his tap shoes in the shammy cloth and puts everything away carefully in the storage trunk. They tell him they wish they could have seen them in the good old days. He says he "wouldn't trade a million good old days for the days he spends with us." But the children watch as he turns off the attic light and "glances back up the stairs." They "wonder how much he really misses that time on the vaudeville stage, when he was a song and dance man." They sense how important that time was and what a loss it is to him.

Anholt, Laurence. *Degas and the Little Dancer: A Story about Edgar Degas.* Hauppauge, NY: Barron's Educational Series, 1996.

Because Marie helps her poor parents by modeling for an ill-tempered artist, she becomes a famous ballerina, but not in the way she had dreamed.

Empathy: Need has thrown Marie and the painter together. She must earn the money he is willing to pay in order to remain a dancing student. But his angry manner is a severe trial. One day she politely tells him, as it was getting late, that she must go home soon. "My father is ill and my family will be worried." He explodes in fury. No one will worry about *him* he shouts. "I have only my work for company and now even my eyesight is leaving me." He explains that to an artist, his eyes are as precious as a dancer's legs. Now he must work with clay instead of paint, because he can hardly see what he is doing anymore. "Suddenly Marie felt very sad for the bad-tempered artist. Could this be why he was always angry?" She, who knows she has lost her chance to become a great dancer, feels the terrible loss facing the artist.

Other character traits shown: *Cooperation, Discernment, Forgiveness*

Borden, Louise. *A. Lincoln and Me.* Illus. by Ted Lewin. New York: Scholastic Press, 1999.

A boy who is tall for his age and awkward learns about the great possibilities for his future by studying the life of the person who shares his birth date.

Empathy: The boy remembers Lincoln when his big, clumsy feet never see "wet paint" signs until it's too late. The kids call him "Butterfeet." Then the teacher shares some of the names Lincoln was called, like "gorilla" and "backwoods hick." The boy thinks about Lincoln when he's line leader at school, when he's reading a good book he doesn't want to end, when he's singing in the back row a head above his friends, and when he's making jokes that cause kids to laugh. He understands Lincoln and feels he has Lincoln's potential.

Other character traits shown: *Respect*

Bruchac, Joseph. *The Great Ball Game: A Muskogee Story.* Illus. by Susan L. Roth. New York: Dial Books for Young Readers, 1994.

Bat, who has both wings and teeth, plays an important part in a game between the Birds and the Animals to decide which group is better.

Empathy: Neither team really wanted Bat on their side. But, after Bat tells Bear, the Animals' leader, that "The Birds laughed at me and would not accept me," Bear feels empathy for Bat's hurt feelings and takes pity on him. He tells Bat that even though he is not very big, "sometimes even the small ones can help." Because of his understanding kindness, Bear's team wins the game.

Other character traits shown: *Helpfulness, Kindness, Patience, Respect, Responsibility, Tolerance*

Bunting, Eve. *Summer Wheels.* Illus. by Thomas B. Allen. New York: Harcourt Brace Jovanovich, 1992.

The Bicycle Man fixes up old bicycles and offers both his friendship and the use of the bikes to the neighborhood kids.

Empathy: The Bicycle Man appears to be allowing himself to be taken advantage of by the tough boy who checks out bikes and doesn't even sign his real name. Still, the Man keeps letting him check out bikes. The Bicycle Man recognizes this fatherless boy's need to become involved in the shop work. One of the shop's rules says that if something breaks when you have it, you have to come to the shop and fix it. The tough boy makes sure there is always something to fix. He smashes up one of the bikes he checks out. The Bicycle Man knows why the boy did what he did, and why he deliberately checked out a bike that needed fixing anyway. The Bicycle Man and the boy decide to fix it the next day. A relationship has begun, cemented by the fact that the tough boy brings the Man a jelly donut, his favorite treat, along with the trashed bike.

Other character traits shown: *Courage, Forgiveness, Generosity, Justice, Kindness, Responsibility, Respect, Tolerance*

Bunting, Eve. *Train to Somewhere.* Illus. by Ronald Himler. New York: Clarion Books (Houghton Mifflin), 1996.

In the late 1800s, Marianne travels westward on the Orphan Train with other children who hope to be placed with caring families.

Empathy: Miss Randolph, who accompanies the children from St. Christopher's, knows their fears and that their placements might not all end happily. She worries when people appear concerned that "they took all the biggest boys" at earlier stops. When Marianne is the last child and is afraid at the last stop, Miss Randolph comfortingly holds her hand as they get down together from the train. There is only one couple waiting. They are old. Marianne is disappointed. When the waiting woman begins, but does not finish asking if Marianne is all that's left, she knows that she is also not what they had wanted. The woman is holding a wooden toy meant for a boy, but Marianne sees a softness in her face. "Somehow this woman understands about me, how it felt that nobody wanted me, even though I was waiting inside myself for my mother to come. Somehow she understands the hurt." The woman admits she had wanted a boy. Quickly her husband adds, "But we like girls fine." They recognize in each other that, "Sometimes what you get turns out to be better than what you wanted in the first place." There is acceptance as well as understanding in this new family relationship.

Other character traits shown: *Courage, Hope, Kindness, Patience, Prudence, Respect*

Chocolate, Debbi. *The Piano Man.* Illus. by Eric Velasquez. New York: Walker & Co., 1998.

A young African American girl recalls the life story of her grandfather, who performed in vaudeville and played piano for the silent movies.

Empathy: The girl's mother enjoyed her father's accompaniment to the silent movie Saturday matinees. She buys the very piano he used to play at the old Rialto Theater. And now, the granddaughter watches old cowboy movies on television with the volume turned low while her grandfather plays piano to accompany the story action.

Other character traits shown: *Resourcefulness*

De Felice, Cynthia. *Willy's Silly Grandma.* Illus. by Shelley Jackson. New York: Orchard Books, 1997.

Willy doesn't believe in any of his grandmother's superstitions, until he ventures down by the Big Swamp one dark night and comes to realize how smart Grandma is.

Empathy: Willy feels certain that Grandma's superstitious beliefs are all untrue. She tells him not to go walking by the Big Swamp at night: "Something could give you a fearsome fright." Willy confidently believes the swamp warning is as silly as are her other warnings. But the longer he walks the more frightened he becomes. Mist like a chilly finger touches his back. Noises and sounds and bright lights could signal the bogeyman. Willy runs to his Grandma, and she understands just what he's feeling and explains. The wind made the moans and groans. The willow branches were the fingers reaching for him. The flickering lights were the stars. And, though it surely does seem like the bogeyman is there, there is no bogeyman.

Other character traits shown: *Helpfulness*

Fleming, Candace. *The Hatmaker's Sign: A Story Told by Benjamin Franklin.* Illus. by Robert Andrew Parker. New York: Orchard Books, 1998.

To heal the hurt pride of Thomas Jefferson as Congress makes changes to his Declaration of Independence, Benjamin Franklin tells his friend the story of a hatmaker and his sign.

Empathy: Jefferson does not like his writing being edited. In like manner, the hatmaker in Franklin's story prepared words that he thought would make a good sign message for his new shop: "John Thompson, hatmaker. Fashionable hats sold inside for ready money." Everyone he meets cuts out a word or phrase. His wife doesn't think he needs "for ready money." He won't be selling them for anything else. The Reverend Brimstone recommended he drop his name from the sign. Customers won't care who sells them as long as they're good hats. Someone else wants "fashionable" removed. He surely wouldn't sell unfashionable hats. And, of course, the merchandise is inside, not being sold outside on a street cart. Soon, there are no words on the sign. The sign painter looks at an empty piece of paper. Poor Mr. Thompson doesn't know what the sign should say; "No one had thought it was perfect enough." Then the sign maker suggests exactly the wording John Thompson had originally planned. Ben Franklin tells Jefferson, "If the public is going to read it, you can be sure they will want to change it."

Other character traits shown: *Fortitude, Helpfulness*

*Frasier, Debra. *Out of the Ocean.* New York: Harcourt Brace, 1998.

A young girl and her mother walk along the beach and marvel at the treasures cast up by the sea and the wonders of the world around them.

Empathy: Mother and daughter share an appreciation for the "gifts" of the ocean. Each day they "help each other look" so that they do not miss either the small things, like a fisherman's glass ball washed up on the beach overnight, or the big things like the morning's rising sun or the replenishing rain of a cloudburst. Mutually, they felt the importance of acknowledging these grand wonders and, together, make certain they will never forget to see them.

Other character traits shown: *Respect*

George, Jean Craighead. *Snow Bear.* Illus. by Wendell Minor. New York: Hyperion Books for Children, 1999.

Bessie and a polar bear cub named Snow Bear play on the ice, while her older brother and Snow Bear's mother watch to make sure everyone is safe.

Empathy: Two watchful pairs of eyes keep track of the bear cub and the child as they innocently play together. The cub's mother senses that the human child will cause her baby no harm. The older brother knows that the cub will not hurt his sister. The joy the little ones display together pleases both their instincts of child welfare. Neither the mother bear nor the big brother will interfere as the two young ones slide down the ice, dig a snow cave and sit side by side. The adult bear and big brother also watch each other and understand each other. Powerful bears can kill. Gun-carrying humans can kill. They respect each other's abilities. But, each willingly tolerates the other in behalf of their mutural interests. Neither will display aggression so long as their young one is not threatened.

Other character traits shown: *Patience, Prudence, Discernment, Respect*

Goble, Paul. *Love Flute.* New York: Bradbury Press (Macmillan), 1992.

A gift to a shy young man from the birds and animals helps him to express his love to a beautiful girl.

Empathy: The animals in this story recognize that the young man cannot express with words his feelings for the girl. They fashion a means for him to say just the right things. They make songs. He listens. He copies them closely with the flute they gave him. But he also weaves their tunes into his own melodies. The girl meant to receive his music responds as though the songs "were speaking to her."

Other character traits shown: *Helpfulness*

Goffstein, M.B. *Our Snowman.* New York: Harper & Row, 1986.

The snowman two children build looks so lonely when night comes that a little girl and her father go out to make a snow woman to keep him company.

Empathy: So sad are the children as the night darkens and the snowman is alone that they even think, "We never should have made him." Father knows how the children feel. He goes out with the porch light on to help the older sister create a companion for the lonely snowman. Back inside, little brother is glad. "Now they each have company," he says.

Other character traits shown: *Kindness*

*Gregory, Valiska. *Through the Mickle Woods.* Illus. by Barry Moser. Boston: Little, Brown & Co., 1992.

After his wife's death, a grieving king journeys to an old bear's cave in the mickle (thick) woods, where he hears three stories that help him go on living.

Empathy: The boy knows the king is in a depression because of the death of his wife, and refuses to be comforted. He coaxes the king out of his funk by taking him on a journey and, on the way, pointing out the good things that still exist in the king's world. "The snow looks like sugar in the moonlight." And he draws out the king's memories of his wife by sharing some of his own. "She told me I didn't have to be scared, because she would always take care of me.". . ."The queen used to tell me stories." The bear tells stories to show his understanding of the way the king is suffering. The boy and bear help the king accept that life must have both the "woe and gladness." And, "so it will forever be." As their journey ends, the king has accepted closure. He can again hear the morning bells and mark "how merrily they ring."

Other character traits shown: *Discernment, Forgiveness, Generosity, Helpfulness, Hope, Kindness, Perseverance*

Hazen, Barbara Shook. *Wally, the Worry-Warthog.* Illus. by Janet Stevens. New York: Clarion Books (Houghton Mifflin), 1990

Wally worries about everything but discovers that the terrifying Wilberforce has as many fears as he does.

Empathy: Once the two warthogs share their fears, they begin to understand each other much better. Wally keeps his hands in his pocket not to hide something dangerous; instead, he carries rocks in his pocket in case he needs to throw them at the trolls under the bridge. Wilberforce wears gloves not to hide long claws but to cover his bitten nails. Once they understand each others' fears, they become good friends.

Other character traits shown: *Courage, Honesty*

Hendry, Diana. *Back Soon.* Illus. by Carol Thompson. New York: BridgeWater Books (Troll Associates), 1995.

A kitten does not like it when his mother goes away without him, but after enjoying some time by himself, he understands why she does it.

Empathy: Herbert tries to show his mother how scary it can feel to hear "Back Soon!" and not know how long she will be gone. At first she doesn't understand, then he tells her he is going into the garden and will be back soon. He has such a good time he forgets his promise to come back inside soon. This time mother notices his absence and calls to him. Herbert hears the worry in her voice and rushes back. Together they agree that "it's very nice having some time to yourself," as long as each always remembers to come back. Both mother and son learn something about the way the other one feels hearing, "Back soon!"

Other character traits shown: *Respect, Tolerance*

Hest, Amy. *Mabel Dancing.* Illus. By Christine Davenier. Cambridge, MA: Candlewick Press, 2000.

Mabel doesn't want to go to sleep while Mama and Papa are having a dance party downstairs.

Empathy: Mabel watches her parents dress in their special party clothes in preparation for the dance. Later, she enjoys hearing the rhythmical music downstairs. Here she is all alone and bored in bed in the dark. Soon it occurs to her that she, too, could dance. She sweeps a blanket around her shoulders and finds herself spinning and leaping down among the party guests. Her parents are not mortified. They do not scold. They do recognize her need to experience a bit of the magic. Her father asks, "Shall we dance?" Together they lift her in a dancing-embrace and swish off across the ballroom. Then she is danced back upstairs to bed, satisfied to receive blown kisses and clapping from the party guests.

Hest, Amy. *The Purple Coat.* Illus. by Amy Schwartz. New York: Four Winds Press, 1986.

Despite her mother's reminder that "navy blue is what you always get," Gabby begs her tailor grandfather to make her a beautiful purple fall coat.

Empathy: Grandpa has a dilemma. His granddaughter's and his daughter's wishes do not match. He would like to please his granddaughter without angering her mother. He rationalizes the child's desire for the outlandish coat by recalling that, "Your mother wanted a tangerine-colored dress once, when she was six or so." The grandfather reminds his daughter of the tangerine dress. He makes a coat that will be reversible so that the child can turn the coat from purple to navy.

Other character traits shown: *Courage, Prudence, Tolerance*

Koller, Jackie French. *No Such Thing.* Illus. by Betsy Lewin. Honesdale, PA: Boyds Mills Press, 1997.

A boy is afraid there is a monster under his bed, until he meets a monster who is afraid there is a boy above his bed.

Empathy: When the boy and the monster find out that neither wishes to eat the other, they begin to realize how much they have in common. Their respective mothers don't believe them when they try to tell them about the monster under the bed and the boy on top of the ed. They come up with a plan to show their mothers how mistaken they are. The monster crawls on top of the bed and the boy crawls under the bed. Then they each proceed to call their Mommies to "come quick."

Lasky, Kathryn. *Marven of the Great North Woods.* Illus. by Kevin Hawkes. New York: Harcourt Brace, 1997.

When his Jewish parents send him to a Minnesota logging camp to escape the influenza epidemic of 1918, 10-year-old Marven finds a special friend.

Empathy: Marven learns his job well and by the second week is ready to explore the countryside. He puts on his skis and follows the sled paths into the woods. He hears something like a growl. Tree branches tremble, and a shower of snow falls. Marven fears a grizzly bear is in the tree. He tries to stand as still as possible and cries silently, thinking he will never see his family again. Then a huge shadow slides from behind the trees. It is Jean Louis with his ax, marking trees to cut next season. The big man sees tears on Marven's cheek. "You miss your mama? Your papa?" Marven admits this is true and then says, "I thought you were a grizzly bear!" Jean Louis, admittedly a very big man, laughs at the thought of his being mistaken for a large bear. More snow falls from the tree, "for his laugh was as powerful as his ax." Together they join the lumberjacks returning to camp in the evening. The big man understands the boy's loneliness, and they are soon companions.

Other character traits shown: *Diligence, Kindness*

Lears, Laurie. *Ian's Walk: A Story about Autism.* Illus. by Karen Ritz. Morton Grove, IL: Albert Whitman, 1998.

A young girl realizes how much she cares about her autistic brother when he gets lost at a park.

Empathy: When the girl realizes her brother, Ian, is lost, she squeezes her eyes shut and tries to think like him. He loves bells. And that is where she finds him, "making the big gong move back and forth" at the bell in the park. She is so relieved he's safe that she is happy to walk home the way he likes to do it. He lies on the walkway lining up stones in a straight row, while she stands guard, so no one steps on his fingers. He sniffs the post office bricks as much as he wants. She waits patiently when he stops to listen to something no one else can hear. And, she, too, stares at the fan in the diner until she's dizzy. Her reward is a flash of a smile from Ian when they return home, and she tells him it was a good walk.

Other character traits shown: Loyalty, Patience

Moyer, Marshall M. *Rollo Bones, Canine Hypnotist.* Berkeley, CA: Tricycle Press, 1998.

Although he has won worldwide success with his ability to hypnotize human beings, Rollo, a soulful yellow dog, takes a stand for what he really wants to be and do.

Empathy: Money and fame has gone to his handler's head. The star of the act, Rollo, does not feel he's being treated respectfully. He's warned to hurry, pay attention, not make a mess, stop shedding, and many more admonishments. Rollo misses walks, late-night snacks, laundry day tugs-of-war, and hugs and biscuits. After a short walkabout to think things over, he decides to "work things out" with the Brain. He hypnotizes the Amazing Brain and orders him to fetch, bring biscuits and bones, and to sit, roll over, and beg. Now, the Amazing Brain understands how it feels to be performing. So, they "blow off the gig at the Palace and take a vacation." They are soon back to romping in the grass just like the old days.

Other character traits shown: *Respect*

Rylant, Cynthia. *The Bird House.* Illus. by Barry Moser. New York: Blue Sky Press (Scholastic), 1998.

A young girl without family is fascinated by a house that draws birds around it.

Empathy: When the old woman and the girl are finally brought together by the efforts of the birds, "the old woman talked with her, all through the night." There is understanding and acceptance. And "since that time, the girl has always lived with the old woman." Together they tend flowers or pumpkins or just take a walk.

Other character traits shown: *Generosity, Kindness*

*Say, Allen. *Grandfather's Journey.* Boston: Houghton Mifflin, 1993.

A Japanese American man recounts his grandfather's journey to America, which he later also undertakes, and experiences the same feelings of being torn by a love for two different countries.

Empathy: As a young man, the author's grandfather comes to America. He settles in California among mountains and rivers that are as beautiful as those in Japan. He returns to Japan to bring his bride back to California. They have a baby girl, whom he tells all about Japan. He surrounds himself with songbirds but cannot forget his homeland. When the daughter is nearly grown they return to Japan, and he finds things just as he remembered. There the daughter marries and the author is born. His grandfather tells him stories about California. "He raised warblers and silvereyes, but he could not forget the mountains and rivers of California." As a nearly grown young man, the author does visit his grandfather's adopted land. He stays on and also has a daughter. But he, too, misses the mountains and rivers of his childhood. He returns now and then to Japan. "The funny thing is, the moment I am in one country, I am homesick for the other. I think I know my grandfather now. I miss him very much."

Other character traits shown: *Discernment*

*Say, Allen. *Tea with Milk*. Boston: Walter Lorraine Books (Houghton Mifflin), 1999.

After growing up near San Francisco, a young Japanese woman returns with her parents to their native Japan, but she feels foreign and out of place.

Empathy: Masako has graduated from high school in America and does not wish to repeat her education in Japan. She sees no use to studying calligraphy and tea ceremony and flower arranging. And she certainly does not want the services of a matchmaker. She would rather "have a turtle than a husband." But when she meets a young man who is also transplanted from his homeland, they find they share an understanding of feeling like foreigners, and they realize that a home is wherever they live together.

Other character traits shown: *Fortitude, Perseverance*

Schertle, Alice. *Down the Road*. Illus. by E.B. Lewis. New York: Browndeer Press (Harcourt Brace), 1995

Hetty is very careful with the eggs she has bought on her first trip to the store, but she runs into trouble when she stops to pick apples.

Empathy: Papa finds a forlorn Hetty up in an apple tree and the basket of broken eggs on the ground. He surmises her shame and disappointment in her failure to complete her errand. He saves her dignity by remarking that "You climbed up into the tree to think it over." Then he climbs up with her and they eat apples together. No mention is made of the lost eggs. When Mama arrives a bit later, she notes the broken eggs. "I'm waiting for twelve beautiful eggs, and what do I find? Shells!" Hetty explains about trying to pick some apples to take home with the eggs. Papa quickly adds, "Fine, sweet apples" to set for Hetty's Mama the joking tone he feels fits the situation. Mama quickly catches on and plays along. "Well, well," she says, "just look at the two big birds in the apple tree." Papa whistles like a magpie. Hetty, who is feeling a little better, contributes "Tweet, tweet, tweet." And pretty soon there are three big birds up in the apple tree. Mama puts her arm around Hetty and tells her, "I'd almost forgotten how lovely the world looks from a tree." Hetty knows her accident is forgiven.

Other character traits shown: *Forgiveness, Honesty, Kindness, Responsibility*

Stanley, Diane. *The Gentleman and the Kitchen Maid.* Illus. by Dennis Nolan. New York: Dial Books for Young Readers, 1994.

When two paintings hanging across from each other in a museum fall in love, a resourceful art student finds a way to reunite the lovers.

Empathy: The art student notices that as she paints the young gentleman's eyes and follows his "longing gaze across the room," she sees 'The Kitchen Maid.' "Oh, I see what you're looking at!" she says, adding, "She is lovely. Just perfect for you!" But when she comes to finish her painting the next day, she looks from her copy to the gentleman and back again. Something is different. "So sad!" she murmured. "Not like yesterday…" When she follows his gaze across the room, she understands why. The kitchen maid has been moved away. In her place is a painting of fruit and goblets. The art student knows what to do to make the young man happy. She paints the kitchen maid into her copy of the young gentleman. The two art pieces are at last together.

Other character traits shown: *Helpfulness*

Steig, William. *Pete's a Pizza.* New York: Michael Di Capua Books (HarperCollins), 1998.

Pete is in a bad mood because it rains when he wants to play ball with his friends, so his father makes him into a pizza.

Empathy: His father recognizes Pete needs distraction. He invents an elaborate game to cheer him up. He lays him down on the kitchen table and begins kneading the dough, stretching it this way and that, whirling the dough and twirling it up in the air. "Oil" (water) is applied, "flour" (talcum powder), "tomatoes" (checkers). Then his mother enters into the game. No tomatoes his mother says; she doesn't like tomatoes on her pizza. So, the "tomatoes" are swept away and "cheese" (bits of paper) is added instead. Maybe some pepperoni. Pete laughs when he's tickled. He is placed in the oven (the couch). When he's "nice and hot" he is placed on the table to be sliced. The pizza runs away. The pizza-maker chases him. The pizza gets captured and hugged. Then, the sun comes out. The pizza decides to go look for his friends.

Other character traits shown: *Resourcefulness*

Stiles, Martha Bennett. *Island Magic.* Illus. by Daniel San Souci. New York: Atheneum Books for Young Readers (Simon & Schuster), 1999.

When Grandad comes to live with David and his family on their island, he and David enjoy sharing the wonders of the natural world.

Empathy: David senses that his grandfather misses the cows he had on his Wisconsin farm. David remembers liking to hear all the things that Grandad told him about the farm. So, he tries to relate the new island life to the familiar things Grandad understood with dairy farming. All of Grandad's cows were named, so as they feed the wild geese that shelter on the island, they name them together and feed them corn, just like the cows were fed. The fog that drifts over the island reminds Grandad of cows drifting along eating grass. And the damp fog on their hands was like a cow's breath. Even the shape of the fog seemed to "split into three pieces, one big and two little." The big one browsed up the yard; the two little ones followed. "Like a cow with twins." David is rewarded at last when Grandad finally tells him, "I like living here where you can tell me things."

Yolen, Jane. *Owl Moon.* Illus. by John Schoenherr. New York: Philomel Books, 1987. (Caldecott–1988)

On a winter's night under a full moon, a father and daughter trek into the woods to see the Great Horned Owl.

Empathy: The daughter understands the momentous nature of her outing with her father. "I had been waiting to go owling with Pa for a long, long time." Their first efforts bring no answering call from an owl. Pa shrugs and she shrugs. Her brothers have all said "sometimes there's an owl and sometimes there isn't." She doesn't allow the discomfort of cold to cause her to break the silence they must maintain. "If you go owling you have to be quiet and make your own heat." The wait and icy cold make the appearance of the owl all that more rewarding. The answering owl call to Pa's call makes them smile together. It flies right over them. They watch silently "with the heat of all those words we had not spoken." Pa's flashlight "caught the owl just as it was landing on a branch." Then, "for one minute, three minutes, maybe even a hundred minutes, we stared at one another." When the owl at last pumps its great wings and leaves without a sound, they can talk out loud. "But I was a shadow as we walked home." There is no need to break the spell of their evening with words.

Other character traits shown: *Hope, Self-discipline*

Zagwyn, Deborah Turney. *Turtle Spring.* Berkeley, CA: Tricycle Press, 1998.

The changing seasons bring surprises to Clee, including a new baby brother and a turtle.

Empathy: Clee's relatives come with hellos and goodbyes, but "her new red-faced baby brother stays for good." From their "orbits around the crib," the relatives insist, "Aren't you the lucky one?" Clee feels "like a lost moon." But one of the visitors understands how she feels, Uncle Fishtank Hal. He comes bearing a gift, but it's not for the baby. He brings a turtle and whispers, "She ain't a gift for a baby. She's too big and would only pinch it."

Other character traits shown: *Responsibility*

FAIRNESS. *SEE* JUSTICE

FORGIVENESS

To give up resentment against and stop being angry with someone so that it is possible to pardon or release another for an offense.

Anholt, Laurence. *Degas and the Little Dancer: A Story about Edgar Degas.* Hauppauge, NY: Barron's Educational Series, 1996.

Because Marie helps her poor parents by modeling for an ill-tempered artist, she becomes a famous ballerina, but not in the way she had dreamed.

Forgiveness: When Marie learns that the painter is losing his eyesight, she understands why he is angry and short-tempered. She tells him she is sorry for his loss and no longer holds his behavior against him. She, too, will not become a great dancer. Her family has no more money for her to continue lessons. Mr. Degas surprises her by saying he is also sorry for her loss. But there is the sculpture, the best work he has done. "Thank you, my little dancer." Marie gives him her peach-colored hair ribbon, then she puts away her dancing clothes. At the art show Marie sees, "Degas had dressed the sculpture in real clothes. In her hair was the peach-colored ribbon."

Other character traits shown: *Cooperation, Discernment, Empathy*

Bang, Molly. *When Sophie Gets Angry—Really, Really Angry.* New York: Blue Sky Press (Scholastic), 1999.

When Sophie gets angry, she runs out and climbs her favorite tree.

Forgiveness: After kicking, screaming, and roaring her anger, Sophie is mad enough to explode like a volcano. Then she runs and runs until she can't run anymore. She is in the woods. There are rocks, trees, ferns. She climbs a special old beech tree and feels the breeze blow her hair. She watches the water and the waves. "The wide world comforts her." Sophie is calm and ready to go home. Her house smells good. It's warm. Everyone is glad she's home. Sophie is no longer angry with her family.

Other character traits shown: *Self-discipline*

Bunting, Eve. *Smoky Night.* Illus. by David Diaz. New York: Harcourt Brace, 1994. (Caldecott–1995)

When the Los Angeles riots break out in the streets of their neighborhoods, a young boy and his mother learn the value of getting along with others no matter their background or nationality.

Forgiveness: Two cats, who formerly fought, show their human owners how to resolve old ethnic tensions. When a fireman finds the cats during the fire, they are hiding together under a stairway. The fireman says, "They were so scared they were holding paws." When the two cats drink together out of the same bowl, people are amazed. "I thought those two didn't like each other." But the cats have obviously forgiven each other their past transgressions. In the face of a serious outside threat, they are joining forces. He notes that when he strokes the big old mean cat that had fought with his cat, it purrs, just like his cat purrs. The people take a lesson from the animals and invite each other to visit when things settle down.

Other character traits shown: *Courtesy, Discernment*

Bunting, Eve. *So Far From the Sea.* Illus. by Chris K. Soentpiet. New York: Clarion Books (Houghton Mifflin), 1998.

When seven-year-old Laura and her family visit Grandfather's grave at the Manzanar War Relocation Center, the Japanese American child leaves behind a special symbol.

Forgiveness: Laura feels keenly the injustice of her parents' families being locked up in detention camps. But, her father reminds her, "It wasn't fair that Japan attacked this country either." He tells her, "It was more than thirty years ago. We have to put it behind us and move on." Laura still feels it was wrong. Finally, her father tells her, "Sometimes in the end there is no right or wrong; it is just a thing that happened long years ago. A thing that cannot be changed." Laying the cub scout neckerchief at her grandfather's grave is an act of both respect and forgiveness.

Other character traits shown: *Justice, Respect*

Bunting, Eve. *Summer Wheels.* Illus. by Thomas B. Allen. New York: Harcourt Brace Jovanovich, 1992.

The Bicycle Man fixes up old bicycles and offers both his friendship and the use of the bikes to the neighborhood kids.

Forgiveness: The Bicycle Man does not seem to mind that the tough boy checks out bicycles without signing his real name and fails to return them. He doesn't even get angry when the boy trashes one of the bikes on purpose. All he remarks is, "It's bad, but it can be fixed." He is more interested in getting the boy into the shop to begin working with him. That's because the Man understands something about this grouchy boy. And Lawrence finally sees it too, "I think he wanted to hang out with the Man but he was too cool to ask." Lawrence rightly guesses that "there is something the Man likes even more than his bikes." He likes kids. He can forgive a little attitude if it means that a boy gets the attention he needs.

Other character traits shown: *Courage, Empathy, Generosity, Justice, Kindness, Respect, Responsibility, Tolerance*

Cooper, Helen. *Pumpkin Soup.* New York: Farrar, Straus & Giroux, 1998.

Cat and Squirrel come to blows with Duck in arguing about who will perform what duty in preparing their pumpkin soup, and nearly lose Duck's friendship when he decides to leave them.

Forgiveness: Duck runs away but has no place to go. Cat and Squirrel are so happy to have Duck back safe and sound they forgive his messiness when (because he is only trying to help) he stirs the soup "so fast that it slopped right out of the pot."

Other character traits shown: *Cooperation, Generosity*

Cummings, Pat. *Carousel.* New York: Bradbury Press (Macmillan), 1994.

Alex's father misses her birthday party, and everything is spoiled, until the animals on his gift of a tiny carousel come to life.

Forgiveness: Alex tries to be nice to her aunts, but can't hide her true feelings. And when her mother tells her that her father wanted her to have the gift carousel "just in case he didn't get back from his trip in time," Alex believes he knew all along that he wouldn't be home. She is furious and ends up being sent to bed without birthday cake. The next morning she awakens to find her father home. He tells her he, too, was angry when his plane was late. But the thought of coming home made him happy. Suddenly, Alex gives up her anger and resentment. She forgives his absence, and even the gifts from her aunts seem so much better in the morning, now that all is back to normal.

Daly, Niki. *Jamela's Dress.* New York: Farrar, Straus & Giroux, 1999.

Jamela gets in trouble when she takes the material intended for a new dress for Mama, parades it in the street, and allows it to become dirty and torn.

Forgiveness: Mama can't think what she will wear to the wedding now that the fabric is ruined. "Mama was so upset that she couldn't even look at Jamela." Everyone "felt sorry for Mama and cross with Jamela. Even Jamela was cross with Jamela." Until Archie shares the big bucks from his prize-winning photograph of Jamela proudly wearing the fabric the day it got ruined. "When Mama saw it, she gave Jamela a big hug." Together they wash the new fabric and play games together while it dries on the line. Then Mama shows Jamela how to fold it, just as she had learned to do when she was a little girl. Jamela's act of carelessness is forgiven, and Mama remembers that a daughter needs her attention.

Other character traits shown: *Generosity, Self-discipline*

*Gregory, Valiska. *Through the Mickle Woods.* Illus. by Barry Moser. Boston: Little, Brown & Co., 1992.

After his wife's death, a grieving king journeys to an old bear's cave in the mickle (thick) woods, where he hears three stories that help him go on living.

Forgiveness: A king cannot get on with his life until he "forgives" his wife for dying and leaving him bereft. Even when offered a seat by a warm stove, he sits "rigid and dark" near the door. "I am used to the cold." He rejects any means to ease his suffering. It takes a very large, venerable bear, who growls menacingly when he attempts to avoid hearing the lessons he needs. Finally, his stubbornness breached, the king tentatively begins to forgive the forces that have removed his beloved, so that he is able to express love again. He forgives himself for not being able to prevent her death. "Do you remember how she loved all things?" he says to the boy. And then the king cradles the boy in his arms "as through the long night they slept, their dreams entwined like holly branches in a wreath."

Other character traits shown: *Discernment, Empathy, Generosity, Helpfulness, Hope, Kindness, Perseverance*

*Hoestlandt, Jo. *Star of Fear, Star of Hope.* Illus. by Johanna Kang. Trans. by Mark Polizzotti. New York: Walker & Co., 1995.

Nine-year-old Helen is confused by the disappearance of her Jewish friend during the German occupation of Paris.

Forgiveness: Helen feels angry and hurt because it seemed her best friend Lydia doesn't want to stay the night of her birthday party with her. Why does she suddenly ask to go home? Helen shouts, "I don't care! You're not my friend anymore!" Slowly, she begins over the next few days to better understand the fear that had caused Lydia to act as she did. But now it is too late. Lydia is gone, perhaps is among the long line of people with yellow stars on their coats being marched away. And Helen is sorry that she could not tell her "she was my best friend." She hopes that over the years Lydia lived to become a grandma somewhere in the world. Mostly, she wants her friend to know she forgave her those long years ago and that, in turn, she, too, was forgiven.

Other character traits shown: *Courage, Discernment, Hope*

Lorbiecki, Marybeth. *Sister Anne's Hands.* Illus. by K. Wendy Popp. New York: Dial Books for Young Readers (Penguin), 1998.

Seven-year-old Anna has her first encounter with racism in the 1960s when an African American nun comes to teach at her parochial school.

Forgiveness: Though personally hurt and angered by the cruelty of a student who sailed a paper airplane at her with a racist poem printed on it, Sister Anne "seemed to warm up to us a little." After shocking them with wall pictures of pain and suffering experienced by black people, she tells them, "I'd rather open my door enough to let everyone in than risk slamming it shut on God's big toe." Anna realizes, "It was clear. Sister Anne was giving us another chance." Sister Anne forgives their youthful ignorance and goes on to provide the best teaching experience any of them had known.

Other character traits shown: *Courage, Respect, Tolerance*

Naylor, Phyllis Reynolds. *Sweet Strawberries.* Illus. by Rosalind Charney Kaye. New York: Atheneum Books for Young Readers (Simon & Schuster), 1999.

A wife and her grumpy husband go to market.

Forgiveness: The last straw is the man's refusal to purchase the strawberries his wife is looking forward to tasting. She cries out that he is "the most stingy, selfish, lazy, impatient, complaining man I have ever seen!" Then she climbs into the wagon and refuses to speak to him the rest of the way home. This is so unlike her behavior, he assumes she must have been upset by all the "unpleasant" people they met on market day. He calls out to the girl, moving her geese across the road, "Fine day to you, Miss!" instead of shouting angrily at her to get out of the way. When he finds the gatekeeper asleep at the job, he sings loudly to awaken him instead of shouting about his laziness. And, when someone takes his favorite parking spot, he calmly announces that "one tree is as good as another" and parks somewhere else. Then, he buys "the largest basket of strawberries his wife had ever seen," because he doesn't want her upset again. He is astonished how much "everyone has so changed in only a week." And the woman, "who had been his wife for a good long time, just smiled and said nothing. Her husband wasn't the nicest man in the world, she knew, but he wasn't the worst one either."

Other character traits shown: *Courtesy, Self-discipline, Tolerance*

Pomerantz, Charlotte. *You're Not My Best Friend Anymore.* Illus. by David Soman. New York: Dial Books for Young Readers (Penguin), 1998.

Molly and Ben are best friends and share everything until they have a fight.

Forgiveness: Despite a bitter argument about the kind of camping tent to buy, the two agree to go through with a shared birthday celebration they have every year to please the grownups. By evening's end, after sharing with each other a special gift, they become reconciled. As they lay in their new sleeping bags together out under the tree, Molly asks Ben if he's asleep. He says he is. She replies, "Me too." Then he says that, "it's a good thing we are both asleep," because he is "willing to have a pup tent." And she replies, " I was just thinking that an umbrella tent is OK with me." They will talk about it tomorrow "when we are both awake." They have forgiven each other.

Other character traits shown: *Courtesy, Generosity*

Schertle, Alice. *Down the Road.* Illus. by E.B. Lewis. New York: Browndeer Press (Harcourt Brace), 1995.

Hetty is very careful with the eggs she has bought on her first trip to the store, but she runs into trouble when she stops to pick apples.

Forgiveness: When Hetty doesn't return when expected Papa, "whose sharp eyes never missed a thing" goes looking for her. He finds her up in a tree and the broken eggs at the tree base. Then, instead of harshly judging her for failing to bring the eggs home safely, "his face wrinkled into a smile" and he says, "There's no finer place than an apple tree to think things over." Mama comes along. Hetty tells her the eggs were broken when she tried to pick some apples. Papa, who is now also sitting up in the tree, adds quickly, "Fine, sweet apples." Mama takes in the scene and pronounces, "Just look at the two big birds in the apple tree." "Pretty soon there were three big birds in the apple tree." Mama puts her arm around Hetty. "I'd almost forgotten how lovely the world looks from a tree," she says. They leave with the basket full of apples and have apple pie for breakfast instead of fried eggs.

Other character traits shown: *Empathy, Honesty, Kindness, Responsibility*

*Schur, Maxine Rose. The Peddler's Gift. Illus. by Kimberly Bulcken Root. New York: Dial Books for Young Readers (Penguin), 1999.

A young boy in rural Russia at the turn of the twentieth century learns that appearances are often deceiving after he steals a dreidel.

Forgiveness: The boy is amazed that the peddler, who knows he stole the toy, is not angry with him for the theft. The peddler explains the reason why. "You were angry at yourself. That is what really mattered." Though the peddler leaves a gift of the dreidel at the boy's door on Hanukkah, the real gift was his forgiveness.

Other character traits shown: *Courage, Honesty, Kindness, Respect, Responsibility*

Sendak, Maurice. *Where the Wild Things Are.* New York: HarperCollins, 1963. (Caldecott–1964)

When Max sasses his mother after a wild day of play, he is banned to his room without supper but happily finds it on his table, still warm, after a wild dream of living as king of the wild things.

Forgiveness: Max is angry with his mother for scolding him. She calls him "wild thing" when he is sent to bed without supper. In his dream he is king of all the wild things. He plays happily with them and he exercises his power to send them to bed without their supper. But he is lonely and "wanted to be where someone loved him best of all." So, he gives up being king of where the wild things are. When he finds himself back in his room, he discovers that his mother, too, has forgiven his indiscretion. There is his supper waiting for him, and it's still hot.

Yacowitz, Caryn. *Pumpkin Fiesta.* Illus. by Joe Cepeda. New York: HarperCollins, 1998.

Hoping to win a prize for the best pumpkin at the fiesta, Foolish Fernando tries to copy Old Juana's successful gardening techniques, but without really watching to see how much effort and love she puts into her work.

Forgiveness: Because Fernando failed to learn how to grow big pumpkins by covertly watching her tend her crop, he steals Juana's pumpkins. When his deed is found out at the fiesta, he admits, "I was wrong to take your pumpkins." She quickly forgives him and then tells him if he really wants to grow beautiful pumpkins to "pay attention and do as I say." She shares her skills with a grateful Fernando.
Other character traits shown: *Diligence, Helpfulness, Honesty*

Yorinks, Arthur. *The Flying Latke.* Illus. by William Steig. Photos by Paul Colin and Arthur Yorinks. New York: Simon & Schuster, 1999.

A family argument on the first night of Chanukah results in a food fight and a flying latke that is mistaken for a flying saucer.
Forgiveness: The family fighting seems to be endless, first flinging food around, then arguments. Only after eight days of being cooped up together and only after the flying saucer potato pancake returns home and lands on the plate can the family give up its animosity with one another. One of the combatants admits to the possibility of being wrong. The two original fighters forgive each other. Peace is restored for a happy Chanukah.
Other character traits shown: *Courtesy, Self-discipline, Tolerance*

FORTITUDE

Use for DEDICATION, INTEGRITY
Strength to bear patiently misfortune or difficulty with courage.

Atkins, Jeannine. *Mary Anning and the Sea Dragon.* Illus. by Michael Dooling. New York: Farrar, Straus & Giroux, 1999.

An account of the finding of the first entire skeleton of an ichthyosaur, an extinct sea reptile, by a 12-year-old English girl who went on to become a paleontologist.

Fortitude: The task she has set for herself is not easy. She must be careful of the tide in order not to be caught between the cliffs and the cold, fierce sea. She works with red, chapped hands all winter. Progress is slow, sometimes only an area half the size of her hand is uncovered in one day's effort. She works alone when others lose patience or find the work too dull. She stays with the job until nearly a year later it is complete.
Other character traits shown: *Courage, Diligence, Perseverance*

Auch, Mary Jane. *Bantam of the Opera.* New York: Holiday House, 1997.

Luigi the rooster wins fame and fortune when the star of the Cosmopolitan Opera Company and his understudy both come down with chicken pox on the same night.

Fortitude: Luigi's desire to sing is ridiculed and his life is threatened. But he continues to practice his heart's desire. He tries to hum so the barnyard head rooster won't hear his crowing. He sneaks a ride to the city to hear the opera he enjoys listening to on the radio. At the opera house he is threatened by a jealous tenor and ridiculed by a laughing audience. No hardship stops Luigi from his goal. His fortitude pays off. "Luigi kept singing, in spite of his broken heart." Eventually, the audience is won over as his "sweet voice soared above the jeers."

Other character traits shown: *Courage, Helpfulness, Hope, Perseverance*

Charles, Donald. *Chancay and the Secret of Fire: A Peruvian Folktale.* New York: A Whitebird Book (G.P. Putnam's Sons), 1992

In Peru, as a reward for releasing the beautiful fish he has caught, Chancay is granted his wish of finding a way to relieve his people from the cold and darkness.

Fortitude: Chancay must prove the knowledge of fire is a secret he has earned as well as a secret to be learned. In his search, he finds the strength to bear his difficulties and discouragement with courage. He survives lightning bolts, dangerous insects, animals, and the rage of the sun until he finishes his task.

Other character traits shown: *Courage, Diligence, Kindness, Patience, Perseverance, Prudence*

*Cutler, Jane. *The Cello of Mr. O.* Illus. by Greg Couch. New York: Dutton Children's Books (Penguin Putnam), 1999.

When a concert cellist plays in the square for his neighbors in a war-besieged city, his priceless instrument is destroyed by a mortar shell, but he finds the courage to return the next day to perform with a harmonica.

Fortitude: Mr. O sits in the war-torn street, risking great personal harm. But playing to "feed" the frightened residents is his gift toward the war effort. And, when even his cello is destroyed, he still returns to the street every afternoon to give a harmonica concert instead.

Other character traits shown: *Courage, Generosity, Hope, Perseverance, Resourcefulness*

Davol, Marguerite W. *The Paper Dragon.* Illus. by Robert Sabuda. Atheneum Books for Young Readers (Simon & Schuster), 1997.

The power of the artist's vision and the ever-sustaining nature of love are brought together when a humble artist agrees to confront the terrifying dragon that threatens to destroy his village.

Fortitude: Mi Fei thinks he is no hero. He is "only a simple artist who paints the past." All he knows of heroic deeds has been told to him by others. But he cannot refuse the villagers' plea for help. He faces the dragon. He finds he must perform three tasks, or he will be devoured. Under great stress he studies his precious paintings for ideas that might help him meet the dragon's challenge. Twice he succeeds, but the scrolls do not help him on the last and most difficult task (finding the strongest thing in the world), and he is on his own. He picks up his brush and paints people of his village as he remembers them and finishes with a poem about love. It turns out to be sufficient to answer the dragon's last task. The strongest thing is Love.

Other character traits shown: *Courage, Discernment, Responsibility*

Fleming, Candace. *The Hatmaker's Sign: A Story Told by Benjamin Franklin.* Illus. by Robert Andrew Parker. New York: Orchard Books, 1998.

To heal the hurt pride of Thomas Jefferson as Congress makes changes to his Declaration of Independence, Benjamin Franklin tells his friend the story of a hatmaker and his sign.

Fortitude: Franklin recognizes Jefferson's disappointment and tells a story. A hatmaker writes the message he believes should be on his sign. But everyone whom he sees wants to cut a word or phrase. In the end, there are no words at all. "No matter what you write, or how well you write it, if the public is going to read it, you can be sure they will want to change it." Jefferson ponders the story, and faces the changes made with fortitude. "Then sighing with acceptance, he listened as the Congress argued over the words that rang, the sentences that sang, and the paragraphs that flowed with truth."

Other character traits shown: *Empathy, Helpfulness*

*Hearne, Betsy. *Seven Brave Women.* Illus. by Bethanne Andersen. New York: Greenwillow (William Morrow), 1997.

A young girl recounts the brave exploits of her female ancestors, beginning with her great-great-great-grandmother, who came to America in a wooden sailboat.

Fortitude: Each woman faces with courage difficult circumstances. The first woman has a year-old baby and a toddler with her on the sailboat, and she is pregnant. Food is bad; it is hard to sleep; she is seasick. The second woman travels to Ohio in a covered wagon. She works hard on a farm, keeps a herd of sheep and weaves blankets from their wool. She makes a quilt "so big it covers my bedroom wall" with "stitches so small you can hardly see them." She makes candles and soap, bread and butter, jam and "everything else that now you can buy at the store." She makes medicine from herbs and helps neighbors have their babies. "Once a sharp knife slipped and cut her finger open. She used the other hand to sew it up with a needle and thread." Each of these women, in her own era of time, face life with fortitude.

Other character traits shown: *Resourcefulness, Respect*

Hughes, Monica. *A Handful of Seeds.* Illus. by Luis Garay. New York: Orchard Books, 1993.

Forced into the barrio by her grandmother's death, Concepcion takes with her a legacy of chili, corn, and bean seeds and finds that they hold the key to her survival.

Fortitude: Concepcion wants to show the other children who live in the barrio that they don't need to steal food to survive. She is determined to raise and sell vegetables. Using only the broken handle of a kettle, she digs the hard ground and plants and waters her seeds. They grow well, but the police, in search of thieves, chase the children right through the garden patch. The plants are ruined. Concepcion begins all over again. This time the children help her. Eventually, their efforts pay off. They have produced something to sell and ended reliance upon theft to stay alive.

Other character traits shown: *Diligence, Generosity, Helpfulness, Perseverance, Resourcefulness*

Jones, Rebecca C. *Down at the Bottom of the Deep Dark Sea.* Illus. by Virginia Wright-Frierson. New York: Bradbury Press (Macmillan), 1991.

Andrew hates water and intends to stay away from the ocean while at the beach, but he changes his mind when he needs water for the sand city he is building.

Fortitude: As his sand city grows, Andrew is loath to abandon it just because the friend who has been bringing him wet sand must leave. He doesn't want his skyscraper to crumble. Perhaps he can hurry to the water's edge and fill his bucket before the roaring water swallows him up. He hurries to the edge many times to bring back wet sand. Sometimes his toes or his heels get wet. Once he falls down, but he continues. As difficult as the task is, he persists despite the unpredictable water that could take him "down to the bottom of the deep dark sea."

Other character traits shown: *Courage*

Joosse, Barbara. *Lewis & Papa: Adventure on the Santa Fe Trail.* Illus. by Jon Van Zyle. San Francisco: Chronicle Books, 1998.

While accompanying his father on the wagon train along the Santa Fe Trail, Lewis discovers what it is to be a man.

Fortitude: There are dark clouds of grasshoppers and great, choking clouds of dust, and they miss Mama, but they continue on. A herd of buffalo threaten to stampede through the wagons. Gun shots cause them to swerve, and they continue along the trail. Nothing stops the moving train, not rivers to wade across, not hot dry deserts, not even the loss of their ox.

Other character traits shown: *Courage, Honesty, Responsibility*

Lee, Milly. *Nim and the War Effort.* Illus. by Yangsook Choi. New York: Frances Foster Books (Farrar, Straus & Giroux), 1997.

Nim and a schoolmate are rivals in a contest to collect newspapers for the war effort until the final day when it seems Nim can't possibly win.

Fortitude: Nim's grandfather has set obligations for her which will use up the time she could have been collecting papers after school. Her competitor has stolen some papers that her aunt had set aside for her to collect. She has canvassed Chinatown and now must go afield to Nob Hill. Despite delays and setbacks, she continues toward her goal.

Other character traits shown: *Loyalty, Perseverance, Resourcefulness, Self-discipline*

Lied, Kate. *Potato: A Tale from the Great Depression.* Illus. by Lisa Campbell Ernst. Washington, DC: National Geographic Society, 1997.

During the Depression, a family seeking work finds employment for two weeks digging potatoes in Idaho.

Fortitude: When the farm is lost, Dorothy's father works in a coal mine. When the coal mine closes, they borrow a car and money for gas to go to Idaho to pick potatoes. For two weeks they live in tents. By day they dig potatoes for the company. By night they pick up leftover potatoes for themselves in burlap sacks that cost a penny each. At the end of the harvest, they make room for their potato sacks on the car and come back home to trade the potatoes for other things they needed.

Other character traits shown: *Resourcefulness, Perseverance*

Martin, Jacqueline Briggs. *Snowflake Bentley.* Illus. by Mary Azarian. Boston: Houghton Mifflin, 1998. (Caldecott–1999)

A self-taught scientist photographs thousands of individual snowflakes in order to provide the world with a view of their unique formations.

Fortitude: The scientist must work from start to finish in the cold. Even the shed where the photos are taken must be unheated in order not to melt the specimens. Some of his collections clump together and can't be photographed. Others break apart before an individual snowflake can be used, and sometimes they evaporate before he has time to work. If he twitches a muscle when he is holding a snow crystal on his long wooden pick, it can be damaged. And he can only work during snowstorms. The scientist works for years, hoping always for the most perfect photograph. Some winters he takes very few successful pictures. Local residents scoff at his work. They don't want to buy pictures of snowflakes; they have enough of the real thing! He never earns enough money from snowflake photo sales to support his work, but he continues to take the photos for the rest of his life.

Other character traits shown: *Diligence, Perseverance, Responsibility*

McCully, Emily Arnold. *The Ballot Box Battle.* New York: Alfred A. Knopf, 1996.

Elizabeth Cady Stanton, famous nineteenth-century leader in the struggle for women's rights, inspires Cordelia to overcome all obstacles to carry on the fight for equality.

Fortitude: Mrs. Stanton tries to be all that her brother is so that her father will say she is as good as any boy. Despite her efforts to learn Greek and master horse management, her father never acknowledges her achievements for herself. As Mrs. Stanton tells Cordelia, "You will fight because you are a girl!" Tirelessly Mrs. Stanton works to get women the right to vote and suffers taunts and ridicule when she makes "a spectacle" of herself at polling sites. Cordelia only begins to understand the value of her efforts when she is goaded by her brother to prove her horse riding skills. She is not sure she can ever be as brave as Mrs. Stanton, but she will begin by showing her accomplishments first on a horse.

Other character traits shown: *Courage, Diligence, Discernment, Hope*

Provensen, Alice, and Martin Provensen. *The Glorious Flight: Across the Channel with Louis Blériot, July 25, 1909.* New York: Viking Press, 1983. (Caldecott– 1984)

A man whose fascination with flying machines produces the Blériot XI, crosses the English Cannel in 37 minutes in the early 1900s.

Fortitude: Beginning with a machine too small to sit in, then going through many renditions, Louis works to develop his flying skills and his airplane design. His early designs are a motorless glider, then a glider with a motor that only makes circles in the water, then a machine with wheels that hops over the ground like a rabbit. It takes "breaks, sprains, and bruises over six years" and 11 prototypes for him to develop a model that can fly across the English Channel.

Other character traits shown: *Hope, Perseverance*

Ransom, Candice F. *The Promise Quilt.* Illus. by Ellen Beier. New York: Walker & Co., 1999.

After her father leaves the family farm on Lost Mountain to be General Lee's guide, Addie finds ways to remember him—even when he does not return at the end of the war.

Fortitude: Before he leaves, Addie's Papa promises, "You'll learn to read and write and make your mark in this life." But he does not return, and there is no money in the community to purchase school supplies. There is only Papa's shirt sent back after his death. In a way, this shirt helps carry out the promise. To buy the necessary books, Mama will make a quilt to auction off. There is not enough fabric to finish the quilt, so Addie donates the precious shirt to be cut into strips to make the quilt's border.

Other character traits shown: *Generosity, Helpfulness, Hope*

*Say, Allen. *Tea with Milk.* Boston: Walter Lorraine Books (Houghton Mifflin), 1999.

After growing up near San Francisco, a young Japanese woman returns with her parents to their native Japan, but she feels foreign and out of place.

Fortitude: Masako feels rejected as a foreigner at the Japanese school, and has no interest learning the tea ceremony and flower arranging and becoming a proper Japanese lady. She wants to go to college, have her own apartment, and not be forced into an arranged marriage. Finally, to escape her family's expectations, she takes a bus to the nearest city, determined to live on her own. Her job application at a store is ignored. She insists on an interview. Her first job is stultifying, but she shows her value as an interpreter for English-speaking customers and is promoted to become the store's guide for foreign businessmen. In time, she learns that it is up to her to make a home for herself. Home "isn't a place or a building that's ready-made and waiting."

Other character traits shown: *Empathy, Perseverance*

Shea, Pegi Deitz. *The Whispering Cloth: A Refugee's Story.* Illus. by Anita Riggio. Stitched by You Yang. Honesdale, PA: Boyds Mills Press, 1995.

A young girl from Laos, Cambodia in a Thai refugee camp during the Vietnam war finds the story within herself to create her own Pa'ndau (story cloth).

Fortitude: Mai wants to make her own story cloth, but she needs to learn the method. For many weeks she practices stitching, short and straight, looped inside others, twirled into long strands, made like dots. Next, Mai embroiders drawings of herbs and animals on the borders. Her work is excellent. Soon she wishes to make a whole pa'ndau by herself. She chooses to tell her own refugee story. But her grandmother tells her such a thing will not sell to the traders, because the story can't be finished. Angrily Mai goes off to think. Finally, she begins adding what she wishes to be the story's conclusion. The finished piece shows flying inside an airplane and landing where villages have homes as "big as mahogany trees." She will build "men with white crystals." She will swim "in curling salt water." She will "read books with beautiful pictures." At night she will snuggle "with Grandmother in a yellow bed with a silky roof." Now, the pa'ndau is finished.

Other character traits shown: *Hope, Respect*

Steig, William. *Sylvester and the Magic Pebble.* New York: Simon & Schuster, 1969. (Caldecott–1970)

In a moment of fright, Sylvester asks his magic pebble to turn him into a rock, but then can not wish himself back to normal again.

Fortitude: As the days and weeks pass into seasons, Sylvester prepares himself to remain a rock. He sleeps longer and longer. His parents try to go on with their lives, too. They are miserable. "Life had no meaning for them any more." Still, they force themselves on a picnic outing. "Let's cheer up. Let us try to live again and be happy even though Sylvester, our angel, is no longer with us." With determined fortitude, they are prepared to go on alone.

Other character traits shown: *Hope*

Wallace, Ian. *Boy of the Deeps.* New York: DK Ink, 1999.

James, the son of a coal miner, goes with his father for the first time to work in the mines of Cape Breton.

Fortitude: It is daunting to go a thousand feet down into the earth, but James bravely gets inside the steel cage with the other miners. He works all morning with his father learning how to bore holes in the wall, pack the hole tight with gunpowder, and set the fuses. He shovels coal onto carts all morning. His hands are blistered and his back aches, and he is so tired that even chewing his lunch is exhausting. Suddenly, the timbers crack and the roof collapses as the layers of rock overhead shift. James and his father are trapped. They hack away slate and coal, sweat running "in rivers beneath their clothes." They work to cut a narrow tunnel ("a yellow light glimmered in the distance"), which they can crawl through. They head toward "the steel cage, the light, and home." But "tomorrow they would go down into the deeps again, for they were miners and that was their job."

GENEROSITY

Use for CHARITY, GIVING, SHARING
Unselfish willingness to give or share.

Aardema. Verna. *Koi and the Kola Nuts.* Illus. by Joe Cepeda. New York: Anne Schwartz Book, Atheneum Books for Young Readers (Simon & Schuster), 1999.

An African folktale in which the son of the chief must make his way in the world with only a sack full of Kola nuts.

Generosity: All the boy has are the nuts, but he freely shares them along the way with others, who have need. Eventually, these fellow travelers, in turn, share their abilities with him during his times of need, causing him to remark, "Do good and good will come back to you—in full measure and overflowing."

Other character traits shown: *Helpfulness, Kindness*

Appelt, Kathi. *Someone's Come to Our House.* Illus. by Nancy Carpenter. Grand Rapids, MI: Eerdmans Books for Young Readers, 1999.

Members of a family celebrate the arrival of a new baby.

Generosity: There is abundant joy as the family receives relatives and friends to share their delight with the new baby. Spirits are loving, and faces show pleasure with one another. Words like: come see, come join, come gather, come hug, come share, come be glad, come play, come sing, come give thanks, and come rejoice indicate the giving among those paying respect to the new life.

Other character traits shown: *Respect*

Best, Cari. *Three Cheers for Catherine the Great.* Illus. by Giselle Potter. New York: DK Ink, 1999.

Sara's Russian grandmother has requested that there be no presents at her seventy-eighth birthday party, so Sara must think of a gift from her heart.

Generosity: It takes special generosity and thinking to give a gift that is not an object. "Any present for Grandma had to be great—just like she was." Finally, each guest knows what to give. There is a fine new hairdo, a waltz, a family photo, and, from Sara, the gift of learning to read and write English.

Other character traits shown: *Resourcefulness*

Bogart, Jo Ellen. *Jeremiah Learns to Read.* Illus. by Laura Fernandez and Rick Jacobsen. New York: Orchard Books, 1997.

Elderly Jeremiah decides that it's finally time to learn to read.

Generosity: The school does not object to teaching one more student, who is much older than the norm. The children help Jeremiah practice his reading and letters during recess. To thank them, he shows them how to chirp like a chickadee and honk like a goose. He shows the Miller twins how to whittle with a pocketknife. He teaches the instructor Mrs. Trumble how to make applesauce and how to whistle through her teeth. There are many useful things that Jeremiah does know how to do, and he shares them generously.

Other character traits shown: *Diligence, Respect*

Bunting, Eve. *December.* Illus. by David Diaz. New York: Harcourt Brace, 1997.

A homeless family's luck changes after they help an old woman who has even less than they do at Christmas.

Generosity: Simon and his Mom share a cardboard box home. Under their makeshift Christmas tree is a paper Santa plate with two cookies, one red for Mom and one green for Simon. Simon had collected 32 soda pop cans to buy the cookies. When an old woman comes to the door to share their warmth, they invite her in. It is obvious she needs shelter. They offer her the coat that both use as a blanket. Then, though it is hard to do, Simon offers her the green cookie. In return she takes the fake rose off her old hat for display on their tree. They have all shared what little they have to offer.

Bunting, Eve. *Summer Wheels.* Illus. by Thomas B. Allen. New York: Harcourt Brace Jovanovich, 1992.

The Bicycle Man fixes up old bicycles and offers both his friendship and the use of the bikes to the neighborhood kids.

Generosity: The Bicycle Man will even let a needy boy trash a bike if it means he can get the boy inside the shop to work with him.

Other character traits shown: *Courage, Empathy, Forgiveness, Justice, Kindness, Respect, Responsibility, Tolerance*

Christelow, Eileen. *The Five-Dog Night.* New York: Clarion Books (Houghton Mifflin), 1993.

Cantankerous Ezra keeps rebuffing his nosy neighbor Old Betty when she tries to give him advice on how to survive cold winter nights, until she finally discovers that his five dogs are his private source for warmth.

Generosity: Old Betty goes the extra mile to see to the welfare of her unappreciative neighbor. She checks in on him despite the inconvenience of cold and inclement weather. He insults her efforts. She brings him cookies, hot chocolate, and a blanket to keep him warm, because she is sure he must be uncomfortable.

Other character traits shown: *Courtesy, Helpfulness, Kindness, Perseverance, Respect*

*Collington, Peter. *A Small Miracle.* New York: Alfred A. Knopf, 1997.

The figures of a nativity scene come to life to help an old woman in need at Christmas.

Generosity: Even though the old woman has no food, has had to pawn her concertina, which is her means of earning a living, and has lost her money to a thief, she still takes time following a burglary at a church to replace the upset pieces of a crèche set and return the charity kettle to its spot. Her generosity is rewarded. The characters from the nativity scene find her fallen in a snowy field due to weakness. They carry her home. They go to a pawn shop and pawn their gold, frankincense, and myrrh. They retrieve the old woman's concertina. With money left over, they buy her a Christmas tree and food. Back at her gypsy wagon, the carpenter character fixes a hole in the wooden floor of her house and cuts firewood for her. They cook her Christmas dinner and decorate her tree. When the woman awakes, her home is warm, her box has money in it again, and dinner awaits. The nativity figures are gone, but their generosity is left behind.

Other character traits shown: *Kindness*

Cooper, Helen. *Pumpkin Soup.* New York: Farrar, Straus & Giroux, 1998.

Cat and Squirrel come to blows with Duck in arguing about who will perform what duty in preparing their pumpkin soup and nearly lose Duck's friendship when he decides to leave them.

Generosity: Duck creates havoc trying to do a portion of the soup-making task without the necessary skills. The others tell him he can't stir the soup because is too small and makes a mess, so he leaves. Soon Cat and Squirrel worry about Duck's safety when he doesn't return by soup time. They search for him. When they fail to find him, they finally discover him back home. Even though it is late, they decide to make soup. This time Cat and Squirrel generously let Duck stir no matter how messy he is, even when he burns the pot with soup that slops over. And, for his part, Duck generously teaches his companions his task—how to measure out just the right amount of salt to put into the soup.

Other character traits shown: *Cooperation, Forgiveness*

*Crimi, Carolyn. *Don't Need Friends.* Illus. by Lynn Munsinger. New York: Doubleday Books for Young Readers (Random House), 1999.

After his best friend moves away, Rat rudely rebuffs the efforts of the other residents of the junkyard to be friendly, until he and a grouchy old dog decide that they need each other.

Generosity: Both Rat and Dog hide their true need for friendship. When they yell at each other to stay away, they are really assuring themselves that the other is nearby. When Dog doesn't respond to Rat's taunts anymore, Rat is alarmed. He drags a large sandwich over to the sick Dog, even while muttering that he doesn't need friends. And Dog hollers for him not to bring that sandwich to him, even while his tail is thumping against the side of his barrel. Soon they are both eating from opposite ends of the sandwich. Then Rat crawls into the barrel with Dog, who tells him "Don't expect me to let you do this again." But, of course, Rat does return night after night. Soon they are making their morning rounds together, searching for scraps. So upbeat is their mood these days that they have good will to spare, even dropping a few french fries for the smaller animals. "Hate french fries," grumbles Rat. "Who needs 'em," says Dog.

Other character traits shown: *Courtesy, Helpfulness*

*Cutler, Jane. *The Cello of Mr. O.* Illus. by Greg Couch. New York: Dutton Children's Books (Penguin Putnam), 1999.

When a concert cellist plays in the square for his neighbors in a war-besieged city, his priceless instrument is destroyed by a mortar shell, but he finds the courage to return the next day to perform with a harmonica.

Generosity: There is so little to share during these bad times. This peculiar man plays his cello every afternoon in the street to "feed" the residents after the supply truck is destroyed. And, even after his cello is gone, he still finds a means of sharing music by playing the harmonica for everyone. A child who participated in teasing the cellist in the past is now respectful of his talent. Where once she would blow up a paper bag outside his door to frighten him, she now paints a picture for him on the bag and slips it quietly under his door.

Other character traits shown: *Courage, Fortitude, Hope, Perseverance, Resourcefulness*

Daly, Niki. *Jamela's Dress.* New York: Farrar, Straus & Giroux, 1999.

Jamela gets in trouble when she takes the material intended for a new dress for Mama, parades it in the street, and allows it to become dirty and torn.

Generosity: Archie shares his prize money for the photograph he takes of Jamela's enjoyment of the dress fabric. This makes all the difference. Thanks to his generosity, Mama will have a new dress to wear to the wedding after all, and Jamela's sad story will have a happy ending.

Other character traits shown: *Forgiveness, Self-discipline*

Friedrich, Elizabeth. *Leah's Pony.* Illus. by Michael Garland. Honesdale, PA: Boyds Mills Press, 1996.

A young girl sells her pony and raises enough money to buy back her father's tractor, which is up for auction on this Depression-era farm.

Generosity: Though she loves her pony more than anything, to help her family during the drought years, Leah sells it in order to bid on her father's tractor at the sale. Her father cannot plant another crop without it. The neighbors recognize her gesture and soon are bidding small amounts of cash for the farm goods, which they then hand back to the family. Their generosity enables the family to keep their farm.

Other character traits shown: *Helpfulness, Responsibility*

Gackenbach, Dick. *Alice's Special Room.* New York: Clarion Books (Houghton Mifflin), 1991.

Alice tells her mother about her special room, where she enjoys a warm beach in January, goes sledding on a hot summer day, and does anything she has already done in the past.

Generosity: This child wants her mother to enjoy the special room she has. After a search of the house, one last clue enables her mother to guess that the special room is her memory. She says, "Would you like to go there with me?" Mother would, very much. So, now they remember things together sharing memories during happy discussions.

Gill, Janet. *Basket Weaver and Catches Many Mice.* Illus. by Yangsook Choi. New York: Alfred A. Knopf, 1999.

A little gray cat saves the day when Basket Weaver is ordered into a competition to make the perfect basket for the Emperor's newborn daughter.

Generosity: The competition requires that the winner become the official palace basket weaver and that the losers be condemned to work in the underground mines. The winner also receives three wishes. When Basket Weaver does win, he requests to be allowed to return to his beloved home to make the palace baskets there. Then he asks that his cat be returned. And, finally, he asks that his fellow weavers be spared the mines. They "did their best for our future Empress. Why should they be punished?" He risks the Emperor's wrath to be generous in his winning.

Other character traits shown: *Diligence, Honesty, Loyalty, Responsibility*

*Gregory, Valiska. *Through the Mickle Woods.* Illus. by Barry Moser. Boston: Little, Brown & Co., 1992.

After his wife's death, a grieving king journeys to an old bear's cave in the mickle (thick) woods, where he hears three stories that help him go on living.

Generosity: The wife, knowing well how her spouse would grieve and shut himself off from those who love him, writes a note to him that would be delivered after her death. She sends him on a journey that she knew would be to his benefit. It will accomplish what his close friends could not. On the way he meets a small boy, who acts as his minder, an old woman, who has nothing to give but the warmth of her hut and a bit of bread, and a mysterious bear, who knows what stories the king needs to hear and has the ability to keep the king's attention. These good souls in the king's path back from grief share what they have unselfishly.

Other character traits shown: *Discernment, Empathy, Forgiveness, Helpfulness, Hope, Kindness, Perseverance*

Howard, Elizabeth Fitzgerald. *Virgie Goes to School with Us Boys.* Illus. by E.B. Lewis. New York: Simon & Schuster 2000.

In the post-Civil War South, a young African American girl is determined to prove that she can go to school just like her older brothers.

Generosity: Except for her brother C.C., the others try to discourage Virgie from going to school. When Nelson says, "Girls don't need school," C.C. tells him that's not so. "Girls need to read and write and do 'rithmetic too. Just like us boys." Then, though Virgie picks pole beans and weighs grain for Papa, sews quilt squares and stirs soap for Mama, the family decides, "All free people need learning." It will be a hardship on the parents, but they allow her to go to school with the boys. But Virgie doesn't forget home when she sees all the books on the school shelves. She suggests that when they go home each weekend, "We'll tell Mama and Papa all we've learned. That way might seem like they've been to school too. Learning to be free, just like us."

Other character traits shown: *Courage, Perseverance*

Hughes, Monica. *A Handful of Seeds.* Illus. by Luis Garay. New York: Orchard Books, 1993.

Forced into the barrio by her grandmother's death, Concepcion takes with her a legacy of chili, corn, and bean seeds and finds that they hold the key to her survival.

Generosity: When her grandmother dies, the neighbors ask Concepcion to live with them even though they have seven children to feed. Concepcion chooses not to burden them and goes instead to live at the edge of the city. The orphan children in the barrio invite her to live with them and share whatever they can scrounge to survive. Concepcion tells them they will not need to steal food, because she will plant vegetables to grow and sell. But, before they can mature, her plants are smashed when the police chase the children through the garden. When she plants her seeds again, the children offer to help her. This time they are successful. There is enough to eat and to sell. When another gang of hungry children appear, they share with them, too. Then Concepcion shares seeds with the other children so they, too, can plant their own food and have vegetables to sell.

Other character traits shown: *Diligence, Fortitude, Helpfulness, Perseverance, Resourcefulness*

Ketteman, Helen. *I Remember Papa.* Illus. by Greg Shed. New York: Dial Books for Young Readers (Penguin), 1998.

After saving to buy a baseball glove, a young farm boy takes a memorable trip to town with his father.

Generosity: Audie loses the envelope of money he has carefully saved over the weeks. His chance to buy the coveted baseball glove is lost. But then, without a word, his father, stern in outward demeanor, purchases the glove for the boy, using the money he had planned to spend on new work shoes. His generosity is remembered for a lifetime.

Other character traits shown: *Responsibility*

Krupinski, Loretta. *Best Friends.* New York: Hyperion Books for Children, 1998.

When a settler's young daughter learns that soldiers will force the Nez Perce off the nearby land, she uses a doll to warn her Indian friend of impending danger.

Generosity: The young homesteader has nothing but a doll to remind her of a life she has left behind. She guards her doll "a little jealously," because the Indian girl's doll is not "nearly as fine as Mary." But when danger threatens, the girl forgets her possessiveness and hides a vital message inside her doll's head and sends her doll with the traveling medicine man to the Indian village. This message will warn the Indians that soldiers mean to round them up to live on a reservation. She has given her precious doll to a higher cause.

Other character traits shown: *Helpfulness, Justice, Kindness, Loyalty, Resourcefulness, Respect*

Leodhas, Sorche Nic. *Always Room for One More.* Illus. by Nonny Hogrogian. New York: Henry Holt, 1965. (Caldecott–1966)

A friendly man and his family always have space to share in their house until the house finally bursts with the load.

Generosity: The man, his wife, and 10 children share "whatever we've got." Inside, family and guests frolic. When the house tumbles down, those who enjoyed the hospitality decide "we'll raise up a bonny new house." So they build one "double as wide and as high." When it's finished, they shout, "There's room galore! Now there will always be room for one more, always room for one more!"

Miller, William. *The Piano.* Illus. by Susan Keeter. New York: Lee & Low Books, 2000.

A young black girl's love of music leads her to a job in the house of an older white woman, who not only teaches her to play the piano, but also the rewards of intergenerational friendship.

Generosity: Miss Hartwell refuses to teach Tia in exchange for Tia giving up her maid's wages. Despite her arthritic hands, she will help Tia for the love of sharing music. Tia tries to do both her duties and another employee's manual labor to demonstrate how grateful she is to receive instruction from Miss Hartwell.

Other character traits shown: *Helpfulness, Kindness, Respect*

Pomerantz, Charlotte. *You're Not My Best Friend Anymore.* Illus. by David Soman. New York: Dial Books for Young Readers (Penguin), 1998.

Molly and Ben are best friends and share everything until they have a fight.

Generosity: Though they are angry with each other and not best friends anymore, Molly and Ben both, unknown to the other, buy each other a birthday gift anyway. So attuned are they to each other's desires, that they each select a sleeping bag for the other. What's more, they each take care to buy one that will especially please the other. Molly gets Ben a bag with a puppy patch on it, because she knows he would like to have a dog. Ben gets Molly a sleeping bag with Raggedy Andy on it, because he knows her favorite doll is Raggedy Andy. "You spent your whole allowance on me." "So did you." Their separate acts of generosity thaw the anger between them and begin the healing of their torn friendship.

Other character traits shown: *Courtesy, Forgiveness*

Rael, Elsa Okon. *What Zeesie Saw on Delancey Street.* Illus. by Marjorie Priceman. New York: Simon & Schuster, 1996.

A young Jewish girl living on Manhattan's Lower East Side attends her first "package party" where she learns about the traditions of community giving among Jewish immigrants in the early 1900s.

Generosity: During the excitement of bidding for food packages, Zeesie listens as a man comes up to Papa and tells him, "It's your turn." She sees Papa get up and go through a door. When she asks to go along, she's told, "No, it's not permitted. I must go alone." Zeesie wonders why she can't go. When Papa comes back, he taps Uncle Yussie's shoulder. It is his turn to go. Zeesie begs her father to tell her what's behind the door. Her father explains that behind the door is the money room. Men go in one at a time. If a man has money to give, he leaves it. If he needs money, he takes it, but only as much as he needs. No one is supposed to know who has given or who has received. No one ever tells. Zeesie wants to peek in the room. She waits until no one is looking and no one is in the room. She sneaks inside. The room is bare and unattractive. A metal cash box on a table contains a section for bills and slots for coins. Then, someone taps on the door and she must quickly hide behind a stack of newspapers. She watches the private prayers of a man who counts out eight dollar bills from the box. She knows this jolly, funny, beloved old Max. But now she sees his need. He pockets the money and leaves. Zeesie knows she was where she should not have been and had seen what she should not have seen. She has a dollar that her grandparents have given her to spend on her birthday. There is something she can do to help make right the wrong she has done. She puts the dollar in the money box. "None of this could be told, she knew, remembering Papa's words. No one ever, ever, ever must know."

Other character traits shown: *Justice, Responsibility*

Ransom, Candice F. *The Promise Quilt.* Illus. by Ellen Beier. New York: Walker & Co., 1999.

After her father leaves the family farm on Lost Mountain to be General Lee's guide, Addie finds ways to remember him—even when he does not return at the end of the war.

Generosity: All Addie has left of her Papa is the red shirt he wore when he left. Now there is not enough money to buy books to begin school. A decision is made to raffle off a quilt. But there is not enough fabric left to complete the quilt's border. It is up to Addie to donate the red shirt to be cut into strips. She can't give it up. Then, she realizes "the quilt wasn't just for me. It was for all the children who wanted to go to school and make their mark in this world." She will still have memories of her father, and the mountain children will all be able to go to school.

Other character traits shown: *Fortitude, Helpfulness, Hope*

Robbins, Ruth. *Baboushka and the Three Kings.* Illus. by Nicolas Sidjakov. Adapted from a Russian folktale. Boston: Houghton Mifflin, 1960. (Caldecott–1961)

When three kings ask an old woman to join them in their search for the Christ Child, she declines because her day's work is not finished. In vain, she tries to follow them the next day.

Generosity: By the time the woman reconsiders the invitation to join in the quest, it is too late to bring her gifts to the Christ Child. But it is not too late to pass them out to other children along the way.

Other character traits shown: *Diligence*

Rylant, Cynthia. *The Bird House.* Illus. by Barry Moser. New York: Blue Sky Press (Scholastic), 1998.

A young girl without family is fascinated by a house that draws birds around it.

Generosity: The birds first notice the homeless girl. They set about sharing their sanctuary with her by drawing the old woman's attention to her. They write GIRL across the sky in formation flying. And, when this does not produce results, their leader, the great barred owl, physically restrains the shy girl by catching his talons in her shirt and holding her until the old woman finds them. The old woman "was not really that surprised to see a girl. She took the child into the bright blue house, and she washed the dirt from the girl's face and fed her bread and beans." The girl is drawn to this safe place and, "since that time, the girl has always lived with the old woman."

Other character traits shown: *Empathy, Kindness*

Say, Allen. *Allison.* Boston: Walter Lorraine Books (Houghton Mifflin), 1997.

> When Allison realizes that she looks more like her favorite doll than like her parents, she comes to terms with this unwelcome discovery with the help of a stray cat.

Generosity: At first Allison is very angry when she discovers her parents are not her "real" mommy and daddy. She behaves badly, vandalizing her mother's old doll and her father's baseball and mitt. But when she finds a cat that needs a home, she begins to realize how important it is to care for someone in need. As she generously provides for the cat, she understands what a loving generous act it was for her parents to take her in.

Other character traits shown: *Discernment, Empathy, Tolerance*

Siekkinen, Raija. *Mister King.* Illus. by Hannu Taina. Trans. by Tim Steffa. Minneapolis: Carolrhoda, 1987.

> A lonely king searches his seaside kingdom for subjects.

Generosity: The king is so pleased to have a "subject" he "didn't even notice that, although he was king, he served the cat." He makes the cat a bed, builds him a fire, and feeds him. They watch sunsets together. The cat purrs his pleasure. To the king it sounds like "hurrah, hurrah, hurrah" in deference to his kingship.

Other character traits shown: *Cooperation*

*Stewart, Sarah. *The Gardener.* Illus. by David Small. New York: Farrar, Straus & Giroux, 1997.

> A series of letters relates what happens when Lydia Grace goes to live with her Uncle Jim in the city but takes her love for gardening with her.

Generosity: Lydia Grace plants flower seeds and bulbs in any container she can find. She shares plants with customers at the bakery and with neighbors. Soon the store is drawing in more customers. Lydia Grace plans a special Fourth of July surprise for her Uncle Jim that is bound to bring a smile to his face. Uncle Jim never smiles. When she shows him the rooftop, covered with growing flowers and vegetables, he responds in the only way he knows how. A few days later, he closes the store early, sends her to the roof garden, and brings up "the most amazing cake I've ever seen—covered in flowers! I truly believe that cake equals one thousand smiles."

Other character traits shown: *Diligence, Discernment, Patience*

*Waldman, Neil. *The Starry Night.* Honesdale, PA: Boyds Mills Press, 1999.

Vincent Van Gogh befriends a young boy in New York City in this fantasy about art and creativity.

Generosity: One boy among a pack running together stops to stare at an artist's "brightly colored canvas" and pronounces, "The Big Apple never looked better!" Quickly a relationship develops. The boy shows the man "some amazing places" to paint and the artist delights the boy with his beautiful paintings. Each unselfishly shares what he knows. And, finally, the artist shows the boy one of his own works among the "walls covered with beautiful paintings" at the art museum. This last generous act is enough to stimulate the boy to buy a sketch pad and a box of colored pencils. He, too, "begins to draw."

Other character traits shown: *Helpfulness, Hope*

GIVING. *SEE* GENEROSITY

HELPFULNESS

Use for CARING, CIVILITY, COMPASSION, THOUGHTFULNESS

To give one in need or trouble something beneficial to provide relief or assistance.

Aardema. Verna. *Koi and the Kola Nuts.* Illus. by Joe Cepeda. New York: Anne Schwartz Book, Atheneum Books for Young Readers (Simon & Schuster), 1999.

An African folktale in which the son of the chief must make his way in the world with only a sack full of Kola Nuts.

Helpfulness: When the animals the boy meets along the way ask for help, he is able to provide just what is needed. They in turn are able to return the favor when he is in need. For example, the snake needs kola nuts for medicine for his sick mother. Later, the snake calls upon his cousins, the pythons, to make sure a tree the boy cuts down lands the right direction.

Other character traits shown: *Generosity, Kindness*

Aardema, Verna. *The Lonely Lioness and the Ostrich Chicks.* Illus. by Yumi Heo. New York: Alfred A. Knopf, 1996.

In this Masai tale, a mongoose helps an ostrich get her chicks back from the lonely lioness who has stolen them.

Helpfulness: Two animals try different approaches to get back the ostrich's chicks. The jackal tries gentle persuasion to appeal to the lioness's common sense. Surely the lioness would have to acknowledge that creatures with two legs cannot belong to one with four legs. But the lioness brushes off this argument. She "went right on past the jackal," with chicks in tow. The mongoose, however, succeeds by taunting the lioness's ego. "You are a bigger fool than I thought you were," he says. This, of course, gets the lioness's attention. She springs at him in anger, forgetting to guard her stolen babies. But the mongoose has stationed himself right beside his burrow and proceeds to immediately "skedaddle" down the hole. In the manner of hunting cats, the lioness waits and waits for the mongoose to come out of his burrow, forgetting entirely about the ostrich chicks. Because of the mongoose's helpful trick, the ostrich has plenty of time to round up her chicks and leave with them.

Other character traits shown: *Courage, Honesty, Justice, Perseverance, Prudence, Self-discipline*

Arnold, Marsha Diane. *The Chicken Salad Club.* Illus. by Julie Downing. New York: Dial Books for Young Readers (Penguin), 1998.

Nathaniel's great-grandfather, who is 100 years old, loves to tell stories from his past but seeks someone to join him with a new batch of stories.

Helpfulness: The old man knows his great-grandson likes to hear his old stories, but he needs to hear a few new stories himself. He and his great-grandson set out to find others who might have stories to share. They try to engage Nathaniel's school class, but the kids are soon bored. They decide to host a party for all people over 100. Nathaniel's mother tries to warn him not to expect too many. In fact, nobody at all comes. Greatpaw is depressed. Nathaniel tries a new plan. He places an ad in the "confidentials" section of the newspaper asking for a storyteller. This gets results. One applicant is interviewed, and Nathaniel believes he has found the perfect person. "Greatpaw, I've been thinking, maybe you don't need lots of storytellers to share stories with you. Maybe just one would do." And she does.

Other character traits shown: *Discernment, Resourcefulness*

Auch, Mary Jane. *Bantam of the Opera.* New York: Holiday House, 1997.

Luigi the rooster wins fame and fortune when the star of the Cosmopolitan Opera Company and his understudy both come down with chicken pox on the same night.

Helpfulness: Though Luigi persists in his goal to sing, he could have failed in his chance if it had not been for the helpfulness of Carlotta Tetrazzini, the soprano, who comes to his aid just when he needed it. She first steps in to shame the tenor Baldini for bullying the "perfect opera mascot" when the jealous singer threatens to make noodle soup of Luigi. She recognizes Luigi's "lovely voice" and his "perfect pitch." Again, when Luigi is the only tenor available to perform when the others come down with chicken pox, she stands up for the rooster. So what if he "doesn't sing words." Carlotta points out, "Who understands the words?" So what if he's "terribly short." Carlotta says, "So he sits on my shoulder." Because she speaks up in his behalf, Luigi gets his opportunity to sing.

Other character traits shown: *Courage, Fortitude, Hope, Perseverance*

Babbitt, Natalie. *Bub or the Very Best Thing.* New York: Michael di Capua Books (HarperCollins), 1994.

Nobody except the little prince himself knows what is the very best thing for the prince.

Helpfulness: As the king and queen ask those at the palace what is the best thing for the prince, each one questioned helpfully responds according to the kind of occupation they have. The prime minister believes the answer is in books. The day nursemaid says the best thing is vegetables. The night nursemaid believes the best thing is sleep. The Gardener believes the answer is sunshine. The court musician, of course, pronounces the best thing for the prince is a song. The lord and lady believe talking and listening are the best things for the prince. But are these the very best things? The cook's daughter says the prince will tell them what is the best thing. And he does. But do they understand what he says?

Other character traits shown: *Discernment*

Brenner, Barbara. *The Boy Who Loved to Draw: Benjamin West.* Illus. by Olivier Dunrea. Boston: Houghton Mifflin, 1999.

The Pennsylvania artist who begins drawing as a boy eventually becomes well known on both sides of the Atlantic.

Helpfulness: When family and friends realize Benjamin's talent, they help at just the right time to further his skills. First, the local Indians help him acquire paint from the river bank clay. His mother gives him some bluing from her stock of laundry supplies. Even his father makes the great sacrifice of sending him away to be schooled.

Other character traits shown: *Diligence, Perseverance, Resourcefulness*

Bruchac, Joseph. *The Great Ball Game: A Muskogee Story.* Illus. by Susan L. Roth. New York: Dial Books for Young Readers, 1994.

Bat, who has both wings and teeth, plays an important part in a game between the Birds and the Animals to decide which group is better.

Helpfulness: Bat wants to be a team member. When given the chance, he proves to be helpful to the extent that he enables a flagging, losing team to win the day. His fellow team members have exhausted their own skills. Bat gives them assistance when it is vitally needed. His beneficial ability of not needing light to find his way as darkness descended is just what the team requires, and without him, they couldn't have won.

Other character traits shown: *Empathy, Kindness, Patience, Respect, Responsibility*

Caseley, Judith. *Mickey's Class Play.* New York: Greenwillow (William Morrow), 1998.

With the help of his family, Mickey enjoys being a duck in the class play. *Helpfulness:* Mickey is easily upset and discouraged. First, he isn't sure he wants to be a duck in the class play. Then, he worries about getting his part just right. And, finally, his costume is ruined when he leaves it out in the rain. Efforts to create a replacement costume don't please him either. "I don't look like the others," he complains. It is the special helpfulness of his loving family that saves the day. Jenna, his older sister, is there to provide just the right assistance. When he is reluctant to play a duck, she reassures him. "You get to sing a song and hop and flap your wings . . . and you even get to hatch." Mickey rehearses with Jenna and his father. Jenna claps loudly in encouragement. She helps make a new costume. She points out there are colored markers, a cardboard box, and an old feather duster to make a replacement. When Mickey doesn't like the result, Jenna searches in a book for a duck that looks like the costume they made. So, Mickey participates in the school play wearing a sign across his chest that says, "I am a blue-winged teal from Saskatchewan, Ontario, Kansas, Missouri, Illinois, Ohio, and New Jersey.

Other character traits shown: *Patience*

Christelow, Eileen. *The Five-Dog Night.* New York: Clarion Books (Houghton Mifflin), 1993.

Cantankerous Ezra keeps rebuffing his nosy neighbor Old Betty when she tries to give him advice on how to survive cold winter nights, until she finally discovers that his five dogs are his private source for warmth.
Helpfulness: Old Betty believes Ezra is being deliberately stubborn about his own welfare. He needs a warm blanket, even though he claims he doesn't. Eventually, over his protestations, when the weather turns frigid, she brings him one. She also regularly checks in on him, bringing other beneficial winter season provisions. She helps him as best she can, despite his rude behavior.

Other character traits shown: *Courtesy, Generosity, Kindness, Perseverance, Respect*

*Crimi, Carolyn. *Don't Need Friends.* Illus. by Lynn Munsinger. New York: Doubleday Books for Young Readers (Random House), 1999

After his best friend moves away, Rat rudely rebuffs the efforts of the other residents of the junkyard to be friendly, until he and a grouchy old dog decide that they need each other.

Helpfulness: When Dog is sick with a cold, Rat is concerned and brings to him what he needs. Dog hasn't been able to forage for himself. The long sandwich Rat brings is just right. Rat needs a warm spot out of the winter's snow. Dog allows Rat to crawl in next to him so that both animals can keep warm. Each reluctantly comes to realize the other's value. Later, in their newfound friendship, they are contented enough with life to go together hunting for scraps. They even drop a few french fries for the other smaller animals.

Other character traits shown: *Courtesy, Generosity*

Daly, Niki. *Bravo Zan Angelo! A Commedia Dell'arte Tale with Story and Pictures.* New York: Farrar, Straus & Giroux, 1998.

In Renaissance Venice, Angelo, longing to be as famous a clown as his grandfather, decides to do something special with his small part in his grandfather's act during Carnival.

Helpfulness: Before he can perform, Angelo must rely upon the helpfulness of good souls who help him get outfitted with just the right pieces for a rooster costume. There is the mask maker, who quickly makes a rooster's face of "bits of red and yellow leather." The seamstress has a neck ruffle for him and skillfully turns his own red coat into a rooster's tail. An elegantly dressed gentleman even gives him one of his gloves to put on his head. "A fine cockscomb for an elegant fowl!"

Other character traits shown: *Courage, Courtesy, Hope, Kindness, Perseverance, Resourcefulness*

De Felice, Cynthia. *Willy's Silly Grandma.* Illus. by Shelley Jackson. New York: Orchard Books, 1997.

Willy doesn't believe in any of his grandmother's superstitions, until he ventures down by the Big Swamp one dark night and comes to realize how smart Grandma is.

Helpfulness: Willy's Grandma says silly things. Willy doesn't believe them until he becomes frightened in the Big Swamp and rushes to her for safety. Suddenly, her words aren't silly anymore. She tells him the wind made the moans and groans and the flickering lights he saw were the stars. And, though it surely does seem like the bogeyman is there, there is no bogeyman. She knows just the right thing to say to help him. "There's no bogeyman, little Willy, I can tell you that for true."

Other character traits shown: *Empathy*

Duncan, Alice Faye. *Miss Viola and Uncle Ed Lee.* Illus. by Catherine Stock. New York: Atheneum Books for Young Readers (Simon & Schuster), 1999.

A young boy helps his two neighbors, one as neat as a pin and the other as junky as a packrat, become friends.

Helpfulness: Before the two would-be friends can become acquainted, someone needs to introduce them. Bradley's house is between theirs. He knows them both. So, he serves as messenger for Uncle Ed Lee, telling Miss Viola that his uncle would like to make friends with her. He reports her response to Uncle Ed Lee. Then, when the moment arrives for their meeting, Bradley serves as chaperone for the two.

Other character traits shown: *Courtesy, Honesty, Kindness, Respect, Tolerance*

Fleming, Candace. *The Hatmaker's Sign: A Story Told by Benjamin Franklin.* Illus. by Robert Andrew Parker. New York: Orchard Books, 1998.

To heal the hurt pride of Thomas Jefferson as Congress makes changes to his Declaration of Independence, Benjamin Franklin tells his friend the story of a hatmaker and his sign.

Helpfulness: Franklin provides Jefferson the one thing he needs most, realization that, "if the public is going to read it, you can be sure they will want to change it." The hatmaker writes the message he thinks is just right for his shop sign. But everyone who sees it edits out a word or phrase until there are no words left. Finally, in confusion, the hatmaker takes his would-be sign to a sign painter, who suggests the original wording the hatmaker had planned. In the end, the original version is almost always "exactly right."

Other character traits shown: *Empathy, Fortitude*

Fowler, Susi Gregg. *Beautiful.* Illus. by Jim Fowler. New York: Greenwillow (William Morrow), 1998.

A young gardener and Uncle George collaborate on a garden, so that when a very sick Uncle George comes home from the doctor he is greeted with beautiful flowers.

Helpfulness: First, Uncle George, a professional gardener, helps the boy establish a flower garden so that when Uncle George leaves for medical treatment, "you won't feel I'm so far away." Encouraging postcards and phone calls keep the two in touch. When Uncle George returns, he is too sick to go out to the garden, but the boy brings him a bouquet of cut flowers just in time for one last photograph of the gardeners together.

Other character traits shown: *Courage, Honesty, Tolerance*

Friedrich, Elizabeth. *Leah's Pony.* Illus. by Michael Garland. New York: Boyds Mills Press, 1996.

A young girl sells her pony and raises enough money to buy back her father's tractor, which is up for auction on this Depression-era farm.

Helpfulness: All the farm animals and the family's pickup truck are sold at auction to help pay back money borrowed to buy seed corn that never produced a crop. But the one item most needed and most missed is the tractor. Without it they can never plant corn again and will have to leave the farm. There is one way Leah believes she can be helpful during these hard times. The grocery store owner admires her beloved pony. She sells it to him. At the auction she bids $1.00 to buy the tractor. Neighbors get the message. They do not raise the bid. Without a higher bid, the auctioneer sells it to Leah. Soon, a flock of chickens go for 10¢. The pickup goes for 25¢. All the neighbors who bid on things return their purchased items to Leah's family. Between Leah and the good-hearted neighbors, the family is not forced off their farm.

Other character traits shown: *Generosity, Responsibility*

Gibbons, Faye. *Mountain Wedding.* Illus. by Ted Rand. New York: Morrow Junior Books, 1996.

The children from two rival mountain families about to be joined in a wedding change their minds about each other only after they face the loss of their household goods.

Helpfulness: The feuding children will have nothing to do with each other or the impending wedding until honey bees cause the near destruction of their mutual possessions. Run-away mules cause things to drop off the wagon; everyone races behind to pick up whatever has fallen. No one pays any attention to whose things are being rescued. They work equally hard gathering up all their belongings. By the time the mules stop at the creek, the children have become one mixed-together family, who have saved their things and are finally ready for the wedding.

Other character traits shown: *Cooperation*

Gillerlain, Gayle. *The Reverend Thomas's False Teeth.* Illus. by Dena Schutzer. BridgeWater Books (Troll Associates), 1995.

On his way to have dinner with Gracie and her family, the preacher loses his teeth in the Chesapeake Bay.

Helpfulness: While the others try diving, netting, and tonging under water to try to find the false teeth, Gracie keeps saying she knows how to find them. When the others fail to retrieve the teeth, Gracie decides to show them how helpful she can be. She remembers having heard the Reverend Thomas say, "he could not keep his teeth out of good fried chicken." So, Gracie goes to get a piece of her Mama's chicken for bait. Sure enough, those teeth under the water clamp on to the piece of chicken that Gracie has tied to string and lowered in the water. "You out-thought us all," the preacher says in praise.

Goble, Paul. *Love Flute.* New York: Bradbury Press (Macmillan), 1992.

A gift to a shy young man from the birds and animals helps him to express his love to a beautiful girl.

Helpfulness: Words fail the young man. He seems incapable of expressing his love to a particular girl and is likely to lose her to others who can speak better. The animals of the forest help him by giving him the one thing that will enable him to catch the girl's attention. The wooden flute is endowed with the animals' special songs, which he has copied from them. She recognizes his message of love in these combined melodies and hears what his words could not say.

Other character traits shown: *Empathy*

*Gregory, Valiska. *Through the Mickle Woods*. Illus. by Barry Moser. Boston: Little, Brown & Co., 1992.

> After his wife's death, a grieving king journeys to an old bear's cave in the mickle (thick) woods, where he hears three stories that help him go on living.

Helpfulness: The wife, boy, old woman, and the bear each offer something beneficial to help the king recover from his loss. The wife, in her letter, sends him to hear stories from the wise bear. The boy, in his exuberance over life and his determination to make the king remember the queen's ways, persists in remaining cheerful and keeping the king focused on the journey. The old woman gives the king warmth and something besides himself to think about. The bear's stories help the king understand how he can go on living without his wife.

Other character traits shown: *Discernment, Empathy, Forgiveness, Generosity, Hope, Kindness, Perseverance*

Guarnieri, Paolo. *A Boy Named Giotto*. Illus. by Bimba Landmann. Trans. by Jonathan Galassi. New York: Farrar, Straus & Giroux, 1998.

> Eight-year-old Giotto the shepherd boy confesses his dream of becoming an artist to the painter Cimabue, who teaches him how to make marvelous pigments from minerals, flowers, and eggs and takes him on as a pupil.

Helpfulness: Were it not for the artist Cimabue, little Giotto might never have become the famous fresco painter who made life-like paintings of Saint Francis on the church walls in Assisi and the Scrovengni Chapel in Padua. Cimabue willingly shares his knowledge of pigments with the child and then waits seven years for him to come study with him. "I will make him into a great painter." He tells the parents the boy's sketches are not scribbles. Though needed to watch the father's sheep, the youth is given permission by his parents to study in the master's workshop, leaving behind his life as a shepherd. Cimabue teaches how to cover a wall with a mixture of lime and very fine sand and to draw figures quickly and apply paint before the mixture dries. Giotto's work is good, causing Cimabue to note, without jealousy, "The pupil has outdone the master."

Other character traits shown: *Diligence, Patience*

Hendrick, Mary Jean. *If Anything Ever Goes Wrong at the Zoo*. Illus. by Jane Dyer. New York: Harcourt Brace Jovanovich, 1993.

After a young girl tells the zookeepers to send the animals to her house should anything go wrong at the zoo, a zoo emergency results in some unusual houseguests for the girl and her family.

Helpfulness: Leslie tells each of the caretakers that her home has just what the animals need. The fenced-in zebras would have a "nice fenced yard" at her place. The monkeys, who need lots of room to exercise, would have "a very large swing set." Her large garage could house the elephants. When rain floods the zoo grounds, zookeepers bring their charges to Leslie's house.

Hogrogrian, Nonny. *The Cat Who Loved to Sing*. New York: Alfred A. Knopf, 1988.

A cat trades one thing for another until he finally gains a mandolin.

Helpfulness: As the cat journeys along, he meets folks who trade him something they have to give for something he has previously received. Each trade gives what the other most needs.

Hopkinson, Deborah. *Sweet Clara and the Freedom Quilt*. Illus. by James Ransome. New York: Alfred A. Knopf, 1993.

A young slave stitches a quilt with a map pattern, which guides her and other slaves to freedom in the North.

Helpfulness: She uses the skill she has to create the single most important thing slaves need to gain their freedom, a map. When the quilt is finished, she leaves it behind so that others may use it to find their way north.

Other character traits shown: *Diligence, Resourcefulness*

Hughes, Monica. *A Handful of Seeds*. Illus. by Luis Garay. New York: Orchard Books, 1993.

Forced into the barrio by her grandmother's death, Concepcion takes with her a legacy of chili, corn, and bean seeds and finds that they hold the key to her survival.

Helpfulness: The orphan children living in the barrio need to be weaned off stealing for their survival. They are constantly running into trouble with the police. Concepcion shows them how planting a garden will provide food to eat and produce to sell. When the garden is ruined, she replants, and the other children help her this time.

Other character traits shown: *Diligence, Fortitude, Generosity, Perseverance, Resourcefulness*

Krupinski, Loretta. *Best Friends*. New York: Hyperion Books for Children, 1998.

When a settler's young daughter learns that soldiers will force the Nez Perce off the nearby land, she uses a doll to warn her Indian friend of impending danger.

Helpfulness: The only way to get a message to the Indians in time is through secrecy. The young girl gives up her precious doll to use as a carrier for the warning. It is the one helpful means of reaching the Indians before the soldiers round them up to live on a reservation. The traveling medicine doctor will take the doll as a "gift" from one friend to another when he makes his rounds at the Indian village.

Other character traits shown: *Generosity, Justice, Kindness, Loyalty, Resourcefulness, Respect*

Levitin, Sonia. *Nine for California.* Illus. by Cat Bowman Smith. New York: Orchard Books, 1996.

Amanda travels by stagecoach with her four siblings and her mother from Missouri to California to join her father.

Helpfulness: Amanda's mother packs a sack to take along on the 21-day journey. Inside is "everything we'll need." As the days pass the sack does, indeed, seem to contain just the right items to help restless children and irritated adults survive a difficult journey in a cramped stagecoach. There are sugar lumps to quiet kids with hiccups. There are prunes to use for dessert with the daily ration of beans. There is corn pone enough for hungry attacking Indians. There are licorice whips to warm the bones after getting stuck in the mud during a cold rain storm. There is pepper to throw in the faces of charging buffalo to make them turn away. And there is a loud whistle to frighten away outlaws attempting to rob the passengers.

Other character traits shown: *Resourcefulness*

Manson, Christopher. *Two Travelers.* New York: Henry Holt, 1990.

The emperor's messenger Isaac must accompany a gift elephant from Baghdad to France, and during the difficult journey, an unexpected friendship develops between man and beast.

Helpfulness: Though the elephant and the messenger are not sure they like each other, they soon begin to mutually look out for each other's needs. Isaac shows the elephant how to stand on a raft, protects his ears from the cold, and provides him clean straw and water. The elephant picks him up with his trunk and saves Isaac from falling overboard off the boat, shades him from the sun with his big ears, and tramps big footprints through the deep snow for Isaac to follow. Each has the ability and willingness to help the other in the manner most needed at the time.

Other character traits shown: *Cooperation, Kindness, Tolerance*

McCully, Emily Arnold. *Mirette on the High Wire.* New York: G.P. Putnam's Sons, 1992. (Caldecott–1993)

Mirette learns tightrope walking from Monsieur Bellini, a guest at her mother's boardinghouse, not knowing that he is a celebrated tightrope artist who has withdrawn from performing because of fear.

Helpfulness: After opening up the world of high-wire performance to her, he suddenly becomes reluctant when she asks him to show her how to do some of the magnificent acts he has done in the past. The master hates to disappoint her and decides one last time to try to overcome his fear. He orders a wire strung between two tall buildings and begins his performance. Mirette knows what is wrong when he does not progress across the wire but instead remains frozen in place. She does the one helpful act that will enable Monsieur Bellini to regain his skills. She begins at the other end of the wire and walks toward him holding out her hands. He smiles and begins to walk toward her. Suddenly the crowd is shouting, and plans begin for a world tour starring the master and his pupil.

Other character traits shown: *Courage, Perseverance*

Miller, William. *The Piano.* Illus. by Susan Keeter. New York: Lee & Low Books, 2000.

A young black girl's love of music leads her to a job in the house of an older white woman, who not only teaches her to play the piano, but also the rewards of intergenerational friendship.

Helpfulness: When Miss Hartwell is unable to use her hands at the piano due to painful arthritis, Tia bathes them in a warm water salt solution. When Tia is unable to play due to abusing her hands with hard manual labor, Miss Hartwell brings her a warm salt water solution. Mutually, they support and comfort each other in their new venture as teacher and pupil.

Other character traits shown: *Generosity, Kindness, Respect*

Perkins, Lynne Rae. *Home Lovely.* New York: Greenwillow (William Morrow), 1995.

Hoping for trees or a flower garden, Tiffany transplants and cares for some seedlings she finds and is surprised by what they become.

Helpfulness: The mail carrier points out that Tiffany's transplants are vegetables. He knows she had hoped for flowers, so a day or so later he stops by with a flat of marigolds, pansies, and petunias, just what she wanted. Later he helps with advice on the vegetable plants. In late summer he remembers she had also wanted a tree. One day he leaves one in the driveway, wrapped in burlap, ready to plant.

Ransom, Candice F. *The Promise Quilt.* Illus. by Ellen Beier. New York: Walker & Co., 1999.

After her father leaves the family farm on Lost Mountain to be General Lee's guide, Addie finds ways to remember him—even when he does not return at the end of the war.

Helpfulness: The only physical thing Addie has to remember her father is the red shirt he wore when he went to war. But her mother needs the shirt now to complete the quilt that will be raffled to purchase school books. Addie realizes that she still has memories of her father. She can give up the shirt to make the binding border for the quilt.

Other character traits shown: *Fortitude, Generosity, Hope*

Sisulu, Elinor Batezat. *The Day Gogo Went to Vote: South Africa, April 1994.* Illus. by Sharon Wilson. New York: Little, Brown & Co., 1997.

Thembi and her beloved great-grandmother, who has not left home for many years, go together to vote on the momentous day when black South Africans are allowed to vote for the first time.

Helpfulness: The venerable old woman intends to vote regardless of her age and infirmities. "This is the first time we have a chance to vote for our own leaders, and it might be my last. That is why I must vote, no matter how many miles I have to walk, no matter how long I have to stand in line!" But she gets help. A rich township man sends his own car and driver to take her to her precinct. He tells the precinct workers about her, and they are waiting for her when she arrives. A presiding officer guides her to the voting office so she will not have to stand in line. They help her inside, too. Everyone is proud of the oldest person leading the way for the others.

Other character traits shown: *Justice, Respect, Responsibility*

Stanley, Diane. *The Gentleman and the Kitchen Maid.* Illus. by Dennis Nolan. New York: Dial Books for Young Readers, 1994.

When two paintings hanging across from each other in a museum fall in love, a resourceful art student finds a way to reunite the lovers.

Helpfulness: Art gallery personnel move 'The Kitchen Maid' to another room, leaving behind a bereft 'The Gentleman.' When the art student working on copying the 'The Gentleman' sees his sad eyes, she discovers, as she follows his gaze across the room, that a painting of fruit and goblets is hanging where 'The Kitchen Maid' used to be. She rushes through her painting of 'The Gentleman' without filling in the background and hurries to the room where 'The Kitchen Maid' is hanging. Instead of painting her on a new canvas, the art student blends her "right into her painting of the young gentleman. His outstretched arm seemed to reach around her waist. She is looking over her shoulder, into his eyes. They smile at one another with perfect contentment." The art student has provided something beneficial in time of need.

Other character traits shown: *Empathy*

*Waldman, Neil. *The Starry Night.* Honesdale, PA: Boyds Mills Press, 1999.

Vincent Van Gogh befriends a young boy in New York City in this fantasy about art and creativity.

Helpfulness: In the single best way that he can offer assistance to an underprivileged city child, the artist quietly shows what he does by painting the sights. The boy exhibits his helpfulness to the foreign artist by showing him "some amazing places" to paint. Together, they appreciate the beauty of the city. Before he leaves, the artist shows the boy one special place he knows about in the city. The Museum of Modern Art has "walls covered with beautiful paintings." The boy is led to one "blue and yellow painting of a country village at night." It impresses the boy and, because it was painted by the foreign artist, it inspires him to sit down across from the "swirling stars, the orange moon, and the sleeping village" and begin to draw it.

Other character traits shown: *Generosity, Hope*

*Wiesniewski, David. *Golem.* New York: Clarion Books (Houghton Mifflin), 1996. (Caldecott–1997)

A saintly rabbi miraculously brings to life a clay giant who helps watch over the Jews of sixteenth-century Prague.

Helpfulness: Even though the giant knows his life will end after the Jews are safe, he helps them by using his strength to fight off the attackers.

Other character traits shown: *Justice, Loyalty*

Yacowitz, Caryn. *Pumpkin Fiesta.* Illus. by Joe Cepeda. New York: HarperCollins, 1998.

Hoping to win a prize for the best pumpkin at the fiesta, Foolish Fernando tries to copy Old Juana's successful gardening techniques, but without really watching to see how much effort and love she puts into her work.

Helpfulness: When Fernando proves unable to learn from watching Old Juana work, she offers to provide him the one thing he needs to be able to grow large pumpkins. She asks him if he really wants to grow beautiful big pumpkins. He replies that he does. She tells him to "pay attention and do as I say."

Other character traits shown: *Diligence, Forgiveness, Honesty*

HONESTY

Use for INTEGRITY, TRUSTWORTHINESS, TRUTHFULNESS
Free of deceit and untruth.

Aardema, Verna. *The Lonely Lioness and the Ostrich Chicks.* Illus. by Yumi Heo. New York: Alfred A. Knopf, 1996.

In this Masai tale, a mongoose helps an ostrich get her chicks back from the lonely lioness who has stolen them.

Honesty: The lioness takes the chicks because she wants to and she can. She is dishonest with herself and the jungle animals by claiming to be the chicks' mother. She must be tricked into letting them go.

Other character traits shown: *Courage, Helpfulness, Justice, Perseverance, Prudence, Self-discipline*

Alborough, Jez. *Watch Out! Big Bro's Coming.* Cambridge, MA: Candlewick Press, 1997.

Terror spreads through the jungle as animals hear the news that rough, tough Big Bro is coming.

Honesty: Even though Big Bro turns out to be a mouse, the jungle animals from frog to elephant find honesty in little mouse's claim that Big Bro is indeed very big and very tough. Only mouse has actually seen Big Bro, but in mass hysteria, they have been bolstering their imaginations and running, Chicken Little-like, in fear of the unknown. When Big Bro is finally revealed to be mouse's big brother, at first they are puzzled. Then, Big Bro draws himself up, "looked up at them all, took a deep breath, and said,....BOO!" His rough and tough attitude confirms what little mouse has been saying. Big Bro takes mouse firmly in tow because, "Mom wants you back home *now!*" Mouse looks over his shoulder and says to the jungle animals, "I *told* you he was big!"

Duncan, Alice Faye. *Miss Viola and Uncle Ed Lee.* Illus. by Catherine Stock. New York: Atheneum Books for Young Readers (Simon & Schuster), 1999.

A young boy helps his two neighbors, one as neat as a pin and the other as junky as a packrat, become friends.

Honesty: Bradley doesn't believe that Uncle Ed Lee and Miss Viola could be friends because, "Y'all are totally different." Uncle Ed Lee honestly admits they are not alike. Even so, "just because folks are different, don't mean they can't be friends." That's true, the boy acknowledges. But if they are going to be friends, says Miss Viola, Ed Lee will have to "do something about that messy yard." That, too, is true. And Uncle Ed Lee spruces up his place for the special meeting that proves different kinds of folks can become friends.

Other character traits shown: *Courtesy, Helpfulness, Kindness, Respect, Tolerance*

Ernst, Lisa Campbell. *When Bluebell Sang.* New York: Bradbury Press (Macmillan), 1989.

Bluebell the cow's talent for singing brings her stardom, but she soon longs to be back at the farm and away from her greedy manager.

Honesty: Big Eddie, the manager has promised Bluebell and farmer Swenson that they will only be on the road a month. But he dishonestly ignores the plan and keeps them touring long after. When they tell him they want to return home, he becomes so angry they agree to continue to perform for one more month. Big Eddie replies, "Whatever you say," but he really has no intention of letting them go. He lies to them.

Other character traits shown: *Prudence*

Fowler, Susi Gregg. *Beautiful.* Illus. by Jim Fowler. New York: Greenwillow (William Morrow), 1998.

A young gardener and Uncle George collaborate on a garden, so that when a very sick Uncle George comes home from the doctor he is greeted with beautiful flowers.

Honesty: Uncle George tells the boy honestly that he is sick and can't get the care he needs locally. He's going away for treatment but will return when the flowers are ready to bloom. When he calls to say he's coming back, the boy assumes he's better. His mother tells him, "We don't think Uncle George is going to get well." Then she says that though Uncle George is coming home, "he's getting sicker." The doctors "can't help anymore." Uncle George "now just wants to be with us." The boy accepts the reality, but when Uncle George moves in and can't sit at the table with them, he admits, "I miss Uncle George the way he used to be." The family does not hide the sad truth of Uncle George's illness.

Other character traits shown: *Courage, Helpfulness, Tolerance*

Gill, Janet. *Basket Weaver and Catches Many Mice.* Illus. by Yangsook Choi. New York: Alfred A. Knopf, 1999.

A little gray cat saves the day when Basket Weaver is ordered into a competition to make the perfect basket for the Emperor's newborn daughter.

Honesty: Basket Weaver would like to avoid the competition. He does not want to live at the palace if he wins and doesn't want to work in the underground mines if he loses. But to run away would mean terrible punishment. He makes the basket and presents himself to the Emperor. When his cat and her kitten are found in the bottom of the basket meant for the newborn baby, he admits with "thumping of his heart" that the cats are his. And, when he wins the competition, he asks to return to his own home and to spare the other basket makers from the mines, because "they did their best for our future Empress." He does not hide from the truth.

Other character traits shown: *Diligence, Generosity, Loyalty, Responsibility*

Hazen, Barbara Shook. *Wally, the Worry-Warthog.* Illus. by Janet Stevens. New York: Clarion Books (Houghton Mifflin), 1990.

Wally worries about everything but discovers that the terrifying Wilberforce has as many fears as he does.

Honesty: Once the two honestly admit their mutual fears, they find much in common. Each had feared the other, and each feared what might be lurking under a bridge. Happily, their honesty has shown them each has nothing to fear from the other. And, when they face the bridge together, there is nothing there at all to fear. Their mutual honesty has enabled two lonely creatures to become friends

Other character traits shown: *Courage, Empathy*

Himmelman, John. *Honest Tulio.* New York: BridgeWater Books (Troll Associates), 1997.

As he pursues the man in the big red hat who dropped a copper coin, Tulio accumulates an unusual following, including a chicken that lays square eggs.

Honesty: Tulio is determined to return the dropped coin. He follows him on an adventure-filled long journey trying to catch up with the owner in order to give him back his coin. But when they finally meet, Tulio finds he has, by now, lost the coin and honestly admits this to the coin's owner.

Other character traits shown: *Perseverance*

Hutchins, Hazel. *Believing Sophie.* Illus. by Dorothy Donohue. Morton Grove, IL: Albert Whitman, 1995.

When a little girl is unjustly accused of shoplifting, she bravely tries to prove her innocence.

Honesty: Sophie is not satisfied that the store owner believes her explanation. How can she prove that she had bought the cough drops during an earlier trip to the store when another clerk had been at the cash register? She is free to go home, but feels the need to do something more to convince the store owner. Then, she remembers she had put the receipt in her sock when she started home on her bike earlier. Everyone in the store now knows the truth.

Other character traits shown: *Courage, Resourcefulness*

Jackson, Isaac. *Somebody's New Pajamas.* Illus. by David Soman. New York: Dial Books for Young Readers (Penguin), 1996.

When two boys from different backgrounds become friends and sleep over at each other's homes, they exchange ideas about sleepwear as well as about family life.

Honesty: Jerome's family has no extra money to waste on pajamas. He feels embarrassed about this until Dad explains why an old faded and stained tablecloth is still treasured. "There's been so much laughing around this tablecloth, it could tell its own jokes." When Jerome asks why they're using such an old tablecloth for Grandma's visit, his Dad says, "Grandma wouldn't have it any other way." This family has its own traditions. When Jerome's friend Robert comes to stay the night, he tells him honestly he won't need pajamas, because in their house they sleep in their underwear. Then, because Robert had earlier offered Jerome pajamas to wear at his house, he now returns the favor and offers to loan Robert extra underwear to use at his house. He says it in such a matter-of-fact way that Robert acts as if it is the most natural thing to do and leaves his pajamas packed.

Other character traits shown: *Courtesy, Loyalty, Respect*

Joosse, Barbara. *Lewis & Papa: Adventure on the Santa Fe Trail.* Illus. by Jon Van Zyle. San Francisco: Chronicle Books, 1998.

While accompanying his father on the wagon train along the Santa Fe Trail, Lewis discovers what it is to be a man.

Honesty: Papa honestly shares his feelings with Lewis when they hear a coyote howl for the first time. He admits he misses Mama just as Lewis does. A buffalo stampede makes Papa's legs shake "like Mama's grape jelly." He says, "There's no shame in feeling scared." Finally, when Papa has to shoot their ox Big Red because they have run out of water, it is Lewis who sees Papa crying and must help him. Papa says, "Big Red and I have been together a long time. The shame would be in feeling nothing for such a good friend."

Other character traits shown: *Courage, Fortitude, Responsibility*

Keller, Holly. *That's Mine, Horace.* New York: Greenwillow Books (HarperCollins), 2000.

Horace loves the little yellow truck that he finds in the schoolyard, but he has a problem when a classmate tries to claim it.

Honesty: No one sees Horace find the special toy, and no one sees him pocket it. Later, though, the owner does see him playing with it and says loudly that it's his. When his teacher asks, Horace says it belongs to him. His teacher tells him that she knows he would never lie. His mother, too, asks Horace about the new truck. Horace says Walter gave it to him. She says she knows Horace would never take something that did not belong to him. Only Horace knows he has lied about stealing another child's toy. This knowledge makes him feel so bad he is too ill to go to school the next day. His class sends him get-well cards. Their kindness makes him feel worse. He dreads reading Walter's card. Then, he discovers that Walter has unknowingly saved his dignity. Walter's note said that Horace could keep the truck until he was all better; then he would have to give it back. Horace happily accepts these terms and feels much better. Back at school he and Walter play with the truck together, making tunnels and roads in the sandbox. When recess is over, Walter puts the truck in his pocket, and the two run back to class together.

McKissack, Patricia. *The Honest to Goodness Truth.* Illus. by Giselle Potter. New York: Atheneum Books for Young Readers (Simon & Schuster), 2000

After promising never to lie, Libby learns it's not always necessary to blurt out the whole truth either.

Honesty: Libby felt much better when she admitted to her mother that she had tried to visit her friend before finishing her morning chore of feeding the horse. Because truth is best, she points out a hole in her friend's sock, tells teacher that a classmate didn't do his homework, and tells a neighbor that she doesn't like the look of her flower garden. Surprisingly, this honesty doesn't have good effects. She forgets that in human relationships, kindness must accompany honesty. There may be a better way to handle unpleasant truths that won't hurt feelings.

Meddaugh, Susan. *Martha Blah Blah*. Boston: Houghton Mifflin, 1996.

When the current owner of the soup company breaks the founder's promise to have every letter of the alphabet in every can of soup, Martha, the talking dog, takes action.

Honesty: Martha learns that the new owner thinks "fewer letters mean bigger profits." Martha confronts the owner in her office and accuses her of dishonesty. As she sits on the floor in front of the owner's desk, (out of sight), the only other thing visible in the room is a portrait on the wall of the business founder. The new owner thinks the founder is speaking through her picture. She is being accused of having broken her promise to include every letter in every can. The new owner tries to plead that it is good for business. Martha counters that "Good soup is your business." Quickly, the new owner makes the calls that get those missing letters back into the soup. What would people do without dogs, Martha wonders.

Other character traits shown: *Justice*

Ness, Evaline. *Sam, Bangs & Moonshine*. New York: Holt Rinehart Winston, 1966. (Caldecott–1967)

Lonely Sam's Moonshine talk nearly results in the loss of her young friend and her cat.

Honesty: Sam doesn't mean to tell lies. But her lonely life is just more interesting when she can imagine her cat talks to her when her father is gone all day fishing, and her mother is a mermaid instead of dead, and she has a pet kangaroo, and she can ride to interesting places in a chariot drawn by dragons. Hardly anyone believes her. But there is someone who does believe her "moonshine" tales. A neighbor child, little Thomas, asks every day to see the pet kangaroo. And every day she sends him off all over looking for it, because it always happens to be gone just when he comes over to her place. One day she sends him to a cave beyond a narrow spit of tide land. Momentarily she thinks about the danger of the tide rising and notes her cat stalking off in the direction Thomas has gone. But she forgets to warn the child as she drifts off in her imaginary world. Too late, she realizes the terrible danger both Thomas and Bangs are in when a fierce rain storm comes up. The moment her father comes home, she screams, "Bangs and Thomas are out on the rock! Blue Rock! Bangs and Thomas!" It is time for the truth. When the danger is over and the boy and cat are safe, her father brings her something, a gerbil, not a baby kangaroo. Sam is pleased to share her pet with Thomas. She also tells her father that, of course, she knows the difference between a cat that talks and one who would be apt to say certain things if he could talk. To symbolize her new honesty, she names the gerbil "Moonshine."

Other character traits shown: *Kindness*

Schertle, Alice. *Down the Road*. Illus. by E.B. Lewis. New York: Browndeer Press (Harcourt Brace), 1995.

Hetty is very careful with the eggs she has bought on her first trip to the store, but she runs into trouble when she stops to pick apples.

Honesty: Hetty plans to go straight home after she picks just three apples. But the basket tips as she reaches high for an apple. All the eggs fall out and break. She is so ashamed she failed her parents' trust that she "wanted to climb up into the apple tree and never, ever come down." While she is thinking, her Papa comes along. Hetty tells him honestly what happened to every single egg. And, again, when Mama comes along, "I dropped the eggs. I was trying to pick some apples." Hetty does not try to hide her catastrophe. And her parents wisely find no reason to scold.

Other character traits shown: *Empathy, Forgiveness, Kindness, Responsibility*

*Schur, Maxine Rose. *The Peddler's Gift.* Illus. by Kimberly Bulcken Root. New York: Dial Books for Young Readers (Penguin), 1999.

A young boy in rural Russia at the turn of the twentieth century learns that appearances are often deceiving after he steals a dreidel.

Honesty: The boy at first feels justified in taking the toy that has fallen from the peddler's bag and rolls under a chair. The fool won't miss it anyway. But the boy imagines how being branded a thief will be. He determines to return the top and goes out into a terrible storm to find the peddler and admit his theft. Besides personal shame for his thievery, he is surprised to find growing awareness that the peddler does not deserve his scorn.

Other character traits shown: *Courage, Forgiveness, Kindness, Respect, Responsibility*

Shannon, Margaret. *Gullible's Troubles.* Boston: Houghton Mifflin, 1998.

Although Gullible Guineapig believes everything his aunt, uncle, and cousin tell him, they, unfortunately, dismiss his warning to them about what is in the basement.

Honesty: Gullible's relatives deliberately tell him things that are untrue. His cousin says there are monsters in the garden ready to eat him. She gives him "soccer boots" that are really high-heeled lady's shoes. Then she tells him if he walks on his hands down in the cellar, the monsters there won't eat him. His aunt tells him eating 50 carrots will make him invisible. Then she gives him moldy ones. When he asks to help his uncle, he is given the task of washing dirty pieces of coal clean. Gullible accepts all this without question and, in perfect honesty, warns them, in turn, about the monster he saw in the basement. They go down to the basement, pretending to be victims of the monster. When they fail to come back up after a long time, Gullible runs home. Meanwhile, too late, they come back up, planning to admit they were just kidding him. But the real joke is on this nasty family. They are soon to become victims as a real monster can be seen lurking over their shoulders at the top of the basement stair steps.

Other character traits shown: *Justice*

Soto, Gary. *Too Many Tamales.* Illus. by Ed Martinez. New York: G.P. Putnam's Sons, 1993.

Maria tries on her mother's wedding ring while helping make tamales for a Christmas family get-together. Panic ensues when, hours later, she realizes the ring is missing.

Honesty: Maria enlists her cousins to help her find the ring, which she assumes has been baked in the tamales. They systematically eat their way through them. But no ring do they find. The youngest cousin thinks maybe he swallowed something hard. Now, there is no way to avoid admitting to her mother what probably happened to the missing ring. As Maria speaks to her mother she sees the missing ring on her mother's hand and realizes it was not accidentally baked in the tamales after all. But she needs to explain honestly why there are no tamales and why. The adults do not scold. They do, however, insist that everyone troop into the kitchen to make a second batch of tamales, because "Everyone knows the second batch of tamales always tastes better than the first, right?"

Other character traits shown: *Self-discipline*

Yacowitz, Caryn. *Pumpkin Fiesta.* Illus. by Joe Cepeda. New York: HarperCollins, 1998.

Hoping to win a prize for the best pumpkin at the fiesta, Foolish Fernando tries to copy Old Juana's successful gardening techniques, but without really watching to see how much effort and love she puts into her work.

Honesty: Though he tries to pass off Juana's pumpkins as his own, she proves they are not his. Caught as a thief, he quickly admits he was wrong to take them and tells her he is sorry. She rewards him for his belated honesty by teaching him the right way to grow large pumpkins.

Other character traits shown: *Diligence, Forgiveness, Helpfulness*

HOPE

Desire accompanied by expectation.

Auch, Mary Jane. *Bantam of the Opera.* New York: Holiday House, 1997.

Luigi the rooster wins fame and fortune when the star of the Cosmopolitan Opera Company and his understudy both come down with chicken pox on the same night.

Hope: Luigi receives no encouragement from his barnyard family when he tries to exercise his singing voice. Neither is he welcomed at the opera house by the jealous leading tenor. Still, he remains hopeful that there is more to life than cock-a-doodle-doo. He has the "soul of a musician." When his big chance comes, things do not seem promising. The crowds jeer at him. But he does not give up hope. He forges ahead with "his sweet voice." The audience is won over. He had expected to sing, and he does.

Other character traits shown: *Courage, Fortitude, Helpfulness, Perseverance*

Brown, Margaret Wise. *The Little Scarecrow Boy.* Illus. by David Diaz. New York: Joanna Cotler Books (HarperCollins), 1998.

Early one morning a little scarecrow whose father warns him that he is not fierce enough to frighten a crow away goes out into the cornfield alone to try his luck. *Hope:* The task is difficult, but the little scarecrow boy is certain he can make a face frightening enough to scare away the crows. Five times he makes a face more fierce than the previous time. The crows continue to come, but he hopes and fully expects that he can do the job. The sixth face stops the crows in fear. His father is proud of all his efforts.

Other character traits shown: *Perseverance, Responsibility*

Bunting, Eve. *Train to Somewhere.* Illus. by Ronald Himler. New York: Clarion Books (Houghton Mifflin), 1996.

In the late 1800s, Marianne travels westward on the Orphan Train with other children who hope to be placed with caring families. *Hope:* Marianne is on the train to find a home, but she hopes at one of the stops it will be her own mother, who comes to take her. Her mother had left to make a new life for them. She was to come for Marianne "before Christmas." Many Christmases have passed. Now, Marianne is going west herself. At each stop she hopes to see her mother waiting for her. It keeps up her spirits as she faces an uncertain future. A time finally comes when she can no longer keep up the pretense. "There's a sort of crumbling inside of me." Her mother is not waiting for her anywhere. As an old hope is laid aside, a new one is appropriately exchanged for it. The defining moment for Marianne comes when she gives to the woman, who will adopt her, the feather she has been saving to give to her mother.

Other character traits shown: *Courage, Empathy, Kindness, Patience, Prudence, Respect*

*Cutler, Jane. *The Cello of Mr. O.* Illus. by Greg Couch. New York: Dutton Children's Books (Penguin Putnam), 1999.

When a concert cellist plays in the square for his neighbors in a war-besieged city, his priceless instrument is destroyed by a mortar shell, but he finds the courage to return the next day to perform with a harmonica. *Hope:* Destruction of their supply truck is the lowest moment for the town's residents. Playing daily afternoon concerts in the street is an act of hope in the face of great odds. It symbolizes a bit of civilized living where all else is grubby survival. As long as there are music and music makers, there is hope for a future different from the present. Mr. O will do his part to make it happen.

Other character traits shown: *Courage, Fortitude, Generosity, Perseverance, Resourcefulness*

Daly, Niki. *Bravo Zan Angelo!* A Commedia Dell'arte Tale with Story and Pictures. New York: Farrar, Straus & Giroux, 1998.

In Renaissance Venice, Angelo, longing to be as famous a clown as his grandfather, decides to do something special with his small part in his grandfather's act during Carnival.

Hope: Angelo has no costume and no real part in his grandfather's act. Still he hopes to make a good performance. He secures a few bits and pieces to assume the role of a rooster and is ready at showtime. Then, because he wants so badly to get in the act, he shows his face before it is time, when the plan was to stay behind the curtain until the final moment. Buoyed by the audience's amused response, he is emboldened to break into a rooster strut and swagger across the stage, "swishing his tail and pumping his arms just like Bardolino" the real rooster he imitates. When he lets go with a mighty Cock-a-doodle-doo, his grandfather is suddenly aware of the boy's intrusion into his act and the chase is on. The delighted audience thinks it's all part of the act. Hoping to become a clown has made it happen.

Other character traits shown: *Courage, Courtesy, Helpfulness, Kindness, Perseverance, Resourcefulness*

dePaola, Tomie. *The Legend of the Indian Paintbrush.* New York: G.P. Putnam's Sons, 1988.

Little Gopher follows his destiny, as revealed in a Dream-Vision, of becoming an artist for his people and eventually is able to bring the colors of the sunset down to earth.

Hope: Little Gopher paints the deeds of the People and the dreams of the shaman, because that is his job. He hopes, for himself, to one day also paint the sunset's true colors. But his paints are not bright enough. Still he continues true to his gift and works faithfully in behalf of the People. Finally, he is rewarded with some special brushes containing the colors he needs to accurately paint the sunset.

Other character traits shown: *Diligence, Loyalty, Patience, Perseverance, Responsibility, Self-discipline*

*Edwards, Pamela Duncan. *Honk!* Illus. by Henry Cole. New York: Hyperion Books for Children, 1998.

A ballet-loving swan wins acclaim when she manages to join the dancers in a performance of Swan Lake.

Hope: Mimi's vision is to be a ballet performer. She practices her ballet pose when she lands on the pond. She watches the Paris Opera from the ledge at the top of the opera house and then practices every day the beautiful leaps and twirls. It is not enough. She must sit inside. But birds are not allowed in the Opera House. She is turned out. She manages to not only get inside but, eventually, to enter the performance. Her complete confidence in her dream enables her to remember everything she's practiced. Audience reaction is gratifying. They cheer and clap and demand more. She is part of the show.

Other character traits shown: *Perseverance, Resourcefulness, Tolerance*

*Garland, Sherry. *The Lotus Seed.* Illus. by Tatsuro Kiuchi. New York: Harcourt Brace Jovanovich, 1993.

A young Vietnamese girl saves a lotus seed and carries it with her everywhere to remember a brave emperor and the homeland that she has to flee.

Hope: Throughout her youth and as a young married woman, she keeps the seed of hope. When finally she is forced to leave her homeland, she preserves the seed and takes it to her new adopted country. It remains a symbol of hope for a land that used to be. All her working years the seed remains undisturbed until one day her grandson, who had never seen a lotus bloom or an emperor, steals it and plants it in a pool of mud near the woman's onion patch. She grieves its loss, because it seems the final closure on her beloved old way of life. But in the spring the seed sprouts and become a beautiful pink lotus, a "flower of life and hope." She realizes "no matter how ugly the mud or how long the seed lays dormant, the bloom will be beautiful." She has many seeds now, for her grandchildren to "remember her by and for herself to remember the emperor by."

Other character traits shown: *Loyalty, Respect*

*Gregory, Valiska. *Through the Mickle Woods.* Illus. by Barry Moser. Boston: Little, Brown & Co., 1992.

After his wife's death, a grieving king journeys to an old bear's cave in the mickle (thick) woods, where he hears three stories that help him go on living.

Hope: The king has lost hope in the goodness of life. His existence is dark and cold. Joy is gone. But, through those who care about him, he learns to continue to enjoy all that is still there for him just as his wife always enjoyed living fully. And he learns that, "Whether we are born high or low, the same things come to us all." Hope is finally back in his heart. He is able, just as she predicted, to mark how merrily the morning bells ring.

Other character traits shown: *Discernment, Empathy, Forgiveness, Generosity, Helpfulness, Kindness, Perseverance*

Haseley, Dennis. *The Old Banjo.* Illus. by Stephen Gammell. New York: Macmillan, 1983.

A hardworking farmer and his son succumb to the enchantment of some very special musical instruments that have been abandoned on their farm.

Hope: In the midst of a dour life of hard work, a boy wonders momentarily if "some band used to live here." The instruments he finds would seem evidence of a possibly happier life than he is living. "I wish we could have heard them," is all he says on the subject before his father reminds him that they're gone now and there's the never ending work to do. But one day when "the sky is the color of a stone" the "old banjo remembers how a smiling old woman and all her sons and daughters used to sit on the porch and fill the night with music." The banjo "gives a quiet little pluck." And slowly the other instruments add their small sounds— the violin, the piano, the trombone, the trumpet. The farmer and the boy "put down their tools." The boy "looks up and smiles." His hope is fulfilled. This farm will unlikely continue to be the place of drudgery it has been.

*Hoestlandt, Jo. *Star of Fear, Star of Hope.* Illus. by Johanna Kang. Trans. by Mark Polizzotti. New York: Walker & Co., 1995.

Nine-year-old Helen is confused by the disappearance of her Jewish friend during the German occupation of Paris.

Hope: Many years have passed since the girls were together for a last birthday party. Helen never saw Lydia after that night. But she has never forgotten her best friend and hopes she lived to become a grandma like herself, somewhere in the world. She would love to get a call on the telephone. "It would make me so happy to hear her voice ... I'll always have hope."

Other character traits shown: *Courage, Discernment, Forgiveness*

Kay, Verla. *Gold Fever.* Illus. by S.D. Schindler. New York: G.P. Putnam's Sons, 1999.

Jasper leaves his family during the gold rush to pursue his dream.

Hope: Jasper forsakes "barnyard, pitchfork, hoe, farmhouse, family" and takes "shovel, pistol, pick, goldpan, bedroll, and walking stick" to seek gold. He is smitten with the hope of becoming rich. He is certain panning for gold will be more profitable than farming. Soon enough his false illusions and foolish hopes are destroyed. He learns the unpleasant reality of his dreams of finding gold. He is only too happy to return to the life of a farmer where lies his true hope for happiness.

Other character traits shown: *Responsibility*

McCully, Emily Arnold. *The Ballot Box Battle.* New York: Alfred A. Knopf, 1996.

Elizabeth Cady Stanton, famous nineteenth-century leader in the struggle for women's rights, inspires Cordelia to overcome all obstacles to carry on the fight for equality.

Hope: Mrs. Stanton never gave up hope that her father would one day accept her as being as good as any boy. She studied Greek and horse management to prove her equality. Neither did she give up trying to win equal rights for women when she became an adult. She went to voting precincts regularly to try to vote and received nothing but ridicule and abuse for her efforts. Failure never dampened her hopes that eventually she would be vindicated. Cordelia begins to see the injustices she as a girl faces. Her brother taunts her at the polling booth and tells her to go home where she belongs. She fears maybe father will be angry that she has come with Mrs. Stanton. But eventually her sense of right and wrong is outraged enough to spur her to action. Her first efforts to prove the equal worth of females is to, on horseback, jump a four-foot fence. There is hope, says Mrs. Stanton, that "the day will come when this girl may vote." Cordelia understands at last something of Mrs. Stanton's fight for equality.

Other character traits shown: *Courage, Diligence, Discernment, Fortitude*

Moss, Marissa. *True Heart.* Illus. by C.F. Payne. New York: Silver Whistle (Harcourt Brace), 1999.

At the turn of the twentieth century, a young woman who works for a railroad accomplishes her yearning ambition to become an engineer when a male engineer is injured and can't drive his train.

Hope: Bee is teased by her co-workers about doing "grunt work" while hoping for an engineer's job. But she is philosophical. She is going to be an engineer someday, but "while I'm waiting, I may as well grunt." She laughs with her friends. "I knew I wouldn't be grunting forever. I waited and kept my eyes open."

Other character traits shown: *Diligence, Perseverance*

Provensen, Alice, and Martin Provensen. *The Glorious Flight: Across the Channel with Louis Blériot July 25, 1909.* New York: Viking Press, 1983. (Caldecott–1984)

A man whose fascination with flying machines produces the Blériot XI, crosses the English Channel in 37 minutes in the early 1900s.

Hope: It is while he was on a family outing in his automobile that an air ship (blimp) went flying overhead. Louis Blériot said, "I, too, will build a flying machine. A great white bird. We will work hard. We will all fly through the air like swallows!" But it takes six years and 11 versions of a flying machine before his skills are good enough and his plane's design is sound enough to fly from France to England across the English Channel. Along the way are accidents and failures. With hope that he will succeed he continues. "We almost flew!" he says when one of his machines goes in beautiful circles on water. "Not so bad!" is the pronouncement when it hits a rock. There is a "slight crash," a "broken rib," a "black eye," and a "list of breaks, sprains, and bruises." But hope prevails until, "a wonderful moment!"

Other character traits shown: *Fortitude, Perseverance*

Ransom, Candice F. *The Promise Quilt.* Illus. by Ellen Beier. New York: Walker & Co., 1999.

After her father leaves the family farm on Lost Mountain to be General Lee's guide, Addie finds ways to remember him—even when he does not return at the end of the war.

Hope: Throughout the war, Addie thinks about the promise her father made that when she is bigger she will learn to read and write and make her mark in life. With the war over and poverty in the mountains, how will this promise be kept? A neighbor donates use of a shed while the community rebuilds the school. Hope is maintained. But they need books, too. They inquire of the woman who had sent back Papa's shirt how they might get books for their school. The woman suggests that she could raffle off a quilt if they would make one. And Addie donates the precious shirt in order to complete the quilt. The books arrive. Papa's promise is kept.

Other character traits shown: *Fortitude, Generosity, Helpfulness, Hope*

*Shannon, George. *This Is the Bird.* Illus. by David Soman. Boston: Houghton Mifflin, 1997.

A cumulative tale about a wooden bird carved by a little girl's maternal ancestor and passed down lovingly from mother to daughter through the generations.

Hope: The bird is first carved from a wagon spoke by a pregnant woman, "while waiting for her baby in a small sod house, and didn't have a single tree to see." Her symbol of hope, becomes, in turn, a similar symbol for future women in the family. One hides it in the butter she was churning when robbers came. One, who couldn't hear a sound, sews it in the hem of her dress when she "went away to school to learn to talk with her hands." Another grabs it on the way to a cellar, when a tornado blows away their new roof. One rubs it for courage and strength when she tells her father she prefers college to the good job he got her at his bank. One loses it for years and feels so sad she "filled the house with small wooden birds" until it is found again in a furnace vent. She then gives away the replacement birds as Halloween treats. Another unpacks it first "when she moved to the Arctic to teach first grade." And, finally, the last girl receives it "to celebrate trying again after falling last week on my first high dive and being too scared to ever dive again." This is the bird that will be kept "till the right time comes to pass it along."

Other character traits shown: *Respect*

Shea, Pegi Deitz. *The Whispering Cloth: A Refugee's Story.* Illus. by Anita Riggio. Stitched by You Yang. Honesdale, PA: Boyds Mills Press, 1995.

A young girl from Laos, Cambodia in a Thai refugee camp during the Vietnam war finds the story within herself to create her own Pa'ndau (story cloth).

Hope: Mai has known no life outside the refugee camp for a long time. She rereads letters from her cousins, who have moved to America. Everyone seems to leave the camp but she. Making and selling story cloths is the means to earn money to buy a ticket to America. She practices her stitchery and helps her grandmother make

Pa'ndaus for traders. But the one she makes of her own story, though well done and worth much, she chooses to keep. It is the story that ends with the new home she expects to have outside the refugee camp, and it is her symbol of hope for a new life.

Other character traits shown: *Fortitude, Respect*

Shulevitz, Uri. *Snow.* New York: Farrar, Straus & Giroux, 1998.

As snowflakes slowly come down one by one, people in the city ignore them; only a boy and his dog think that the snowfall will amount to anything.

Hope: From the first unpromising snowflake, the boy's desire for snow convinces him it is snowing. His expectations are contrary to the rest of the city's prediction. It's nothing. It'll melt. No snow, the television and radio say. But nothing dissuades him. One flake follows another until hope has turned into joyous reality. Just the boy, his dog, and Mother Goose, and some of her storybook characters, who hop off the bookshop storefront, cavort in the white city.

Steig, William. *Sylvester and the Magic Pebble.* New York: Simon & Schuster, 1969. (Caldecott–1970)

In a moment of fright, Sylvester asks his magic pebble to turn him into a rock, but then can not wish himself back to normal again.

Hope: Because Sylvester has to be touching the magic pebble in order for wishes to happen, he knows that, as a rock, his chance of being turned back into himself is "one in a billion at best." Yet, he can't help but hope that "someone would surely find the red pebble—it was so bright and shiny…" Back at home his parents search and have friends search for their beloved child. They conclude that "something dreadful must have happened and that they would probably never see their son again." They are miserable. Sylvester "felt he would be a rock forever and he tried to get used to it." He sleeps a lot because "when he was awake, he was only hopeless and unhappy." On the day that his parents came to have a picnic at the rock site, his father finds the magic pebble. "Sylvester would have loved it for his collection." His mother said, "I have the strangest feeling that our dear Sylvester is still alive and not far away." Hope has returned to the family. Soon, they are reunited as they all wish "he were here with us on this lovely May day."

Other character traits shown: *Fortitude*

Van Allsburg, Chris. *The Polar Express.* Boston: Houghton Mifflin, 1985. (Caldecott–1986)

A magical train ride on Christmas Eve takes a boy to the North Pole to receive a special gift from Santa Claus.

Hope: It is fitting that this child be selected to receive the "first gift of Christmas." He has the Christmas hope. He lies in bed silently waiting to hear a sound "a friend had told me I'd never hear, the ringing bells of Santa's sleigh." The friend has said there is no Santa, but "I knew he was wrong." Still, it is not the sleigh he hears that

Christmas Eve. It is the hissing steam and squeaking metal of the Polar Express, come to collect him for a night's journey to the North Pole. Like the other children in their bedtime wear, he is welcomed aboard and enjoys "candies with nougat centers as white as snow" and "cocoa as thick and rich as melted chocolate bars." The mystical journey ends at Santa's city where all the elves make way for the children's arrival. Santa will choose one of them to receive the first gift. The huge bag of gifts is ready. The boy is enchanted by the magical sound of the sleigh bells. Santa points to the story's narrator and is clearly pleased when this child asks for "one silver bell from Santa's reindeer harness." Back on the train, the other children ask to see it, but it has dropped out of a hole in the boy's bathrobe pocket. It breaks his heart to lose the bell. But back home on Christmas morning, the bell has been delivered by Santa after all. The boy enjoys the bell's sound throughout the years. His parents always assumed the bell was broken; they never heard it. But over the years, the bell is not silent for those who have Christmas hope.

*Waldman, Neil. *The Starry Night.* Honesdale, PA: Boyds Mills Press, 1999.

Vincent Van Gogh befriends a young boy in New York City in this fantasy about art and creativity.
Hope: The boy finds something compelling about the artist's beautiful paintings. He is able to make the ordinary city "never look better." After many days of showing him new sights to paint, the boy is, in turn, shown one special place by the artist. In the art museum are many beautiful pictures. But the one with "the swirling stars, the orange moon, and the sleeping village" makes the boy's eyes widen. Soon he is sitting in front of the picture with his own sketch pad and a box of colored pencils. It is his hope to make the Big Apple look great, too.
Other character traits shown: *Helpfulness, Generosity*

Yolen, Jane. *Owl Moon.* Illus. by John Schoenherr. New York: Philomel Books, 1987. (Caldecott–1988)

On a winter's night under a full moon, a father and daughter trek into the woods to see the Great Horned Owl.
Hope: The night is cold and silent. This is the girl's first owling with her father and she has been waiting for it a long time. When he calls, they pause to listen for a return hoot. At first there is no response. She is prepared, so is not disappointed. Her brothers have all said, "Sometimes there's an owl and sometimes there isn't." They continue walking. The cold deepens. She listens and hopes. Finally there is a faint call in return. The owl comes closer. A shadow flies over their head. It lands on a tree branch. Their flashlight catches the owl and the owl and humans stare at one another. The owl leaves first. It's time to go home. It is ok to talk or laugh now, but she does not break the spell of silence. When you go owling, she thinks, you don't need words or warm or anything but hope. "The kind of hope that flies on silent wings under a shining Owl Moon."
Other character traits shown: *Empathy, Self-discipline*

INTEGRITY. *SEE* FAIRNESS, FORTITUDE, HONESTY, JUSTICE

JUSTICE

Use for INTEGRITY

To uphold what is right, correct, honorable and fair and to be free of prejudice, partiality, discrimination, and dishonesty.

Aardema, Verna. *The Lonely Lioness and the Ostrich Chicks.* Illus. by Yumi Heo. New York: Alfred A. Knopf, 1996.

In this Masai tale, a mongoose helps an ostrich get her chicks back from the lonely lioness who has stolen them.

Justice: The lioness has strength and determination on her side. The ostrich has right and determination on her side. Justice demands that the mother be returned her children. Eventually, along the way, one of the animals, whom the ostrich beseeches to help her, comes up with the correct method to dislodge the stolen babies from a formidable foe.

Other character traits shown: *Courage, Helpfulness, Honesty, Perseverance, Prudence, Self-discipline*

Bunting, Eve. *So Far From the Sea.* Illus. by Chris K. Soentpiet. New York: Clarion Books (Houghton Mifflin), 1998.

When seven-year-old Laura and her family visit Grandfather's grave at the Manzanar War Relocation Center, the Japanese American child leaves behind a special symbol.

Justice: The Japanese aggression against the United States caused paranoid reactions against Japanese Americans. Laura's father and grandfather were relocated into a detention camp. Grandfather had his own home and a tuna boat, but "the government took those things and Grandfather's dignity along with them when they brought him here, so far from the sea." Even though Grandfather asked his son to put on his Cub Scout uniform so "they will know you are a true American and they will not take you, they took me anyway. They took all of us." Laura pronounces this behavior wrong. She is angry at the lack of justice afforded her relatives. But, as her father points out, "It wasn't fair that Japan attacked this country either." He says there was a lot of fear and anger then, but, "We have to put it behind us and move on." This last visit to the grave site is a farewell act of respect. The Cub Scout neckerchief flutters like a boat with sails skimming the wind, heading away from this unhappy place.

Other character traits shown: *Forgiveness, Respect*

Bunting, Eve. *Summer Wheels.* Illus. by Thomas B. Allen. New York: Harcourt Brace Jovanovich, 1992.

The Bicycle Man fixes up old bicycles and offers both his friendship and the use of the bikes to the neighborhood kids.

Justice: It doesn't seem fair to Lawrence that the tough boy is permitted to check out a second bike after failing to return the first one according to the rules. But the Bicycle Man operates a different kind of justice. The boy needs a father figure more than the bike shop needs bikes. The tough boy deliberately trashes a bike to so that he will have to fix it in the shop and ensure that he and the Man will work together.

Other character traits shown: *Courage, Empathy, Forgiveness, Generosity, Kindness, Responsibility, Respect, Tolerance*

Burningham, John. *Whaddayamean.* New York: Crown, 1999.

When God sees what a mess has been made of the world, He gets two children to convince everyone to help make it the lovely place it was meant to be.

Justice: Seen through the eyes and hearts of children, this view of correcting earth's ailments has the children telling grownups that God has told them what should be done, and the people respond. So it comes to pass that the men with money stop cutting trees, dirtying the waters, and fouling the air. Men who speak for God stop quarreling amongst themselves. Men in uniforms threw away bombs and guns that hurt and kill. People who had stood by and took no notice of what was happening begin to notice. As a result, people who did not have enough to eat had enough to eat. "And the world became a better world."

Other character traits shown: *Diligence, Responsibility*

Fleming, Candace. *When Agnes Caws.* Illus. by Giselle Potter. New York: Anne Schwartz Book, Atheneum Books for Young Readers (Simon & Schuster), 1999.

When eight-year-old Agnes Peregrine, an accomplished bird caller, travels with her mother to the Himalayas in search of the elusive pink-headed duck, she encounters a dastardly foe.

Justice: Colonel Pittsnap wants the pink-headed duck to add to his collection of stuffed wildlife. He will stop at nothing to have his way. When he catches the duck, he threatens Agnes if she refuses to "call some birds for my collection." Agnes does indeed call them, all of them at once. They dive bomb the nasty man, "weaving, swatting, crouching, dodging," them. He flees for his "birdpecked" life. Justice has prevailed. Agnes and her mother untangle the pink-headed duck from the colonel's net, restoring its freedom.

Other character traits shown: *Resourcefulness*

Gerrard, Roy. *The Roman Twins.* New York: Farrar, Straus & Giroux, 1998.

Maximus and his twin sister Vanilla, slaves to the cruel and greedy Slobbus Pompius, risk their lives to save a horse and end up helping to save the city of Rome from the Goths.

Justice: The greedy Slobbus is at the chariot race conclusion to demand revenge against his slaves, who have run away with his horse in order to save its life. The law demands that runaways should suffer death. But when the children bravely help save the city against the invaders by cutting the ropes that hold up the bridge over which the Goths intended to cross, the Emperor shows his gratitude to the children instead of punishing them. He "gave them gifts of gold." Then, seeing that Slobbus was vexed, he ordered Slobbus, "by himself, to build the bridge again."

Other character traits shown: *Courage, Loyalty*

Hassett, John, and Ann Hassett. *Cat Up a Tree.* Boston: Walter Lorraine Books (Houghton Mifflin), 1998.

With rapidly increasing numbers of cats stuck in her tree, Nana Quimby asks for help from the firehouse, police, pet shop, zoo, post office, library, and city hall, but no one will help rescue the cats.

Justice: Her problem, they tell her, is not their problem. Call back, says the firehouse, if the cat starts playing with matches. Call back, say the police, if the cats rob a bank. Call back, says the pet shop, if the cats wish to buy a dog. Call back, says the zoo, if one of the cats is the tiger they are missing. And so goes her requests for assistance. When 35 cats are up her tree, Nana throws her phone out the window. The cats walk the telephone line in through her window and "into Nana Quimby's arms." Then, all the sources of help that failed her, suddenly call her for help. "Mice!" they say, are in the firehouse, city hall, the jail, in books, everywhere! But Nana Quimby tells them her cats "do not catch mice anymore. Call back if you wish to hear cats purr." (Poetic) justice in this city has been served.

Jonas, Ann. *Watch William Walk.* New York: Greenwillow (William Morrow), 1997.

William and Wilma take a walk with Wally the dog and Wanda the duck.

Justice: In this very basic story, a fundamental kind of justice is evident when William and his active dog Wally cannot bear to wait for the slower Wilma and waddling Wanda to keep up. They rush ahead leaving them behind. But when they reach the water, it is Wanda the duck who won't wait for the others. Released by earthly confines, she is in her element and races off leaving them behind. As they join her in the water, trying to keep up, they are weary, winded, and weakened. Wanda whirls; her wake widens. She takes waves, whirlpools, and whitecaps with ease.

Krupinski, Loretta. *Best Friends.* New York: Hyperion Books for Children, 1998.

When a settler's young daughter learns that soldiers will force the Nez Perce off the nearby land, she uses a doll to warn her Indian friend of impending danger.

Justice: A traveling salesman tells what he knows about the soldiers' plan to round up the Indians to put them on a reservation. The white girl is outraged by this injustice. "But Lily says the land has belonged to her people forever," she recalls. There is little time to take action. The girl's parents agree with her that something must be done. They say, however, it would be too dangerous to go to the village with the soldiers about to strike. The girl feels it is wrong to do nothing. "Ma and I came up with a plan." She puts a warning message inside her beloved doll's head and asks the traveling medicine doctor to give the doll to her friend as a last parting gift when he visits the village. He will be the unwitting courier. "Pa agreed it was the right thing to do."

Other character traits shown: *Generosity, Helpfulness, Kindness, Loyalty, Resourcefulness, Respect*

Lester, Helen. *Hooway for Wodney Wat.* Illus. by Lynn Munsinger. Boston: Walter Lorraine Books (Houghton Mifflin), 1999.

All his classmates make fun of Rodney because he can't pronounce his name, but it is Rodney's speech impediment that drives away the class bully.

Justice: Rodney's name is drawn to be leader for the game 'Simon Says' at recess. His classmates make allowance for his inability to pronounce R's when he calls out "Weed the sign." But new student, Camilla Capybara, a terrible bully, takes his directive literally. At P.S. 142 Elementary School for Rodents, she begins "pulling up weeds around the sign and wildly flinging them hither and yon till she was clear up to her teeth in dirt." The other students begin to smile. When Rodney calls out to "wap your paws awound your head," she did that, too, "Whap! Whap! Whappity Slappity Whap!" Rodney's directives continue. Camilla tries and tries to "Wake the leaves," but her, "Rise and shine!" gets no results. Finally, when Rodney says, "go west!" the other students sit down to rest while the frustrated bully stomps off in the direction she believes is west, "Forever. She was gone." Rodney is the hero. Camilla Capybara has received the justice she deserves for upsetting the school.

Other character traits shown: *Respect*

Lester, Helen. *Princess Penelope's Parrot.* Illus. by Lynn Munsinger. Boston: Houghton Mifflin, 1996.

An arrogant and greedy princess's chances with a rich prince are ruined when her parrot repeats to him all the rude comments the princess made to the parrot.

Justice: The long-suffering parrot is the victim of the princess's tirades. Before her guest, the prince, arrives, the princess banishes the silent parrot behind her chair. When the parrot finally speaks, it is most untimely that he should choose to repeat the princess's own words while her guest is present. The prince hears "Gimme" as he hands over the roses he brought and "Talk, Big Beak." He assumes the princess is speaking and he soon wishes to be somewhere else. But there is more. "Speak or I'll Rattle Your Cage." "All Righty Then, I'll Put You On a Ball And Chain." These and similar unpleasant comments, quickly convinces the prince he has heard enough.

There is nothing the princess can do to undue her previous rude language. The parrot has learned well. Justice has prevailed. The prince is gone and she is alone.

*Mathers, Petra. *Victor and Christabel.* New York: Alfred A. Knopf, 1993.

The shy guard at an art museum falls in love with the sad young woman in a painting that mysteriously appears one day.

Justice: Christabel's insensitive cousin is demanding, rude, and a nuisance with his inept magic tricks. It wears down her health running all over town for the ingredients he wants, not to mention being a house servant to him with cooking, laundering, and cleaning. It is no wonder she falls ill and goes to bed with a cold. He tries to turn her into a cockroach, and this is the last straw. She throws her cup of tea at him and orders him out of her house and her life. He, in turn, calls her a "good-for-nothing mole tail, crawling in and out of bed with your endless cups of tea, sniffling your life away in your stuffy room. Stay there, then, red-nosed and bleary-eyed for all the world to see, like a picture in a museum." Suddenly, at this inopportune moment his magic works. She and her room are transformed into a framed picture. Cousin Anatole packs his bags and drops her off at the nearest museum. The museum guard is drawn to her look of sadness in the picture. He puts a night light on for her, brings her flowers, and talks soothingly to her. But it is the cup of tea he brings that finally breaks the spell and returns her to life. The girl's misery is ended, and happiness is rightfully restored.

Other character traits shown: *Kindness*

McCully, Emily Arnold. *The Bobbin Girl.* New York: Dial Books for Young Readers (Penguin), 1996.

A 10-year-old bobbin girl working in a textile mill in Lowell, Massachusetts, in the 1830s must make a difficult decision.

Justice: All workers at the cotton mills were women, because men refused to work for such low wages. The mill owners had the habit of not telling the workers about any accidents and didn't stop the machines. One of the working girls is struck by a shuttle that flies off the loom when she turns aside to cough, due to cotton dust. The injured girl is called "careless," and she is fired. The bobbin girl's sense of justice is outraged. This injury is not the girl's fault. She was not careless. On top of this injustice, the mill owners arbitrarily decide to lower wages by 15 percent because they claim the price of cotton has fallen. At this final injustice, the women "turn out," refusing to work. They withdraw their bank savings, which threatens the solidity of the local bank. But justice is not served during this first "strike." The mill owners do not give in. They simply hire new workers as replacements for those who go home. Still, the girls, who had stood up to injustice, are not defeated. They continue their battle at other mills, working to improve conditions. "We showed we can stand up for what is right. Next time, or the time after, we will win."

Other character traits shown: *Cooperation, Courage, Perseverance, Prudence*

*Meddaugh, Susan. *Cinderella's Rat.* Boston: Walter Lorraine Books (Houghton Mifflin), 1997.

One of the rats that was turned into a coachman by Cinderella's fairy godmother tells his story.

Justice: The rat and his sister had been living a marginal life with too many cats about and too little food. That all changed on the fateful evening the fairy godmother turned him into a boy. His sister, still her rat self, hitches a ride on the coach and they soon find themselves in the palace kitchen. One of the servants nearly kills his sister until he shouts that the rat is his sister. The servant takes him and his sister to a wizard to end what the servant assumes has been an awful spell cast on her. The "coachman" cannot explain that it is he, a rat, who has had a spell cast upon him, turning him into a boy. The palace "would turn us both into food for cats." So, the "boy" and his rat sister submit to the wizard's talents. The outcome is mixed. Sister rat is turned into a girl, but one that "Woofs" instead of talks. Then, the spell cast by the fairy godmother ends, of course, at midnight. The coachman is turned back into his rat self. Nowadays, the rat family lives better in their own cottage with sister rat (the girl) looking after them all. And there is no longer any bother with cats, because sister "Woofs" them away. All's fair and a certain justice prevails, because, "Life is full of surprises, so you may as well get used to it."

Other character traits shown: *Tolerance*

Meddaugh, Susan. *Martha Blah Blah.* Boston: Houghton Mifflin, 1996.

When the current owner of the soup company breaks the founder's promise to have every letter of the alphabet in every can of soup, Martha the talking dog takes action.

Justice: The new owner tries to cheat the consumers by taking out some of the alphabet letters. "No one will even notice the difference." But, of course, Martha does. Her words are short the letters that were not in the can and she can no longer speak. She discovers who is responsible and goes on the attack, shaming the new owner with her dishonesty. By the time Martha is finished, the missing letters have been restored and the new owner has learned to honor her promises. Justice has been achieved.

Other character traits shown: *Honesty*

Mosel, Arlene. *The Funny Little Woman.* Illus. by Blair Lent. New York: E.P. Dutton, 1972. (Caldecott–1973)

Chasing a rice dumpling down an underground hole leads to the capture of a laughing woman, who in turn, causes her captors to laugh, which leads to her escape.

Justice: It seems the woman's inability to keep from laughing was her downfall. She is found hiding and is taken by the monsters as a slave to cook their meals. When she tries to escape by boat, they drink up the stream water and the boat founders in the mud. She jumps from the boat and begins running. "Her feet stuck in the mud, her hands stuck in the mud, and she fell in the mud!" The monsters roar with laughter at her appearance, and the water fell from their mouths back into the river, thereby enabling her to paddle off to safety. It is justice that her inability to keep from laughing at the monsters, which leads to her capture, is offset by the monsters' inability to keep from laughing at her, which leads to her escape.

Potter, Beatrix. *The Tale of Peter Rabbit.* London: Frederick Warne & Co., 1902.

Mrs. Rabbit goes out on errands after admonishing her children to stay away from Mr. McGregor's garden.

Justice: Three of the Rabbit children obey their mother and enjoy an afternoon of berry picking followed by a pleasant dinner and delicious dessert. Peter, on the other hand, ignores her warning, eats himself sick in the forbidden garden, loses his clothes, has to run for his life, gets lost, comes down with a cold and gets chamomile tea and early bedtime instead of his dinner. For putting his life unnecessarily in danger, Peter must live with the justice resulting from the consequences of his choices.

Other character traits shown: *Self-discipline*

Rael, Elsa Okon. *What Zeesie Saw on Delancey Street.* Illus. by Marjorie Priceman. New York: Simon & Schuster, 1996.

A young Jewish girl living on Manhattan's Lower East Side attends her first "package party" where she learns about the traditions of community giving among Jewish immigrants in the early 1900s.

Justice: Her curiosity has resulted in Zeesie witnessing what was intended to be a private act. One by one, each man enters the money box room and either takes from the box or adds to it according to need or ability. But no one ever tells. Now, Zeesie, who has snooped where she was told not to go, knows something about one of the party guests. She feels ashamed. But perhaps there is a means to help undue her wrong. She takes the dollar given her by her grandparents to spend on her birthday and puts it into the box. No one will know that she was in the room or that she saw a man in need take out money from the box. She can never tell what she saw or what she did to make amends. Justice has been self-administered.

Other character traits shown: *Generosity, Responsibility*

Scheffler, Ursel. *Stop Your Crowing, Kasimir!* Illus. by Silke Brix-Henker. Minneapolis: Carolrhoda, 1988.

Katy's neighbors appeal to the authorities to silence her extremely loud rooster, but the final result is very different from what they had in mind.

Justice: Katy's neighbors succeed in driving her away. But construction machines move in. The noise of Katy's crowing rooster is nothing compared to the nightly noise of the new disco that sets on the same site. Meanwhile, Katy and her animals have settled into her old farm in the country where each evening they watch the sun go down. Katy sighs in relief that ironically, "Finally, at last, we have some peace and quiet."

Other character traits shown: *Cooperation, Tolerance*

Shannon, Margaret. *Gullible's Troubles.* Boston: Houghton Mifflin, 1998.

Although Gullible Guineapig believes everything his aunt, uncle, and cousin tell him, they, unfortunately, dismiss his warning about what is in the basement.

Justice: Gullible's relatives take advantage of his naiveté. His aunt makes him believe eating 50 carrots will make him invisible, then gives him moldy ones. His uncle sets him the task of washing coal clean. His cousin teases him about monsters in the basement. If he walks on his hands down there, they won't eat him. They even tease him by going down to the basement and staying there so long he thinks the monster has eaten them. What they don't know is that he really did see evidence of a monster down there. He warns them. They ignore him, because they assume he is as deceitful as they have been to him. He runs home to Mama as they try to tell him they were just kidding. But behind them lurks a monster ready to administer justice.

Other character traits shown: *Honesty*

Sisulu, Elinor Batezat. *The Day Gogo Went to Vote: South Africa, April 1994.* Illus. by Sharon Wilson. New York: Little, Brown & Co., 1997.

Thembi and her beloved great-grandmother, who has not left home for many years, go together to vote on the momentous day when black South Africans are allowed to vote for the first time.

Justice: The township people have looked forward to the chance to determine their own political destiny. Now, the old woman must explain why, despite her great age and frailty, she must go to the voting precinct. Her family means well to think about her health, but they don't understand the significance of this event. This is the first time, and for her, may be the last time, she will ever vote for her leaders. And "because she was born in the olden days, Gogo knows a lot of things that happened long ago." She has a sense of history that younger family members do not yet possess. It is her right to lead the way.

Other character traits shown: *Helpfulness, Respect, Responsibility*

*Turner, Ann. *Katie's Trunk.* Illus. by Ron Himler. New York: Macmillan, 1992.

Katie, whose family is not sympathetic to the rebel soldiers during the American Revolution, hides under the clothes in her mother's wedding trunk when they invade her home.

Justice: Katie's friend's father is among those who plundered her family's home. It is he who discovers her hiding as he rummaged about in the trunk. Instead of exposing her to his dangerous companions, he creates a diversion, shouting that the Tories are coming. He doesn't close the trunk lid as they all rush out. "He left the trunk lid up to let me breathe and called the others away." Katie realizes he has acted upon a more basic justice than political differences.

Other character traits shown: *Kindness*

*Van Allsburg, Chris. *The Sweetest Fig.* Boston: Houghton Mifflin, 1993.

After being given two magical figs that make his dreams come true, Monsieur Bibot sees his plans for future wealth upset by his long-suffering dog.

Justice: When Monsieur Bibot eats the first fig, he finds his night dream has become reality the next day. He is indeed walking down the street in his underwear and the Eiffel Tower has drooped over as if it were made of soft rubber. He will not waste the second fig on dreams so foolish. He prepares himself to dream about being rich. Daily he looks in the mirror and tries to mentally hypnotize himself into believing he is the richest man on earth. Soon, in his dreams, that's exactly what he is. He is ready to eat the remaining fig. But he discovers his dog has just gobbled it down, and now the dog's dreams become reality. Monsieur Bibot has been cruel and thoughtless to little Marcel. The dog dreams of exchanging places with Bibot. That becomes reality. Bibot suddenly finds himself under the bed, not in it, the next morning. And a face, his own face appears in front of him. "Time for your walk," it says to him. "A hand reached down and grabbed him. Bibot tried to yell, but all he could do was bark."

*Wiesniewski, David. *Golem.* New York: Clarion Books (Houghton Mifflin), 1996. (Caldecott–1997)

A saintly rabbi miraculously brings to life a clay giant who helps watch over the Jews of sixteenth-century Prague.

Justice: The Jews are forbidden to own weapons and are forced to live in a tiny area of the city. Their means of livelihood is limited. When they become the victims of vicious lies, they have no means of defense. Except, however, they can create a golem. His massive physical strength makes up for the deficiencies in their manner of living. Brute strength defeats overwhelming persecution. It is only fair that, deprived as they are of a means of securing their own welfare, they have special access to a unique defense system.

Other character traits shown: *Helpfulness, Loyalty, Respect*

KINDNESS

Use for CARING, CHARITY, CIVILITY, COMPASSION, THOUGHTFULNESS
Acting with goodwill toward another.

Aardema. Verna. *Koi and the Kola Nuts.* Illus. by Joe Cepeda. New York: Anne Schwartz Book, Atheneum Books for Young Readers (Simon & Schuster), 1999.

An African folktale in which the son of the chief must make his way in the world with only a sack full of Kola nuts.

Kindness: Though he hasn't much in the way of worldly goods, when those along the way need what he can give, Koi universally shares with them all his kola nuts. They remember his kindness to them and return his good will when he must meet the challenges set forth by a chief who promises half his chiefdom and his beautiful daughter.

Other character traits shown: *Generosity, Helpfulness*

Bruchac, Joseph. *The Great Ball Game: A Muskogee Story.* Illus. by Susan L. Roth. New York: Dial Books for Young Readers, 1994.

Bat, who has both wings and teeth, plays an important part in a game between the Birds and the Animals to decide which group is better.

Kindness: Bear could easily have refused to allow Bat to play on the Animals' team, just as the Birds did. But in an act of kindness, he let Bat join with the Animals' team even though, "You are not very big." He may not have expected Bat to be of use to the team, but to the surprise of everyone, it was Bat who won the game.

Other character traits shown: *Empathy, Helpfulness, Patience, Respect, Responsibility, Tolerance*

Bunting, Eve. *Summer Wheels.* Illus. by Thomas B. Allen. New York: Harcourt Brace Jovanovich, 1992.

The Bicycle Man fixes up old bicycles and offers both his friendship and the use of the bikes to the neighborhood kids.

Kindness: The Bicycle Man tells a frustrated Lawrence that he's "not here to suspect" kids that might be thieves. He treats all kids with dignity and lets them all pick out the bikes they want, first come, first served. He doesn't scold when accidents happen to bikes. He doesn't even condemn deliberate acts of vandalism. He does work alongside kids, and if something happens to a bike when a kid has it, they repair it together the next day. Finally, Lawrence realizes that "there's something the Man likes even more than his bikes." He likes kids.

Other character traits shown: *Courage, Empathy, Forgiveness, Generosity, Justice, Responsibility, Respect, Tolerance*

Bunting, Eve. *Train to Somewhere.* Illus. by Ronald Himler. New York: Clarion Books (Houghton Mifflin), 1996.

In the late 1800s, Marianne travels westward on the Orphan Train with other children who hope to be placed with caring families.

Kindness: Miss Randolph allows the children their dignity while shepherding them to their new families. She knows they are frightened, but she maintains a calm loving presence. She knows when to be firm. The girls must not spoil their placements by pretending to go together as sisters. And when there is only one stop left, she does not panic. She tells Marianne, "If there's nobody at this next stop, why, we'll just go on. I'll be glad of the company. And on the journey back." The woman and man who accept Marianne are quick to hide their disappointment that she was not a boy. They tell her the toy locomotive is for her. They like girls fine. They think, "Sometimes what you get turns out to be better than what you wanted in the first place." Marianne is quick to accept this loving couple, too. She recognizes in them a kindness that is worth keeping.

Other character traits shown: *Courage, Empathy, Hope, Patience, Prudence, Respect*

Charles, Donald. *Chancay and the Secret of Fire: A Peruvian Folktale.* New York: A Whitebird Book (G.P. Putnam's Sons), 1992.

In Peru, as a reward for releasing the beautiful fish he has caught, Chancay is granted his wish of finding a way to relieve his people from the cold and darkness. *Kindness:* Chancay catches a fish, whose strangeness and beauty catches him by surprise. "This thing is far too beautiful to be killed and eaten," he says. "Even though I am hungry, I will let this fish go." When the grateful fish asks what reward he can bestow, Chancay seeks nothing for himself. But he would like to relieve his people of their cold and fear of darkness. His kindness ultimately brings the gift of fire to humanity.

Other character traits shown: *Courage, Diligence, Fortitude, Patience, Perseverance, Prudence*

Christelow, Eileen. *The Five-Dog Night.* New York: Clarion Books (Houghton Mifflin), 1993.

Cantankerous Ezra keeps rebuffing his nosy neighbor Old Betty when she tries to give him advice on how to survive cold winter nights, until she finally discovers that his five dogs are his private source for warmth. *Kindness:* Old Betty receives no appreciation for her efforts to look after her stubborn neighbor. But she ignores his rudeness and continues to check in on him, bringing him gifts to ease winter's harshness. Her kindness goes unnoticed until a final rebuff ends her visits. Ezra finds he misses her kind acts. He has even learned from her to reciprocate kindness.

Other character traits shown: *Courtesy, Generosity, Helpfulness, Perseverance, Respect*

*Collington, Peter. *A Small Miracle.* New York: Alfred A. Knopf, 1997.

The figures of a Nativity scene come to life to help an old woman in need at Christmas.

Kindness: Though herself robbed of her money and facing dire circumstances, the old woman returns the charity money kettle that she grabs in a foiled robbery and returns it to the church. She takes none of the money for her own desperate needs but pauses to set the crèche figures that the robber has knocked down back into position. It is kindness that has made her act. And, in equal kindness, the characters from the Nativity set respond to her needs and create a small miracle for her.

Other character traits shown: *Generosity*

Daly, Niki. *Bravo Zan Angelo! A Commedia Dell'arte Tale with Story and Pictures.* New York: Farrar, Straus & Giroux, 1998.

In Renaissance Venice, Angelo, longing to be as famous a clown as his grandfather, decides to so something special with his small part in his grandfather's act during Carnival.

Kindness: Angelo has the will to become a good clown, but he needs the caring attention and good will of others to help outfit him for his rooster role. A mask maker, a seamstress, a gentleman, and his aunt all give attention to his needs, even though they are busy with their own work.

Other character traits shown: *Courage, Courtesy, Helpfulness, Hope, Perseverance, Resourcefulness*

Duncan, Alice Faye. *Miss Viola and Uncle Ed Lee.* Illus. by Catherine Stock. New York: Atheneum Books for Young Readers (Simon & Schuster), 1999.

A young boy helps his two neighbors, one as neat as a pin and the other as junky as a packrat, become friends.

Kindness: The two are not alike, but that is no reason they can't be friends. Uncle Ed Lee admires Miss Viola's bright smile, how sweet she is, how neat, how spotless her place is, how sparkling white her fence is, how neat her grass stays. Miss Viola says she loves making friends. Uncle Ed Lee works hard to clean up his place and make his guest comfortable with a table, chairs, lemonade, and a deck of cards, just like a "good friend would."

Other character traits shown: *Courtesy, Helpfulness, Honesty, Respect, Tolerance*

*Garland, Sherry. *I Never Knew Your Name.* Illus. by Sheldon Greenberg. New York: Ticknor & Fields (Houghton Mifflin), 1994.

A small boy laments the lonely life of a teenage suicide whose neighbors didn't even know his name.

Kindness: A lack of human kindness is at the base of this tragedy. The one person who admires the teenager, a boy who watches him from his apartment window, hasn't the courage to make his acquaintance. Though good at shooting baskets, the teenager isn't invited to play with the other guys. The teenager befriends and feeds a stray dog, but his mom yells at him and the landlord calls the city pound to take it away. The teenager has a crush on the boy's sister, but she calls him names and makes fun of his clothes. The teenager sits on the curb throwing gravel at a lamppost the night the other guys go to the prom. On his last day, the teenager throws bread to the pigeons on the roof. The young boy watches "a boring old movie on TV," instead of joining him as he almost did. No one prevents the needless suicide. And no one but the young boy can think why it happened.

Other character traits shown: *Respect*

Goffstein, M. B. *Our Snowman.* New York: Harper & Row, 1986.

The snowman two children build looks so lonely when night comes that a little girl and her father go out to make a snow woman to keep him company.

Kindness: The children want the snowman to have company. So, even though it is after dark, mother turns on the porch light and father goes out to help the girl make a companion for the snowman. Father doesn't remark on the silly emotion involved or try to convince them it's unnecessary. He simply responds by doing what the children need.

Other character traits shown: *Empathy*

Gove, Doris. *One Rainy Night.* Illus. by Walter Lyon Krudop. New York: Atheneum, 1994.

A boy and his mother go out on a rainy night to collect animals for a nature center that releases its specimens to the wild after two weeks.

Kindness: A toad among other caged animals at the nature center was on display two weeks. It's time now to return it back to its natural habitat because "that's longer than any animal should have to stay in a cage." It takes time and effort to capture fresh animals over and over again. It is uncomfortable to go out on rainy nights. But they do this because it's best for the creatures to live life naturally.

Other character traits shown: *Respect*

*Gregory, Valiska. *Through the Mickle Woods.* Illus. by Barry Moser. Boston: Little, Brown & Co., 1992.

After his wife's death, a grieving king journeys to an old bear's cave in the mickle (thick) woods, where he hears three stories that help him go on living.

Kindness: The king's wife reaches out to him in kindness before her death with the note that sends him on his journey of recovery. The boy ignores the king's coldness and keeps forcing him to speak of his loss, then allows the king to administer comfort to him when the king is ready to give in return. The old woman in the woods invites into her home strangers she does not know simply because they "need a bit of bread." She even wraps a scarf around the boy and admonishes the king to "keep him warm and safe." Through her kindness she reminds the king of his humanity and helps him dwell on something besides his feelings of loss. The bear, who serves as the king's teacher, is patient with the king's lack of willingness to listen. But he insists upon the king's attention and has the authority of presence to demand it. "Consider this," he says as he teaches the king to rejoin the living, and the king does listen.

Other character traits shown: *Discernment, Empathy, Forgiveness, Generosity, Helpfulness, Hope, Perseverance*

Herzig, Alison Cragin. *Bronco Busters.* Illus. by Kimberly Bulcken Root. New York: G.P. Putnam's Sons, 1998.

Three rough, tough bronco busters can't tame a little black pony, but a small, quiet cowboy talks to him, brings his water and food, and then quietly rides away with him.

Kindness: It is obvious that kindness is superior to the effects of traditionally harsh horse-breaking techniques. In condescending swagger, the bronco busters tell the boy to "stand aside, sonny!" Despite their dismal failure, they still adhere to their inferior methods, and, as the boy watches, even foolishly say, "He might learn a thing or two." Good will evaporates, however, by the time two of the three bronco busters have failed. By now, their attitude is "Scram, pip-squeak! Yeah, beat it, squirt! Let the big guys do it." Following each failed attempt, a bronco buster limps away to nurse his bruises, and, in the evening, the boy comes back with kind words, treats, and gentle touches. A relationship of trust slowly develops between the horse and boy over several evenings. When the last bronco buster can't subdue the pony, they pronounce it "plum loco." "No one can ride that horse. Nothing to do but sell him to the rodeo." On this night the boy saddles the "loco" pony easily and they ride together "through the tall grass toward the high blue mountains."

James, Simon. *Leon and Bob.* Cambridge, MA: Candlewick Press, 1997.

Leon and his imaginary friend Bob do everything together until a new boy moves in next door.

Kindness: Leon is a lonely child who relies on "Bob" as his only friend. But when a new family moves in next door, the new boy waves to Leon and Leon waves back. He thinks about the boy and decides to go see him as long as "Bob" comes along. But, just when he needs his imaginary friend most, he isn't there. Still, the prospect of a real friend is strong enough for Leon to overcome his shyness. He rings the bell and finds his initial kindness of approaching a stranger pays off. The new boy is willing to play with him at the park. They share names and are on their way.

Other character traits shown: *Courage*

Krupinski, Loretta. *Best Friends.* New York: Hyperion Books for Children, 1998.

When a settler's young daughter learns that soldiers will force the Nez Perce off the nearby land, she uses a doll to warn her Indian friend of impending danger. *Kindness*: When the two girls accidentally meet, the white girl is startled and drops her treasures, which she keeps inside a doll's head. The Indian girl gathers them up and holds them out to her. The white girl realizes, "I knew then not to be afraid." They begin sharing each other's cultures, learning skills from each other, including the ability to do sign language and to read English. When the white girl learns that the Indians are about to be forcibly removed from their land, she sends a secret message of warning to them inside her own precious doll, knowing that she is unlikely to ever see her friend or the doll again.

Other character traits shown: *Generosity, Helpfulness, Justice, Loyalty, Resourcefulness, Respect*

Lamstein, Sarah Marwil. *I Like Your Buttons!* Illus. By Nancy Cote. Morton Grove, IL: Albert Whitman & Co., 1999.

When a little girl compliments her teacher about the buttons on her outfit, it starts a chain reaction of goodwill, good deeds, and thoughtfulness throughout the day.
Kindness: Good feelings begin and end with Cassandra. Her teacher is so pleased to be told her buttons are pretty that she compliments a custodian, who, in turn, feels so happy she compliments another teacher. The teacher feels so good he begins snack time before spelling is finished. And, so goes the day. Cassandra's father is one of the recipients of the day's compliments. At work he notices a stray kitten hanging around the back door of the restaurant where he is a cook and thinks his daughter might like to have it. Cassandra is delighted with her gift but has no idea that she was the impetus for the day's final positive act. A little bit of thoughtful kindness can have far reaching effects.

Lasky, Kathryn. *Marven of the Great North Woods*. Illus. by Kevin Hawkes. New York: Harcourt Brace, 1997.

When his Jewish parents send him to a Minnesota logging camp to escape the influenza epidemic of 1918, 10-year-old Marven finds a special friend.
Kindness: The big lumberjack Jean Louis senses that the child is lonely for his family. One day Marven is out exploring and hears a growl and sees tree branches shaking. He thinks a grizzly bear is in the tree. He also thinks he will never see his family again. But the bear is only Jean Louis marking trees with his ax for cutting next season. After that encounter Marven skis into the woods every afternoon when his work is finished and falls in beside Jean Louis as the jacks return to camp. He learns the lumberjack songs, plays their games, and dances. Sometimes Jean Louis lifts him up to do a little two-step right there in his stocking feet on his shoulders. Jean Louis gives him a brand new ax. "You are a woodsman now." When Marven's time at the camp is over, Jean Louis goes with him all the way to the train

station, carrying him on his shoulders, skis and all. Marven is at last to return home. The big man's kindness has helped Marven get through the lonely separation from his family.

Other character traits shown: *Diligence, Empathy*

Manson, Christopher. *Two Travelers.* New York: Henry Holt, 1990.

The emperor's messenger Isaac must accompany a gift elephant from Baghdad to France, and during the difficult journey, an unexpected friendship develops between man and beast.

Kindness: The messenger and the elephant have doubts about liking each other, but their basic kindness helps them establish an acquaintance. What Isaac fears does not happen. The elephant doesn't step on him, poke him with his "enormous white teeth," nor eat him up for dinner. And what the elephant fears does not happen. Isaac doesn't beat him with sticks, and he does remember to provide clean straw and water. Soon the two are looking out for each other's welfare. Isaac helps assure the elephant that it can step safely on the raft. He warms the elephant's cold ears with his own cloak. The elephant shades Isaac from the hot sun with his big floppy ears and stops him from falling out of the boat with his trunk.

Other character traits shown: *Cooperation, Helpfulness, Tolerance*

*Mathers, Petra. *Victor and Christabel.* New York: Alfred A. Knopf, 1993.

The shy guard at an art museum falls in love with the sad young woman in a painting that mysteriously appears one day.

Kindness: Victor is drawn to the picture and finds himself doing small acts of kindness, as though a night light or vase of flowers might make the sad girl in the picture more comfortable. He talks to her and is puzzled about the broken teacup on the rug next to her bed. "Must have taken ill quite suddenly, didn't you, dear?" he murmurs. Finally, it is the cup of tea he brings to sip near her that finally breaks the spell and restores Christabel to life.

Other character traits shown: *Justice*

Meddaugh, Susan. *Martha Walks the Dog.* Boston: Walter Lorraine Books (Houghton Mifflin), 1998.

Martha the talking dog rescues the neighborhood from a bully dog with the help of a parrot.

Kindness: Bad Bob lives up to his name, terrorizing everyone with whom he comes in contact. When his chain breaks and he takes after Martha, she calls him every bad name she can think of. "Nothing she yelled had any effect on him." But kind words do. She had taught the parrot to mimic her. Now, in desperation, while hiding from Bob under the bushes, she continues to teach the parrot phrases.

Suddenly, Bad Bob is hearing "Good dog," and "Great dog," and "Bob is soooooo handsome." Bob's tail begins to wag. Kindness has worked wonders.

Other character traits shown: *Prudence, Resourcefulness*

Miller, William. *The Piano*. Illus. by Susan Keeter. New York: Lee & Low Books, 2000.

A young black girl's love of music leads her to a job in the house of an older white woman, who not only teaches her to play the piano, but also the rewards of intergenerational friendship.

Kindness: When the two sit down together for the first time at the piano, Tia sees the pain in Miss Hartwell's face when the old woman tries to spread her hands over the keys. To spare her embarrassment at her frailty and to spare her physical pain, she quickly comments that she should be getting back to work. When Tia suggest that she exchange her maid's wages for piano lessons, Miss Hartwell refuses not to pay her and teaches her for free. When next they sit down together, Tia bathes Miss hartwell's hands in a soothing solution of warm salt water to ease her painful joints. Later, Miss Hartwell does the same for her when she injures her hands doing hard manual labor.

Ness, Evaline. *Sam, Bangs & Moonshine*. New York: Holt Rinehart Winston, 1966. (Caldecott–1967)

Lonely Sam's Moonshine talk nearly results in the loss of her young friend and her cat.

Kindness: Sam sees no harm in her little games of untruth until the prospect of a terrible tragedy awakens her to the reality of lying. Her amusement, she realizes with shame, might have caused Thomas to drown. To make up for the hurt she has caused him, because she knows he would especially like to have it, and because it looks like the pet kangaroo he was searching for, she gives him her precious new gerbil. It is an act of kindness and contrition and symbolizes her new respect for truth.

Other character traits shown: *Honesty*

Nolen, Jerdine. *Raising Dragons*. Illus. by Elise Primavera. New York: Silver Whistle (Harcourt Brace), 1998.

A farmer's young daughter shares numerous adventures with the dragon that she raises from infancy.

Kindness: Though told to leave the mysterious egg alone, the girl keeps checking on it until it finally hatches. "As I stroked his nose, a sweet little purring whimper came from him. As I touched skin to scale, I knew I was his girl and he was my dragon." She proceeds to look after him alone, because "Ma never wanted to know about Hank." Finally, when she learns about a special island where dragons live, she "knew he had found the perfect place to be" and is willing to give him up though she "boohooed a heap."

Other character traits shown: *Cooperation, Diligence, Loyalty, Responsibility*

Ransome, Arthur. *The Fool of the World and the Flying Ship.* Illus. by Uri Shulevitz. New York: Farrar, Straus & Giroux, 1968. (Caldecott–1969)

A third son, little revered by his family, manages to win the Czar's daughter through God's favor of loving the simple folk.
Kindness: His parents have no confidence in their third son. The first two they shower with blessings; the third gets crusts and water as he sets out in the world. No matter. He sings as he goes and trudges along merrily. After all, the main thing on a journey is to have something to eat. The trees are green and there is a blue sky overhead. Along the way he receives abundance. He is kind, and he receives kindness in return. He may be "simple as a child, simpler than some children," but he never does anyone a harm in his life, and God "turns things to their advantage in the end."

Rylant, Cynthia. *The Bird House.* Illus. by Barry Moser. New York: Blue Sky Press (Scholastic), 1998.

A young girl without family is fascinated by a house that draws birds around it.
Kindness: The birds recognize a kindred spirit in need of a good home. They set about introducing her to the old woman. The old woman cleans up the girl and feeds her. "Then the old woman talked with her, all through the night." By morning, the girl has a home.

Other character traits shown: *Empathy, Generosity*

Schertle, Alice. *Down the Road.* Illus. by E.B. Lewis. New York: Browndeer Press (Harcourt Brace), 1995.

Hetty is very careful with the eggs she has bought on her first trip to the store, but she runs into trouble when she stops to pick apples.
Kindness: Hetty is devastated when the eggs break. She crawls up into the tree out of shame. She can't face her parents' disappointment. But they show no criticism of an act for which she is already plenty sorry. Papa's face "wrinkled into a smile." He joins her in the tree. Together they are both soon sticky with apple juice. Mama comes. She has been waiting for 12 beautiful eggs. But when Hetty explains how she was trying to pick apples, Papa's quick "Fine, sweet apples," alerts Mama to the spin they are going to put on this incident. She plays along instantly. Soon they are joking about being birds up in the tree together. Papa and Mama have shown kindness toward their child, who needed no scolding to remind her of the loss.

Other character traits shown: *Empathy, Forgiveness, Honesty, Responsibility*

*Schur, Maxine Rose. *The Peddler's Gift.* Illus. by Kimberly Bulcken Root. New York: Dial Books for Young Readers (Penguin), 1999.

A young boy in rural Russia at the turn of the twentieth century learns that appearances are often deceiving after he steals a dreidel.

Kindness: The community of youngsters have greatly underestimated the peddler they call Shnook. He appears almost half-witted in his approach to selling goods. He never gets it right. He doesn't brag about his wares and even cheats himself on occasion by giving goods away. And, even though the boy's mother has ever only one ruble to spend, her selection of items never costs more than one ruble. But when the boy steals a toy from the fool, his conscience makes him return it. He finds the Shnook at the synagogue where, surprisingly he can sing beautifully. He is really no fool at all. The peddler doesn't show anger about the theft. There is no need, because the boy has showed anger at himself for the wrong he's done. And that is what matters. The peddler invites the boy to stay with him and wait until the storm passes. There is a gift of blue cloth his mother wanted and the dreidel left at their doorstep, which are remembered through the years. But also remembered is the gift of forgiveness.

Other character traits shown: *Courage, Forgiveness, Honesty, Respect, Responsibility*

*Stanley, Diane. *Raising Sweetness.* Illus. by G. Brian Karas. New York: G.P. Putnam's Sons, 1999.

Sweetness, one of eight orphans living with a man who is an unconventional housekeeper, learns to read and write and important letter to improve their situation.

Kindness: The children love their adopted father, but he truly needs a woman's help raising a family. He cleans windows with butter, combs hair with a fork, and makes meals that include combinations like pickle and banana pie (burned black due to his distraction over a letter received). The children, in kindness ask, "Ever thought about gettin' married?" They are motivated to learn to read when they get a letter that might have been sent by their father's missing sweetheart. She might be answering his marriage proposal. The sooner they learn to read the better. When they puzzle out its meaning, they write back for Lucy Locket to "Kum Kwik." They say it's an emergency. Their father wonders what the emergency is. The children don't tell him the reason is his bad housekeeping; they say, instead, "We just didn't want your heart to be broke no more. We thought it was time you got married." Their gentle maneuvering has succeeded.

Other character traits shown: *Loyalty*

*Stanley, Diane. *Rumpelstiltskin's Daughter.* New York: William Morrow, 1997.

Rumpelstiltskin's daughter may not be able to spin straw into gold, but she is more than a match for a monarch whose greed has blighted an entire kingdom.

Kindness: In this version of the old fairytale, Rumpelstiltskin doesn't try to make a deal with the miller's daughter. He just does his thing and accepts for payment a worthless goldtone metal necklace the first time and a cigar-band pinkie ring the next time. By the third time the king expects not only the straw turned into gold, but marriage to her as well. She is so distressed she declares she would rather marry Rumpelstiltskin than live a life with that king. Rumpelstiltskin is pleasantly shocked. Would she really marry him? Yes, she thinks he would make a good provider and she has a weakness for short men. So, he spins a ladder of gold and they escape out the window. The story doesn't end there. They have a daughter who is "sunny and clever." When she gets picked up for passing off some gold strands to the goldsmith, she, too, ends up in the king's clutches. Now, it's her job to turn straw into gold. But she has a plan. She noticed on the carriage ride to the palace, "Nobody in the kingdom had anything anymore, because the king had it all." Before she is finished she has manipulated the king into providing gold coin for the farmers to plant gold (food produce) and yellow wool with which to knit gold (clothes). The people are so pleased they love their munificent king. He doesn't need his guards, who "stand there, gnashing their teeth, clutching their swords, and peering about with shifty eyes." She suggests putting them to work taking down the walls of the moat and building a zoo for the crocodiles that swam in the moat. The king is sorry she can't turn straw into gold, "but you did try." As a reward he decides to make her his queen. "Why don't you make me prime minister instead?" He does. The people of the kingdom never go cold or hungry again. If he started worrying about gold, she would send him on a goodwill tour throughout the countryside, which cheered him right up.

Other character traits shown: *Resourcefulness*

*Turner, Ann. *Katie's Trunk.* Illus. by Ron Himler. New York: Macmillan, 1992.

Katie, whose family is not sympathetic to the rebel soldiers during the American Revolution, hides under the clothes in her mother's wedding trunk when they invade her home.

Kindness: It is an act of kindness that saves Katie's life. While her family rushes off to safety, Katie is outraged that her neighbors intend to plunder their belongings. "It was not right, it was not just, it was not fair." She goes back into their home with some vague notion of trying to save their possessions. But the looters come, and she must hide. It is while she is inside the trunk that her best friend's father stumbles upon her accidentally. He does not expose her presence to the others. Though they need to sell goods to get money to buy guns for their cause, he chooses instead to forfeit the chance to steal valuables in order to protect this child from harm, a girl who is his daughter's former friend. He leaves open the trunk lid, so she can breathe, and he pretends to have heard the Tories returning. His gang runs away. Katie realizes he has chosen good over self-serving gain.

Other character traits shown: *Justice*

Uchida, Yoshiko. *The Bracelet.* Illus. by Joanna Yardley. New York: Philomel Books (Putnam & Grosset), 1976.

Emi, a Japanese American in the second grade is sent with her family to an internment camp during World War II, but the loss of the bracelet her best friend has given her proves that she doesn't need a physical reminder of her friendship.

Kindness: Laurie can't prevent the American government's hysteria that has caused their separation, so her gift of a bracelet with a heart pendant dangling on it will at least remind Emi that her friend hasn't forgotten her, even though they may never see each other again. It is a gift that Emi treasures as a symbol that not all Americans distrust Japanese Americans.

Other character traits shown: *Patience, Tolerance*

LOYALTY

Use for DEDICATION
Faithful support and devotion.

Bang, Molly. *Goose.* New York: Blue Sky Press (Scholastic), 1996.

Adopted by woodchucks at birth, a baby goose never feels she truly belongs, until the day she discovers she can fly.

Loyalty: In this surprise denouement, Goose leaves her loving family, who has taught her "everything they thought a youngster should know." Goose walks off into the world to try to "see what she could figure out by herself." She finds she is lonely and sad. In her distraction she doesn't watch where she is going and walks off a cliff. She drops toward the ocean below and fights to stay aloft. In the process, she discovers she can fly. So she flies and flies "all the way home." She does not go off to live among her own kind. She loyally returns home to her family of woodchucks. Only, now, she can take them up with her on her back for rides in the sky.

Bemelmans, Ludwig. *Madeline's Rescue.* New York: Viking Press, 1953. (Caldecott–1954)

Following an accident on an outing, the rescued girl's school takes in the dog that saved her from drowning despite rules against pets.

Loyalty: The children's teacher first allows the dog to share living space with the girls when it pulls Madeline to safety from the water. Then she calmly explains after the school inspectors banish the dog that as soon as the girls get dressed, the sooner they can begin to search the city for the dog. And, finally, when the dog comes up with puppies, their teacher loyally allows "enough hound to go around."

Bunting, Eve. *I Have an Olive Tree.* Illus. by Karen Barbour. New York: Joanna Cotler Books (HarperCollins), 1999.

After her grandfather's death, eight-year-old Sophia fulfills his last request and journeys to Greece with her mother to see the land where her roots are.

Loyalty: When the family left Greece for California, they sold their land but kept one olive tree as a symbol of their roots in Greek earth. On her birthday, Sophia's grandfather gives the tree to her, even though she would have preferred a skateboard. What would she do with the tree? Later, her mother takes her to Greece to the family tree where they will hang the beads that had belonged to grandmother. Bit by bit, Sophia understands that hanging the beads on the olive tree is not the only reason grandfather had wanted her and her mother to come. "He wanted Mama to remember again, and he wanted me to know." Loyalty to her heritage makes Sophia realize, "I have an olive tree."

Other character traits shown: *Respect*

Bunting, Eve. *A Picnic in October.* Illus. by Nancy Carpenter. New York: Harcourt Brace, 1999.

A boy finally comes to understand why his grandmother insists that the family come to Ellis Island each year to celebrate Lady Liberty's birthday.

Loyalty: The picnic ritual has become a nuisance. The October weather is too cold. Why must the family sit outside? The boy's grandparents embarrass him with their sentimental behavior. The famous words on the statue are memorized by rote. Then, suddenly, the boy sees through the eyes of new immigrants "the way they stand, so still, so respectful, so peaceful." It makes him "choke up." Maybe they've come to the end of a long journey, just as his grandparents did so many years ago. Suddenly, he is no longer ashamed of his family's old country background. He shouts, "Brava, Bella!" to the statue and doesn't care who's watching.

Other character traits shown: *Respect*

Bunting, Eve. *Swan in Love.* Illus. by Jo Ellen McAllister Stammen. New York: Atheneum Books for Young Readers (Simon & Schuster), 2000.

Despite riducule of the other animals, Swan persists in his adoration for a swan-shaped boat named Dora.

Loyalty: Winter and summer throughout the years, Swan remains faithful at the side of Dora. When tourists ride the boat in summer he swims along. When the boat is pulled ashore for winter, he settles down beside her instead of leaving with the other swans for warmer lands. Love is never wrong. They both age together. And, when Dora's useful life is over, Swan, too, lies beside her. They are together to the end, and even beyond.

Other character traits shown: *Patience*

Conrad, Pam. *The Rooster's Gift.* Illus. by Eric Beddows. New York: Laura Geringer Book (HarperCollins), 1996.

Young Rooster thinks his Gift is making the sun rise, until one morning when the sun rises without him.

Loyalty: Rooster is depressed to realize that it is not his efforts that cause the sun to rise each day. Smallest Hen tries to minimize his devastation. Though the sun can come up without him, "it's much better with you," she loyally tells him. He is not comforted. She suggests that maybe his gift is "that you know when the sun is about to come up." He dismisses this as making so sense whatsoever. "Even you know when the sun is about to come up." This is true. She does. "But it's you who call to the sun," she told him. Again, he says that is ridiculous. "Anybody could do it. Even you." So, they set about proving that Smallest Hen can also call the sun. She tries. But the effect is not the same. The sound comes out wrong. Smallest Hen is embarrassed. Rooster suddenly realizes that even though both know when the sun is about to rise, "you can't announce it quite the same." She admits that, "You do it very well, Rooster. I always loved the way you did it."

Other character traits shown: *Discernment*

Cox, Judy. *Rabbit Pirates: A Tale of the Spinach Main.* Illus. by Emily Arnold McCully. New York: Browndeer Press (Harcourt Brace), 1999.

Two old rabbit friends disagree about many things but join forces to deal with a tricky fox who threatens them and their business.

Loyalty: These two tough old mates must learn to adapt to civilian life as restaurant operators. And, though they occasionally get into ego arguments, they quickly back down and generously allow as how the other may be in the right. Their loyalty toward each other eventually enables them to work together to make a kitchen concoction that sends the fox away forever.

Other character traits shown: *Cooperation*

dePaola, Tomie. *The Legend of the Indian Paintbrush.* New York: G.P. Putnam's Sons, 1988.

Little Gopher follows his destiny, as revealed in a Dream-Vision, of becoming an artist for his people and eventually is able to bring the colors of the sunset down to earth.

Loyalty: Little Gopher would like to be a warrior like his friends, but the shaman says he is destined for something else. His Dream-Vision tells him to make paint and brushes and record the deeds of the People and the dreams of his shaman. He remains loyal to his task through the years even as he searches for colors bright enough to paint the sunset.

Other character traits shown: *Diligence, Hope, Patience, Perseverance, Responsibility, Self-discipline*

*Garland, Sherry. *The Lotus Seed.* Illus. by Tatsuro Kiuchi. New York: Harcourt Brace Jovanovich, 1993.

A young Vietnamese girl saves a lotus seed and carries it with her everywhere to remember a brave emperor and the homeland that she has to flee.

Loyalty: First there is invasion by the French. The girl sees the emperor cry on the day he loses his golden dragon throne. She wants something to remember him by and plucks a lotus pod seed from the imperial garden. From that time on she carefully saves the seed, wrapped in a piece of silk in a special place under the family altar. When war comes again, she grabs the seed and leaves behind her mother-of-pearl hair combs. Even in her new country, she remembers the brave young emperor and preserves the seed. When, many years later, her grandchild finds and plants the seed in order to learn what the plant will look like, the former resident of Vietnam is devastated. Its loss seems to her like disloyalty. Later the lotus seed sprouts and blooms. She sees it as "the flower of life and hope." There are many more seeds now, which she shares with her children and grandchildren, so that they, too, may remember not only her but the land of their heritage. She comes to see that "no matter how ugly the mud or how long the seed lays dormant, the bloom will be beautiful. It is the flower of my country."

Other character traits shown: *Hope, Respect*

Gill, Janet. *Basket Weaver and Catches Many Mice.* Illus. by Yangsook Choi. New York: Alfred A. Knopf, 1999.

A little gray cat saves the day when Basket Weaver is ordered into a competition to make the perfect basket for the Emperor's newborn daughter.

Loyalty: Despite his personal fears, Basket Weaver does his duty for the Emperor. He would like to run away from his obligations, but he presents himself at the palace at the appointed time. He neither wants to stay to work at the palace if he wins the contest nor work in the underground mines if he loses. He has prepared a bed that promises a fine future for the Emperor's daughter.

Other character traits shown: *Diligence, Generosity, Honesty, Responsibility*

Gerrard, Roy. *The Roman Twins.* New York: Farrar, Straus & Giroux, 1998.

Maximus and his twin sister Vanilla, slaves to the cruel and greedy Slobbus Pompius, risk their lives to save a horse and end up helping to save the city of Rome from the Goths.

Loyalty: Though badly treated by mother Rome, the children, who are doomed to slavery "from cradle to the grave," nonetheless step forward when the city is threatened. They cut the rope holding up the bridge over which the enemy must cross to burn Rome. Thus, their loyalty and bravery save the city from destruction.

Other character traits shown: *Courage, Justice*

Jackson, Isaac. *Somebody's New Pajamas.* Illus. by David Soman. New York: Dial Books for Young Readers (Penguin), 1996.

When two boys from different backgrounds become friends and sleep over at each other's homes, they exchange ideas about sleepwear as well as about family life.

Loyalty: Jerome feels ashamed when he has no pajamas to wear at his friend's sleepover, but when his Dad talks about family life, he begins to feel loyal to his own traditions. And, when he finally gets pajamas for Christmas, he is pleased but says half the time he'll continue to sleep in his underwear, "'cause this family does things it own way."

Other character traits shown: *Courtesy, Honesty, Respect*

Krupinski, Loretta. *Best Friends.* New York: Hyperion Books for Children, 1998.

When a settler's young daughter learns that soldiers will force the Nez Perce off the nearby land, she uses a doll to warn her Indian friend of impending danger.

Loyalty: Loyalty to her new Indian friend is strong enough for the white settler girl to willingly risk her own family's safety to send a message of warning to the Indian village. As a result, they are able to get away free.

Other character traits shown: *Generosity, Helpfulness, Justice, Kindness, Resourcefulness, Respect*

Lears, Laurie. *Ian's Walk: A Story about Autism.* Illus. by Karen Ritz. Morton Grove, IL: Albert Whitman, 1998.

A young girl realizes how much she cares about her autistic brother when he gets lost at a park.

Loyalty: Though embarrassed in public about his peculiar behavior, the girl is so grateful when she finds her lost brother, she stands guard so people won't step on his fingers when he lies on the ground as he lines up pebbles on the sidewalk. She doesn't mind when he sniffs the post office bricks instead of the flower shop flowers. She joins him staring at the circulating ceiling fan at the café for as long as he wishes to watch it. She doesn't hurry him along when he stops to listen to something no one else can hear. On the walk home, she tells him, "We'll walk home the way you like!"

Other character traits shown: *Empathy, Patience*

Lee, Milly. *Nim and the War Effort.* Illus. by Yangsook Choi. New York: Frances Foster Books (Farrar, Straus & Giroux), 1997.

Nim and a schoolmate are rivals in a contest to collect newspapers for the war effort until the final day when it seems Nim can't possibly win.

Loyalty: Nim's heritage is grist for the boy's cruel taunts about going back to Japan. She is determined to show her loyalty to her country by winning the newspaper collection contest. She even defies her formidable grandfather by daring to be late to her special classes just so she can finish her newspaper project.

He is impressed and allows her to wear his double flag pin, one flag for the old home country, one for the new home country.

Other character traits shown: *Fortitude, Persistence, Resourcefulness, Self-discipline*

Mitchell, Barbara. *Red Bird.* Illus. by Todd Doney. New York: Lothrop, Lee & Shepard, 1996.

Katie, also known as Red Bird, joins her family and other Indians at the annual powwow in southern Delaware, where they celebrate their Nanticoke heritage with music, dancing, and special foods.

Loyalty: Over the generations, the various tribes have learned to live in the modern world and have assimilated into its work life, but once a year they demonstrate their loyalty to their origins by celebrating the powwow. "The heartbeat of The People stays with her all year long."

Other character traits shown: *Cooperation, Respect*

Nolen, Jerdine. *Raising Dragons.* Illus. by Elise Primavera. New York: Silver Whistle (Harcourt Brace), 1998.

A farmer's young daughter shares numerous adventures with the dragon that she raises from infancy.

Loyalty: Despite a warning to stay away from the big egg, the little girl is enthralled. She keeps coming back to check on it until it hatches. Her parents cover their ears when she wants to talk about her baby dragon. So, she takes care of him by herself. She remains loyal to him when "the crowds and attention decided his fate." She takes him to a special island where dragons live. It is hard to part, but "I knew he had found the perfect place to be."

Other character traits shown: *Cooperation, Diligence, Kindness, Responsibility*

*Stanley, Diane. *Raising Sweetness.* Illus. by G. Brian Karas. New York: G.P. Putnam's Sons, 1999.

Sweetness, one of eight orphans living with a man who is an unconventional housekeeper, learns to read and write an important letter to improve their situation.

Loyalty: Nothing would induce the children to speak unkindly of their adopted father. But he certainly could use the help of a wife. They mention that to him every time he hangs clothes on the line without first washing them, combs their hair with a fork, and serves them foods that "don't go over very well." He puzzles why the kids write to his fiancée to "Kum Kwik" because it's an emergency. They tell him "We just didn't want your heart to be broke no more." And, when the good lady arrives, nobody says a word against the secret ingredient in his famous chili recipe, catfish. On the other hand, he would never dream of telling his new bride she didn't "know enuf to put raisins in mashed potatoes," because "a man will do anything for love. And that's the truth."

Other character traits shown: *Kindness*

*Wiesniewski, David. *Golem.* New York: Clarion Books (Houghton Mifflin), 1996. (Caldecott–1997)

A saintly rabbi miraculously brings to life a clay giant who helps watch over the Jews of sixteenth-century Prague.

Loyalty: The giant, who is only clay, has enough of life in him to appreciate the beauty of the sun rising. His human creator does not understand "how simple Golem was. The smallest thing—the scent of a rose, the flight of a pigeon—filled him with wonder." The rabbi is intent only on the service this man of clay can provide the human Jews. He tells the golem that he has been created for one reason, and when that need is over "you will return to the earth from whence you came." The golem knows his purpose and that he will not be allowed to live. He finds "life is precious to me." Despite his joy in living, he performs his duties loyally and protects the human Jews from invasion, knowing that when they are safe and no longer in danger, his time of living will be finished. And so it happens. When the golem is once again a pile of earth, however, the Jews do not throw the clay irreverently outdoors. They remember the loyalty of their benefactor and return that loyalty by bringing wheeled barrows of the clay that was the golem to the synagogue. They put the clay in the attic and cover it with tattered prayer books. "Though Golem had not truly been a man, they recited Kaddish, the prayer for the dead."

Other character traits shown: *Helpfulness, Justice, Respect*

PATIENCE

Waiting or enduring without complaint.

Bruchac, Joseph. *The Great Ball Game: A Muskogee Story.* Illus. by Susan L. Roth. New York: Dial Books for Young Readers, 1994.

Bat, who has both wings and teeth, plays an important part in a game between the Birds and the Animals to decide which group is better.

Patience: Bat wants badly to play in the ball game. But when he is told, "You must hold back and let the bigger Animals play first," he is patient and waits for his chance. The game is a long one. Eventually, the time is right, and he enters the game and leads his team to victory.

Other character traits shown: *Empathy, Helpfulness, Kindness, Respect, Responsibility, Tolerance*

Bunting, Eve. *Swan in Love.* Illus. by Jo Ellen McAllister Stammen. New York: Atheneum Books for Young Readers (Simon & Schuster), 2000.

Despite riducule of the other animals, Swan persists in his adoration for a swan-shaped boat named Dora.

Patience: Swan asks for nothing in return for his love over the years. He swims beside Dora and lies beside her. And, in the end his love is rewarded as they depart this life together for a new existence.

Other character traits shown: *Loyalty*

Bunting, Eve. *Train to Somewhere.* Illus. by Ronald Himler. New York: Clarion Books (Houghton Mifflin), 1996.

In the late 1800s, Marianne travels westward on the Orphan Train with other children who hope to be placed with caring families.

Patience: Marianne's trip west is a patient trek to find her mother. At each stop along the western route she thinks it possible that her mother will be there for her. In the end, though her mother does not come, a loving family does choose her. She has waited a long time without complaint. And she will patiently accept, as well, those who are willing to adopt her.

Other character traits shown: *Empathy, Hope, Kindness, Prudence, Respect*

Caseley, Judith. *Mickey's Class Play.* New York: Greenwillow (William Morrow), 1998.

With the help of his family, Mickey enjoys being a duck in the class play.

Patience: It is not easy getting Mickey through his class play. He is "a grouchy duck until Jenna read him the play" and he decides his part will be ok after all. He wears out his family practicing day and night. But they listen and encourage him. He leaves his costume out in the rain, and it is ruined. They help him construct a last-minute replacement. "No way," he tells them when it's finished. "I don't look like the others!" They patiently help him find a way to accept his new appearance. At the play, he wears a sign identifying his kind of duck as a "blue-winged teal from Saskatchewan, Ontario, Kansas, Missouri, Illinois, Ohio, and New Jersey." Through his family's endless patience, they help this child have a successful experience.

Other character traits shown: *Helpfulness*

Charles, Donald. *Chancay and the Secret of Fire: A Peruvian Folktale.* New York: A Whitebird Book (G.P. Putnam's Sons), 1992.

In Peru, as a reward for releasing the beautiful fish he has caught, Chancay is granted his wish of finding a way to relieve his people from the cold and darkness.

Patience: Though he feels he is being sent on fool's errands, Chancay does not quit his quest to bring fire to his people. He waits on Tambo the fish to finish testing his ability to achieve his goal. Meanwhile he endures without complaint. In his final task, he must wait patiently for "many days and nights" until the Sun and Moon both fall asleep, before he can steal the mirror and return to earth to finish learning the secret of fire.

Other character traits shown: *Courage, Diligence, Fortitude, Kindness, Perseverance, Prudence*

dePaola, Tomie. *The Legend of the Indian Paintbrush.* New York: G.P. Putnam's Sons, 1988.

Little Gopher follows his destiny, as revealed in a Dream-Vision, of becoming an artist for his people and eventually is able to bring the colors of the sunset down to earth.

Patience: Little Gopher never complains about his task of recording the People's deeds and the shaman's dreams even though he would like to be one of the warriors. He tries to find the colors of the sunset, patiently using the materials he has, even though his paintings never satisfy him. They look dull and dark. Still, he continues without complaint doing what his Dream-Vision requires.

Other character traits shown: *Diligence, Hope, Loyalty, Perseverance, Responsibility, Self-discipline*

Doyle, Malachy. *Jody's Beans.* Illus. by Judith Allibone. Cambridge, MA: Candlewick Press, 1999.

From spring to fall with the help of her grandfather, Jody learns to plant, care for, harvest, prepare, and eat some runner beans.

Patience: Jody patiently waits for the small plants to emerge. She waters them daily. She thins out some and waits for the plants to grow big enough to make beans. She picks them regularly. She saves the final large beans for next year's plants.

Other character traits shown: *Cooperation, Diligence*

George, Jean Craighead. *Snow Bear.* Illus. by Wendell Minor. New York: Hyperion Books for Children, 1999.

Bessie and a polar bear cub named Snow Bear play on the ice, while her older brother and Snow Bear's mother watch to make sure everyone is safe.

Patience: While the youngsters frolic, older brother and mama bear watch for any sign that the children are in danger. "The Arctic cannot be rushed." Perhaps there will be no need to interfere.

Other character traits shown: *Discernment, Empathy, Prudence, Respect*

Guarnieri, Paolo. *A Boy Named Giotto.* Illus. by Bimba Landmann. Trans. by Jonathan Galassi. New York: Farrar, Straus & Giroux, 1998.

Eight-year-old Giotto the shepherd boy confesses his dream of becoming an artist to the painter Cimabue, who teaches him how to make marvelous pigments from minerals, flowers, and eggs and takes him on as a pupil.

Patience: The boy Giotto patiently waits for seven years, after being discovered by the painter, before being allowed to realize his apprenticeship. In his turn, the painter patiently abides by the parents' wishes and waits until the child is old enough before being allowed to take on the best student he will ever have. Even the parents realize that they must be patient with the child who doesn't take care of the sheep nearly as well as he paints on the local rocks.

Other character traits shown: *Diligence, Helpfulness*

Henkes, Kevin. *Lilly's Purple Plastic Purse.* New York: Greenwillow (William Morrow), 1996.

Lilly loves everything about school, especially her teacher, but when he asks her to wait a while before showing her new purse, she does something for which she is very sorry later.

Patience: When Lilly's purse and quarters and sunglasses were taken away from her because she couldn't sit quietly for her turn to share, she angrily draws a mean picture of her teacher and slips it into his book bag. Later, she is sorry she wasn't more patient. The next time Lilly brings her purse to share, she has learned to be patient until it's her turn. "Her purse and quarters and sunglasses were tucked safely inside her desk. She peeked at them often but did not disturb a soul."

Other character traits shown: *Self-discipline*

Lears, Laurie. *Ian's Walk: A Story about Autism.* Illus. by Karen Ritz. Morton Grove, IL: Albert Whitman, 1998.

A young girl realizes how much she cares about her autistic brother when he gets lost at a park.

Patience: On the trip to the park, the boy's behavior is an annoying embarrassment. He makes a face smelling flowers but puts his nose against warm, gritty bricks and sniffs the post office wall. She tells him, "Stop that. You look silly." Then she yanks him away before anyone notices. He won't eat pizza for lunch. Instead he munches cereal. When he is lost and then found, the girl's attitude changes. She no longer cares who might be watching his crazy-looking mannerisms. She patiently waits while he listens to something no one else can hear. She watches a spinning ceiling fan with him as long as he wants to. She waits while he sniffs bricks and lies on the ground, lining up pebbles in a straight row on the sidewalk. It no longer matters that he acts differently. "We'll walk home the way you like!" she tells him.

Other character traits shown: *Empathy, Loyalty*

Schertle, Alice. *That's What I Thought.* Illus. by John Wallner. New York: Harper & Row, 1990.

A little girl imagines different, exciting, and dangerous situations and is comforted by her parents' loving reassurance.

Patience: Over and over the child asks "What If" questions. What if it never stops raining? What if a bear comes to our house and wants to eat me up? Each question requires lengthy responses until the child works through to the reality of the situation, and is satisfied enough to say, "That's what I thought." Her parents never give up responding or make her uncomfortable asking.

Other character traits shown: *Respect*

Stewart, Sarah. *The Gardener.* Illus. by David Small. New York: Farrar, Straus & Giroux, 1997.

A series of letters relates what happens when Lydia Grace goes to live with her Uncle Jim in the city but takes her love for gardening with her.

Patience: Lydia Grace notes when she arrives in September, 1935, that Uncle Jim doesn't smile. Each letter home she reports on her gardening ventures and her efforts to get Uncle Jim to smile. He likes the poem she wrote him for Christmas, but he doesn't smile. She plants the seeds and bulbs her family has sent her. In February the bulbs are blooming; she's still hoping for a smile. In March she has discovered a special place on the apartment roof and plans a surprise for Uncle Jim, which is sure to make him smile. Through April she works on the secret roof garden. She gets seedlings in May from her family. More customers are filling the bakery and trading plants with her. In June lettuce and radishes and onions are growing in neighborhood window boxes. In July the secret garden on the roof is ready to show to Uncle Jim. He is surprised. A few days later he closes shop early, sends her to the roof garden and brings her a surprise. It is "the most amazing cake I've ever seen—covered in flowers! I truly believe that cake equals one thousand smiles."

Other character traits shown: *Diligence, Discernment, Generosity*

Uchida, Yoshiko. *The Bracelet.* Illus. by Joanna Yardley. New York: Philomel Books (Putnam & Grosset), 1976.

Emi, a Japanese American in the second grade, is sent with her family to an internment camp during World War II, but the loss of the bracelet her best friend has given her proves that she doesn't need a physical reminder of that friendship.

Patience: Emi is afraid that losing the bracelet means she will forget her best friend. Then she unpacks her suitcase and lifts out her favorite red sweater. This prompts her to remember how she and her friend Laurie had both worn their red sweaters on the first day of school. They'd also had matching lunch boxes. They had gone to fly kites in the vacant lot near home after school. She doesn't need a bracelet to remember her friend. She can remember her "right inside her head." Meanwhile, her mother sweeps out the tiny horse stall that is their temporary camp home. And they put up shelves. Soon they would be shipped to a camp in the Utah desert. But Laurie will still be in her heart, even there. They will endure this physical separation with patience. Emi is at peace. No one can take away her memories.

Other character traits shown: *Kindness, Tolerance*

PERSEVERANCE

Continued persistent effort.

Aardema, Verna. *The Lonely Lioness and the Ostrich Chicks.* Illus. by Yumi Heo. New York: Alfred A. Knopf, 1996.

In this Masai tale, a mongoose helps an ostrich get her chicks back from the lonely lioness who has stolen them.

Perseverance: Unlikely to prevail against such a superior foe, the ostrich mother continues to seek assistance from animals she passes in order to retrieve her chicks. She follows after the lioness, calling for their return. And, when the opportunity finally comes to reclaim them, she is there and ready to step forth to walk them home.

Other character traits shown: *Courage, Helpfulness, Honesty, Justice, Prudence, Self-discipline*

Atkins, Jeannine. *Mary Anning and the Sea Dragon.* Illus. by Michael Dooling. New York: Farrar, Straus & Giroux, 1999.

An account of the finding of the first entire skeleton of an ichthyosaur, an extinct sea reptile, by a 12-year-old English girl who went on to become a paleontologist.

Perseverance: Her aunt hopes she will get over this peculiar interest. Her skirts get wet in the sea water as she works to dislodge the fossil. And who would want to buy a sea dragon for one's parlor anyway? But someone does come along with the promise of payment for her find. Mary continues digging patiently when others tire of the monotonous work in cold winter weather. After nearly a year of slow progress, the creature is unearthed. Mary's life's work has begun.

Other character traits shown: *Courage, Diligence, Fortitude*

Auch, Mary Jane. *Bantam of the Opera.* New York: Holiday House, 1997.

Luigi the rooster wins fame and fortune when the star of the Cosmopolitan Opera Company and his understudy both come down with chicken pox on the same night.

Perseverance: Luigi knows there is "more to life" than cock-a-doodle-doo. He longs to use his voice more beautifully. His efforts in the chicken yard are not welcomed. When he hears opera being sung on a radio, he is thrilled. He hitches a ride to a performance of *Rigoletto* and can "barely keep from bursting into song." But neither does the opera company welcome his singing. Even his perfect pitch doesn't ensure him a role in the performance. Still, he perseveres. Only when the star performers cannot sing, does he don a costume and go on stage. But the audience reaction is disheartening. "Luigi kept singing, in spite of his broken heart." His "sweet voice soared above the jeers." His perseverance pays off. In the end, the audience gives him a standing ovation.

Other character traits shown: *Courage, Fortitude, Helpfulness, Hope*

Brenner, Barbara. *The Boy Who Loved to Draw: Benjamin West.* Illus. by Olivier Dunrea. Boston: Houghton Mifflin, 1999.

The Pennsylvania artist who begins drawing as a boy eventually becomes well known on both sides of the Atlantic.

Perseverance: From the moment Benjamin first draws a picture of his baby niece, for whom he is supposed to be rocking her cradle and flapping away flies, he is never without a notebook and pen. At age nine, he uses homemade paints of river clay and brushes made with cat fur and makes drawings good enough to impress the leading artist of the day, William Williams. He sells his first painting at age 12.

Other character traits shown: *Diligence, Helpfulness, Resourcefulness*

Brown, Margaret Wise. *The Little Scarecrow Boy.* Illus. by David Díaz. New York: Joanna Cotler Books (HarperCollins), 1998.

Early one morning a little scarecrow whose father warns him that he is not fierce enough to frighten a crow away goes out into the cornfield alone to try his luck.

Perseverance: Little scarecrow tries five times with a face more fierce each time. He does not quit. Though it is extremely taxing, finally, on the sixth try, he stops the crow.

Other character traits shown: *Hope, Responsibility*

Charles, Donald. *Chancay and the Secret of Fire: A Peruvian Folktale.* New York: A Whitebird Book, (G.P. Putnam's Sons), 1992.

In Peru, as a reward for releasing the beautiful fish he has caught, Chancay is granted his wish of finding a way to relieve his people from the cold and darkness.

Perseverance: The tasks to prove Chancay is worthy to bring the gift of fire to his people are exhausting and dangerous. Still, though he feels each time he is being sent on a fool's errand, Chancay persists in the quest, following the directives of the fish exactly. He continues until he has achieved his goal.

Other character traits shown: *Courage, Diligence, Fortitude, Kindness, Patience, Perseverance*

Christelow, Eileen. *The Five-Dog Night.* New York: Clarion Books (Houghton Mifflin), 1993.

Cantankerous Ezra keeps rebuffing his nosy neighbor Old Betty when she tries to give him advice on how to survive cold winter nights, until she finally discovers that his five dogs are his private source for warmth.

Perseverance: Despite the poor reception Old Betty receives for her efforts to look after her neighbor, she determinedly continues. She brings him cookies and hot chocolate as the weather turns colder, and a blanket, though he claims he doesn't need one. She even drives through deep snow to make sure he's not frozen to death. He calls her a "nosy old busybody." Her concern survives his callous rejection.

Other character traits shown: *Courage, Generosity, Helpfulness, Kindness, Respect*

Cole, Babette. *Bad Habits (or The Taming of Lucretzia Crum).* New York: Dial Books for Young Readers (Penguin), 1999.

What can be done about a girl with such awful behavior and the kids who want to be just like her?

Perseverance: Parents tell Lucretzia's parents to "keep your daughter under control!" So, Mr. Crum, who is also a mad scientist, devises objects to do that. Unfortunately, when her dad's inventions have been removed, she becomes wilder than ever. The parents persevere. When she demands a birthday party, they readily agree. They have a plan. Children arrive and trash the home. Then there is a knock on the door. "Some really big monsters burst in!" They wreck the party. "They spat, screamed, kicked, farted," and outdid the little monsters. Who are they? They "were children once, but they turned into monsters because they grew up doing what you do!" Lucretzia's parents tell her. Neither Lucretzia nor the other children want to be monsters any more "if that's what happens to us!" Hooray! Mr. and Mrs. Crum call the other parents to tell them the good news. They, however, are taking off their costumes and "having their own party, because their monster trick had worked so well!"

Other character traits shown: *Resourcefulness*

*Cutler, Jane. *The Cello of Mr. O.* Illus. by Greg Couch. New York: Dutton Children's Books (Penguin Putnam), 1999.

When a concert cellist plays in the square for his neighbors in a war-besieged city, his priceless instrument is destroyed by a mortar shell, but he finds the courage to return the next day to perform with a harmonica.

Perseverance: The supply truck can no longer come to the square, so Mr. O fills the space every day with a concert to "feed" the souls of the townspeople. When the enemy destroys his cello, he returns the next day with a harmonica and continues as before.

Other character traits shown: *Courage, Fortitude, Generosity, Hope, Resourcefulness*

Daly, Niki. *Bravo Zan Angelo! A Commedia Dell'arte Tale with Story and Pictures.* New York: Farrar, Straus & Giroux, 1998.

In Renaissance Venice, Angelo, longing to be as famous a clown as his grandfather, decides to do something special with his small part in his grandfather's act during Carnival.

Perseverance: Angelo asks his grandfather why he can't play the various parts in the group act. Each time he asks for a specific role, his grandfather ridicules him for being inappropriate for that part. Angelo persists until his grandfather finally reluctantly makes a small part for him. He will be a rooster that stays behind the curtain and makes only one "cock-a-doodle-do." Angelo finds his own costume, and expands his own part in the act. He struts on stage and shows the audience, as well as his grandfather, he is an excellent clown.

Other character traits shown: *Courage, Courtesy, Helpfulness, Hope, Kindness, Resourcefulness*

dePaola, Tomie. *The Legend of the Indian Paintbrush.* New York: G.P. Putnam's Sons, 1988.

Little Gopher follows his destiny, as revealed in a Dream-Vision, of becoming an artist for his people and eventually is able to bring the colors of the sunset down to earth.

Perseverance: Little Gopher faithfully carries out his task of painting the deeds of the People and the dreams of the shaman, but he keeps trying to find brighter colors that will truly capture the colors of the sunset. And, though he uses the brightest flowers, the reddest berries, the deepest purples from the rocks, still his "paintings never satisfied him. They looked dull and dark." He never stops trying.

Other character traits shown: *Diligence, Hope, Loyalty, Patience, Responsibility, Self-discipline,*

*Edwards, Pamela Duncan. *Honk!* Illus. by Henry Cole. New York: Hyperion Books for Children, 1998.

A ballet-loving swan wins acclaim when she manages to join the dancers in a performance of Swan Lake.

Perseverance: She practices en pointe when she lands on the pond. She practices on the ledge at the top of the Paris Opera House those dance movements she watches through the window. She is determined to get inside the Opera House. She finds a ticket stub and tries to gain admittance. She is turned back. She tries a number of times to sneak in by hiding under a gentleman's cloak, on a lady's hat, in a rubbish bin, and with a costume. But the manager throws her out again and again. She perseveres. When a late ballerina enters through a side stage door, she seizes the opportunity and follows. And she just keeps right on following onto the stage. Her graceful performance wins over the audience. They want more of her. Her efforts have paid off. She is a ballerina.

Other character traits shown: *Hope, Resourcefulness, Tolerance*

Goode, Diane. *Mama's Perfect Present.* New York: Dutton Children's Books (Penguin Putnam), 1996.

Led by the intrepid Zaza, their dachshund, two children troop all over Paris looking for the perfect gift for their mama, oblivious to the havoc Zaza causes along the way.

Perseverance: Despite dumped flowers, mussed dresses, loose birds, dropped cake, and mixed up shoes, the children push on to find the elusive perfect gift. Not until they watch a painter at work do they finally come up with the right gift choice. After buying some watercolors and paper, they paint Mama a birthday picture. They persevered until they knew they had found something just right.

Other character traits shown: *Discernment, Prudence*

*Gregory, Valiska. *Through the Mickle Woods.* Illus. by Barry Moser. Boston: Little, Brown & Co., 1992.

After his wife's death, a grieving king journeys to an old bear's cave in the mickle (thick) woods, where he hears three stories that help him go on living.

Perseverance: The king's companions do not have an easy time bringing him back to sound mental health. He rebuffs the boy many times for trying to help the king talk about his wife and see the delights still available in living. The king is short with the old woman, who tries to offer him comfort on a cold dark night. He even tries to cut short the bear's story lessons. "Can you bear to remember less?" No one gives up on the king. They persist until he finds peace. The king at last "took hold of Michael's small hand as if it were a gift of great price."

Other character traits shown: *Discernment, Empathy, Forgiveness, Generosity, Helpfulness, Hope, Kindness*

Himmelman, John. *Honest Tulio.* New York: BridgeWater (Troll Communications), 1997.

As he pursues the man in the big red hat who dropped a copper coin, Tulio accumulates an unusual following, including a chicken that lays square eggs.

Perseverance: Nothing keeps Tulio from his determination to return the copper coin to the man in the big red hat. He follows him across water, through farms, and even through a circus. His dream is simply to own his own stand in the market. But he trails the stranger in order to return the coin. In doing so, people give him things. By the end of his quest he is left with one chicken and returns to the market where he can set up a stand and sell the chicken's square eggs.

Other character traits shown: *Honesty*

Howard, Elizabeth Fitzgerald. *Virgie Goes to School with Us Boys.* Illus. by E.B. Lewis. New York: Simon & Schuster, 2000.

In the post-Civil War South, a young African American girl is determined to prove that she can go to school just like her older brothers.

Perseverance: The brothers argue that Virgie is too young to go so far to a school that keeps students from Monday through Friday. She will get homesick. But Virgie persists in her plea. Her parents need her to help on the farm, but they, too, realize "all free people need learning—old folks, young folks…small girls, too." She wins her battle and proves she can not only keep up with the boys, but can help them get through the deep dark woods more easily.

Other character traits shown: *Courage, Generosity*

Hughes, Monica. *A Handful of Seeds.* Illus. by Luis Garay. New York: Orchard Books, 1993.

Forced into the barrio by her grandmother's death, Concepcion takes with her a legacy of chili, corn, and bean seeds and finds that they hold the key to her survival.

Perseverance: Concepcion remembers to save enough seed for the next planting as her grandmother has advised. In her new residence, she uses what means are available to her to continue making a garden as she had been taught. She plants seeds in the barrio, but the plants are trampled when the police chase thieving children. She replants, certain that this is the means to self-sufficiency so that stealing is not necessary. This time the orphan barrio children help her toward her goal.

Other character traits shown: *Diligence, Fortitude, Generosity, Helpfulness, Resourcefulness*

Jay, Betsy. *Swimming Lessons.* Illus. by Lori Osiecki. Flagstaff, AZ: Rising Moon (Northland), 1998.

Although she has many excuses for refusing to take swimming lessons, Jane finally finds a reason to face the inevitable and jumps into the water.

Perseverance: Jane tells everyone that she doesn't intend to take lessons. Not even a bathing suit that changes colors when it's wet will entice her into the water. Perhaps she is a cross between a person on the outside and a cat on the inside. She insists she will not take swimming lessons, right up to the moment that Jimmy accuses her of being scared "because girls can't swim." He also said she was a chicken. "Chickens and girls can't swim." Suddenly, she is just as determined to learn to swim as she had been not to learn. "Everyone was very proud of me. I don't know why they made such a big deal out of it. Everybody should learn how to swim."

Lee, Milly. *Nim and the War Effort.* Illus. by Yangsook Choi. New York: Frances Foster Books (Farrar, Straus & Giroux), 1997.

Nim and a schoolmate are rivals in a contest to collect newspapers for the war effort until the final day when it seems Nim can't possibly win.

Perseverance: Despite having so little time available to her to go out collecting, Nim continues to keep searching the neighborhood. Despite being cheated of a newspaper pile her aunt has set aside for her, she seeks other avenues for finding papers. And, despite having found the mother lode of all piles, she still asks her grandfather for the one paper he is reading "for the war effort." Neither failures nor successes stop Nim from continuing to pursue her goal.

Other character traits shown: *Fortitude, Loyalty, Resourcefulness, Self-discipline*

Lied, Kate. *Potato: A Tale from the Great Depression.* Illus. by Lisa Campbell Ernst. Washington, DC: National Geographic Society, 1997.

During the Depression, a family seeking work finds employment for two weeks digging potatoes in Idaho.

Perseverance: Losing their farm and home doesn't stop this family. Father works in a coal mine until it closes. Then they borrow money for gas and a car to dig potatoes out of state. They earn cash picking up potatoes for the company owner in the daytime and at night collect bags of leftover potatoes for themselves to use in trade. By continuing to work hard and make do with little, the family eventually is able to get a real job that lasts.

Other character traits shown: *Fortitude, Resourcefulness*

*London, Jonathan. *Hip Cat.* Illus. by Woodleigh Hubbard. San Francisco: Chronicle Books, 1993.

A hip saxophone-playing cat goes to the big city to seek fame and fortune but finds that the top dogs own the cool clubs and sometimes you have to work in the Doggie Diner to make ends meet while learning to do what you love to do well.

Perseverance: Hip Cat likes to play at Minnie's Can Do, but she can't pay him a living wage. He tries to play at the better bars. They won't hire him. He continues to play "under the bridges, in the fog, on the ridges, all day, all night, for no pay." But "he kept up the fight." He becomes a short-order cook, in order to keep going. He plays for donations in the tourist traps. Back at Minnie's Can Do with polished skills, he begins again. This time, "he blew everybody away with his horn." Then, word gets around. Finally, his abilities attract the attention of the top dogs. His perseverance has enabled him to achieve his goal.

Other character traits shown: *Diligence*

McCully, Emily Arnold. *The Bobbin Girl.* New York: Dial Books for Young Readers (Penguin), 1996.

A 10-year-old bobbin girl working in a textile mill in Lowell, Massachusetts in the 1830s must make a difficult decision.

Perseverance: The women chose to "turn out" rather than continue to work under slave labor conditions. Though their efforts are courageous in support of justice, they are not successful. Mill owners simply hire other workers. Nevertheless, the women do not feel defeated. They find they can "stand up for what is right. Next time, or the time after, we will win." They will persevere for improved working conditions somewhere else.

Other character traits shown: *Cooperation, Courage, Justice, Prudence*

McCully, Emily Arnold. *Mirette on the High Wire.* New York: G.P. Putnam's Sons, 1992. (Caldecott–1993)

Mirette learns tightrope walking from Monsieur Bellini, a guest at her mother's boardinghouse, not knowing that he is a celebrated tightrope artist who has withdrawn from performing because of fear.

Perseverance: Mirette will not allow either herself or the master to quit. She must work to improve her basic skills. He must work to regain his courage to walk across the wire. When she discovers he has performed many magnificent acts, she begs him to teach them to her. He does not wish to disappoint her. So he sets up the high wire one last time between two tall buildings. But when he tries to walk across it, he freezes. His audience is puzzled. Mirette knows what to do. She rushes up the building steps and out the window and enters the wire from the opposite side. She walks toward him, holding out her arms to him. Suddenly, he smiles and begins to come across the wire to her. Together they have persevered. Their agent is already planning a world tour of protegee and master.

Other character traits shown: *Courage, Helpfulness*

McCully, Emily Arnold. *Mouse Practice.* New York: Arthur A. Levine Books (Scholastic Press), 1999.

Monk needs to learn his baseball skills, but his parents aren't natural athletes and can't teach him, so he must rely on his own ingenuity.

Perseverance: The team tells Monk he is too young to play. He isn't ready yet. In this practical tale of a child who must turn to alternative means to perfect his skills, readers might use some of Monk's methods to help themselves if, like him, there is no one else to turn to. Monk tries to get tips from his musician parents, but they clearly aren't able to teach him. So, he must invent his own teaching devices. He throws at a target painted on a fence until his throwing arm is developed. He whacks at a ball hanging from a rope until he can connect with precision. He catches balls tossed against the fence until he can field balls well. He's determined to do what it takes.

Other character traits shown: *Resourcefulness*

Martin, Jacqueline Briggs. *Snowflake Bentley.* Illus. by Mary Azarian. Boston:
Houghton Mifflin, 1998. (Caldecott–1999)

A self-taught scientist photographs thousands of individual snowflakes in order
to provide the world with a view of their unique formations.

Perseverance: "His first pictures were failures—no better than shadows. Yet he
would not quit." Storm after storm, through many winter seasons, Willie perseveres
collecting trays of snowflakes, always looking for the best samples. He tries a new
experiment with a small lens opening and holding it open up to 90 seconds.
Sometimes he manages only a few good photos a year. Townspeople say they don't
need pictures of snowflakes. They have plenty of the real thing. Still he keeps up
his life's work, compiling the singular definitive volume on his topic, which is
studied later by scientists.

Other character traits shown: *Diligence, Fortitude, Responsibility*

Moss, Marissa. *True Heart.* Illus. by C.F. Payne. New York: Silver Whistle (Harcourt
Brace), 1999.

At the turn of the twentieth century, a young woman who works for a railroad
accomplishes her yearning ambition to become an engineer when a male engineer
is injured and can't drive his train.

Perseverance: Bee begins her career by loading freight at the age of 16. It is good
paying work, and she is strong. She sits in the cab whenever she can and closely
watches engineers at work. She also asks lots of questions. And sometimes Ole Pete
will let her couple cars on the side tracks or drive all the way to the next station.
Meanwhile, she patiently loads steel as a "grunt." She knows she won't be grunting
forever. "I waited and kept my eyes open." When the opportunity arrives, she
volunteers to drive the train. The station master isn't sure her experience is sufficient.
He says what she's done was "different from flat-out driving." But the passengers
want to go, and there is no one else to drive them. By carefully persevering in her
knowledge and work ethics, she begins her career as an engineer that day.

Other character traits shown: *Diligence, Hope*

Provensen, Alice, and Martin Provensen. *The Glorious Flight: Across the Channel
with Louis Blériot July 25, 1909.* New York: Viking Press, 1983. (Caldecott–
1984)

A man whose fascination with flying machines produces the Blériot XI, crosses
the English Channel in 37 minutes in the early 1900s.

Perseverance: It takes six years of trial and error before an eleventh prototype
plane is designed well enough to fly from France, across the English Channel, to
England and for the pilot to learn his flying skills. There are, along the way, slight

crashes, total wrecks, and such injuries as a broken rib, a black eye, sprains, and bruises.

Other character traits shown: *Fortitude, Hope*

*Say, Allen. *Tea with Milk.* Boston: Walter Lorraine Books (Houghton Mifflin), 1999.

After growing up near San Francisco, a young Japanese woman returns with her parents to their native Japan, but she feels foreign and out of place.

Perseverance: Though her family sends her to Japanese school where she is called foreign, and she must take classes in how to be a proper Japanese lady, and a matchmaker's services are called upon, Masako does not give up her own dream of living like an American girl, including going to college and having her own apartment.

Other character traits shown: *Empathy, Fortitude*

Tunnell, Michael. *Mailing May.* Illus. by Ted Rand. New York: Greenwillow (William Morrow), 1997.

In 1914, because her family cannot afford a train ticket to her grandmother's town, May gets mailed and rides in the mail car on the train to see her grandmother.

Perseverance: May's parents promise she can visit Grandma "a million miles away through the rough old Idaho mountains." But when May reminds them, they say they can't afford the $1.55 for a ticket. May doesn't want to wait until next year. She tries to get a job in Mr. Alexander's department store, but there are only grown-up jobs available. Then her parents think of a plan. Perhaps they can send her as a mail package. Ma's cousin Leonard works in the train's mail car. He will look after her. The postal code says nothing about mailing children, but it allows baby chicks. May weighs under the 50-pound limit. To mail her from Grangeville to Lewiston will cost 53 cents. The postal officer glues stamps on the back of May's coat and a label, stating she is to be delivered to her grandmother's address.

Other character traits shown: *Resourcefulness*

PRUDENCE

Exercising sound judgment, shrewdness and discretion in personal matters.

Aardema, Verna. *Borreguita and the Coyote: A Tale from Ayutla, Mexico.* Illus. by Petra Mathers. New York: Alfred A. Knopf, 1991.

A little lamb uses her clever wiles to keep a coyote from eating her up.

Prudence: Virtually helpless physically from the much larger coyote, the lamb must prudently use her wits to save herself. In the first encounter she is staked out in a clover field by the farmer when the coyote comes to eat her. She points out how she is "thin as a bean pod." She advises waiting until she has eaten all the clover. When she's fat she will make a better meal. But when she is finally fat, she needs another delay tactic. She says cheese tastes better than lamb, and she knows a large round cheese is in the pond at the end of the pasture. When the coyote swims out to get it, "the image shattered," and the coyote howls in frustration "at the big cheese in the sky." In like manner, lamb convinces coyote she is holding up the mountain as she lies on her back under a ledge of rock, "bracing her feet against the top." She goes to get help while coyote exchanges places with her and assumes the job of holding up the mountain. When he tires and lets go, he realizes again the lamb has fooled him. Finally, his patience worn thin, he opens his mouth wide to eat her right now. She asks him for the kindness of being swallowed whole so she won't "suffer the biting and the chewing." She has flattered him into thinking he can swallow her in one piece by telling him his "mouth is so big you could swallow a cougar." With his mouth open she rushes forward striking "the inside of Coyote's mouth so hard she sent him rolling. His mouth feels like "one big toothache." Lamb is not bothered again.

Other character traits shown: *Courage, Resourcefulness*

Aardema, Verna. *The Lonely Lioness and the Ostrich Chicks.* Illus. by Yumi Heo. New York: Alfred A. Knopf, 1996.

In this Masai tale, a mongoose helps an ostrich get her chicks back from the lonely lioness who has stolen them.

Prudence: When the frantic mother ostrich asks a passing gazelle to help her get back the chicks a lioness has stolen, the gazelle, knowing well the relationship between lions and gazelles, prudently declines the request saying, "I wouldn't argue with a lioness if she said that the moon was her cub." Though not courageous or helpful, the gazelle knows better than to become involved in a no-win situation. The mongoose, who acts more bravely, also behaves with prudence. He confronts the lioness directly. But before provoking her with a taunt so she will abandon the chicks, he sensibly stands beside his burrow for a quick get-away.

Other character traits shown: *Courage, Helpfulness, Honesty, Justice, Perseverance, Self-discipline*

Arnold, Katya. *Duck, Duck, Goose?* New York: Holiday House, 1997.

Based on a story by Vladimir Grigorievich Suteev, a goose who envies the attributes of other birds learns to appreciate her own qualities.

Prudence: Goose wanted to look different from all the other geese. After trading parts with other birds, Goose does not look like any other bird. Soon she discovers Pelican's beak keeps her from grazing in the meadow. Stork's legs keep her from swimming in the shallow pond water. And, worst of all, she is defenseless against fox. She can't run away, because Peacock's tail gets caught in a bush. Fox is easily able to grab her long swan's neck. The other geese come to her rescue, pecking and pinching him from all sides until he lets Goose go. Prudently, she decides, "Now I know what I need to do." She goes back to all the birds and trades back her original parts. She looks like all the other geese again, except she is smarter, kinder, and happier.

Other character traits shown: *Discernment*

Bunting, Eve. *Train to Somewhere.* Illus. by Ronald Himler. New York: Clarion Books (Houghton Mifflin), 1996.

In the late 1800s, Marianne travels westward on the Orphan Train with other children, who hope to be placed with caring families.

Prudence: Marianne does not tell anyone she is really hoping to find her mother at one of the train stops along the way. While looking at the prospects for a new family, she holds in reserve the belief that it won't matter whether she is selected or not, because she has a mother. Later, when her mother fails to materialize, she must look more closely at the one couple who seems to be her last chance for a family. She can imagine that her own mother might have a softness in her face like this woman. And "Sometimes what you get turns out to be better than what you wanted in the first place."

Other character traits shown: *Courage, Empathy, Hope, Kindness, Patience, Respect*

Charles, Donald. *Chancay and the Secret of Fire: A Peruvian Folktale.* New York: A Whitebird Book (G. P. Putnam's Sons), 1992.

As a reward for releasing the beautiful fish he has caught, Chancay is granted his wish of finding a way to relieve his people from the cold and darkness.

Prudence: Chancay's strength and courage are not enough to secure the gift of fire, a task that he must both earn and learn. When he is told he must steal a mirror from the moon and not be caught by the sun, he must look to his sound judgement concerning how to do these things and stay safe. He will have to be cautious. It would be prudent not to allow the Moon and the Sun to know he is present. He waits for "many days and nights." He knows there is a time when "the Moon did not appear in the sky, and he reasoned that on cloudy days, the Sun must also sleep." He watches for his chance when both are asleep before he seizes the mirror and takes it to earth.

Other character traits shown: *Courage, Diligence, Fortitude, Kindness, Patience, Perseverance*

Edwards, Pamela Duncan. *The Worrywarts.* Illus. by Henry Cole. New York: HarperCollins, 1999.

Wombat, Weasel, and Woodchuck won't be wimps when they wander the world using wise means of outwitting not-so-wicked rascals.

Prudence: When one imagines an awful scenario that could happen to them on their wanderings in the world, another quickly explains what action he will take to stay safe. For example, if they should end up washed by a wave so that a wallowing walrus swallows them, weasel will wear water wings in case they can swim away.

Other character traits shown: *Courage, Resourcefulness*

Ernst, Lisa Campbell. *When Bluebell Sang.* New York: Bradbury Press (Macmillan), 1989.

Bluebell the cow's talent for singing brings her stardom, but she soon longs to be back at the farm and away from her greedy manager.

Prudence: When Bluebell and farmer Swenson overhear their manager's phone conversation, in which he says he will never let them go, Bluebell must think of a prudent way to get back to the farm. They have not been paid and have no way to get back. She does not confront the manager about his dishonesty. Instead, she pretends to go along with his scheme to keep touring. She tells him, "This concert life is great. I don't ever want to quit." But she does make a suggested itinerary change. They will go back to Swenson's farm where reporters can see where she came from, and at that time will reveal concert plans for a West Coast tour. Big Eddie recognizes the publicity potential and agrees to the plan. Once on the farm amidst the hubbub of photographers and reporters, Bluebell slips away among the other cows. Big Eddie is unable to identify her from all the others, because when he asks each one to sing, they all "mooo," including the prudent Bluebell.

Other character traits shown: *Honesty*

Feiffer, Jules. *I Lost My Bear.* New York: Morrow Junior Books, 1998.

When she cannot find her favorite stuffed toy, a young girl asks her mother, father, and older sister for help.

Prudence: Her sister tells her to throw another stuffed animal. Where it lands is also sometimes where the missing toy is located. So, the little girl studies her supply of stuffed animals. Prudently, she reasons, "If I throw one of my favorites, what if I lose that one too?" Then she reasons that if she throws one she doesn't care about, "it will know." And "it won't want to find my lost bear." She shuts her eyes and tries to select one randomly. But random selection points to her second favorite stuffed animal after her bear. She can't do it! Not her rabbit. So, she returns to her sister. "This was your idea. Could I throw one of your stuffed animals?" Amazingly, her sister does give her one. And she proceeds to try this method of finding a lost object.

Other character traits shown: *Diligence, Self-discipline*

George, Jean Craighead. *Snow Bear.* Illus. by Wendell Minor. New York: Hyperion Books for Children, 1999.

Bessie and a polar bear cub named Snow Bear play on the ice, while her older brother and Snow Bear's mother watch to make sure everyone is safe.

Prudence: The young ones play in friendly harmony until a very large male bear intrudes. They prudently run back the way they came. Their minders, mama bear and big brother, hurry to save the youngsters from this definite threat. But the large male bear knows a gun can kill. He slips quietly back into the water without threatening anyone's safety. Each arctic creature knows when to turn away from danger.

Other character traits shown: *Discernment, Empathy, Patience, Respect*

Goode, Diane. *Mama's Perfect Present.* New York: Dutton Children's Books (Penguin Putnam), 1996.

Led by the intrepid Zaza, their dachshund, two children troop all over Paris looking for the perfect gift for their mama, oblivious to the havoc Zaza causes along the way.

Prudence: After leaving a trail of crushed flowers, dresses, and cakes, fluttering birds and flying shoes, the children decide prudently that these kinds of gifts are too difficult for them to give to Mama. Wisely, they purchase some watercolor paint and make a picture for her. It's just the perfect gift for children to give, and Mama thinks so too.

Other character traits shown: *Discernment, Perseverance*

Hest, Amy. *The Purple Coat.* Illus. by Amy Schwartz. New York: Four Winds Press, 1986.

Despite her mother's reminder that "navy blue is what you always get," Gabby begs her tailor grandfather to make her a beautiful purple fall coat.

Prudence: Gabby knows what she wants, but she is prudent enough to accept that she must give up some of her choices for the overall goal of getting a purple coat. She asks for a long coat to her ankles but doesn't fuss when grandpa tells her it's not going to be quite that long. She asks for purple lining. He warns her not to push her luck. Mother wants the traditional navy blue coat, but she is prudent enough not to insist. She accepts the inevitable. "I have a sneaky suspicion this is going to be the best purple coat ever." Grandfather is prudent enough to please both his granddaughter and daughter. He agrees to make a purple coat for his granddaughter but offers to make it reversible with a navy blue lining to satisfy his daughter.

Other character traits shown: *Courage, Empathy, Tolerance*

McCully, Emily Arnold. *The Bobbin Girl.* New York: Dial Books for Young Readers (Penguin), 1996.

A 10-year-old bobbin girl working in a textile mill in Lowell, Massachusetts in the 1830s must make a difficult decision.

Prudence: When the "turn out" fails, Judith must go to find a position in another town. Rebecca, the bobbin girl, feels she is deserting their cause. She has led them into battle; now she is abandoning them. But the prudent Judith tells her they aren't defeated. Next time or the time after they will win. For now, "you must go back to work," and save money. Meanwhile Judith will "be working to improve our conditions somewhere else. Can you take my place here in Lowell?" Rebecca will do whatever she can. "Everything you would do!" They will quietly pick their battles and prudently make changes whenever possible. To do this, they must be on the job.

Other character traits shown: *Cooperation, Courage, Justice, Perseverance*

Meddaugh, Susan. *Martha Walks the Dog.* Boston: Walter Lorraine Books (Houghton Mifflin), 1998.

Martha the talking dog rescues the neighborhood from a bully dog with the help of a parrot.

Prudence: Name-calling is fine until Martha notices that Bad Bob's chain is broken. There is nothing to stop him. Running out of words and breath as she is being chased, she hears the parrot mimic her past words. The parrot happened to say, "Good dog," and the effect on Bob is immediate. Martha finds it prudent to encourage more of the same. Quickly, from her hiding spot under the bushes, she teaches the parrot such useful phrases as "Great dog," and "Bob is soooo handsome," and "Be nice." The effect is a miracle. Bob walks calmly home with his owner. It looks like "the beginning of a beautiful friendship."

Other character traits shown: *Kindness, Resourcefulness*

*Thurber, James. *Many Moons.* Illus. by Louis Slobodkin. New York: Harcourt Brace, 1943. (Caldecott–1944)

Though many try, only the court jester is able to fulfill Princess Lenore's wish for the moon.

Prudence: The intellectuals err by presuming they know what is the truth, though each seems to know a different truth. The court jester, who knows no more than they do but does not pretend to, does not dispute them. "They are all wise men, and so they must all be right." He reasons prudently that the truth about the moon's distance and size must be "as each person thinks it is." The thing to do is ask Princess Lenore what she thinks. When he does, she tells him. From her answer he is able to "give" her the moon. But what will happen when she sees the moon, that she is supposed to have, rise in the sky again? The intellectuals can come up with no useful strategy. The court jester again prudently seeks information from the child. "How can the moon be shining in the sky when it is hanging on a golden chain around your neck?" The princess is undeterred. She explains that it is like a lost tooth. Another grows in its place—like daylight, like flowers. Replacements happen.

Other character traits shown: *Respect*

Zemach, Harve. *Duffy and the Devil.* Illus. by Margot Zemach. New York: Farrar, Straus & Giroux, 1973. (Caldecott–1974)

Duffy is hired by the squire to knit his clothes, but because she can neither spin thread nor knit, she must make a deal with the devil in order to retain her position.

Prudence: Duffy angers the devil when she tells him correctly his name and so will not have to leave with him after all. But he retaliates by turning to ash all the clothes he has knitted over the three years of their bargain. Duffy prudently realizes that she is likely to be expected to replace these items and knows she can't do it. How can she avoid being "found out?" She has always done a good job of looking out for her own interests and quickly thwarts any such request of her by telling the squire, "All my work! Gone up in smoke! I swear I'll never knit another thing ever again!" She doesn't. And, of course, who could possibly ask her?

Other character traits shown: *Resourcefulness*

RESOURCEFULNESS

Use for SELF-RELIANCE
Ability to deal promptly and effectively with problems or difficulties

Aardema, Verna. *Borreguita and the Coyote: A Tale from Ayutla, Mexico.* Illus. by Petra Mathers. New York: Alfred A. Knopf, 1991.

A little lamb uses her clever wiles to keep a coyote from eating her up.

Resourcefulness: Though not strong enough to fight off the coyote or run away from him, she is more than a match for her foe. First, she tricks him into letting her eat clover in order to make herself fatter and tastier for him. He agrees. The next time the coyote approaches, she convinces him that cheese tastes better, and she knows where the biggest round cheese can be found. The coyote jumps into the pond one evening to retrieve that big round "cheese" and finds it merely the moon's reflection. When the coyote surprises her on the mountain, she invents a tale about holding up the mountain by lying on her back and bracing her feet on a rock above her. The coyote agrees to hold up the mountain for her while she goes to get help. When he tires of his task and drops his feet, he knows he's been fooled again. Finally, he will endure no more stalling tactics. She acknowledges the inevitable but asks only to be swallowed whole so that she is spared the pain of being chewed. He opens wide his mouth; she rushes forward and rams him. He is in too much pain to continue his quest to make a meal of the lamb.

Other character traits shown: *Courage, Prudence*

Arnold, Marsha Diane. *The Chicken Salad Club.* Illus. by Julie Downing. New York: Dial Books for Young Readers (Penguin), 1998.

Nathaniel's great-grandfather, who is 100 years old, loves to tell stories from his past but seeks someone to join him with a new batch of stories.

Resourcefulness: Nathaniel wants to cheer up his grandfather. He tries to reassure him that he loves hearing the same stories again and again. He brings his dog to listen. His grandfather smiles but tells no stories. He tries to bring his grandfather and the kids in his class together. But the kids are bored and they have nothing to say to each other. Nathaniel sets about organizing a party for people over 100 for the purpose of sharing stories. Unfortunately, the expected crowd doesn't arrive. Finally, Nathaniel thinks of the "Confidentials" section of the newspaper. He places an ad, which states that a 100-year-old man "fiery, fit, and a fine storyteller" is looking for 100-year-old friends who are the same. One person answers the ad and is interviewed. Nathaniel is satisfied. He tells his grandfather, "I've been thinking, maybe you don't need lots of storytellers to share stories with you. Maybe just one would do." And she did do just fine.

Other character traits shown: *Discernment, Helpfulness*

Best, Cari. *Three Cheers for Catherine the Great.* Illus. by Giselle Potter. New York: DK Ink, 1999.

Sara's Russian grandmother has requested that there be no presents at her seventy-eighth birthday party, so Sara must think of a gift from her heart.

Resourcefulness: Each of the guests gives something meaningful that is special to that person. The hairdresser fixes grandmother's hair. The dance instructor waltzes with her. And, Sara has decided, because her grandmother likes to write just as she does, she will teach her grandmother to finally read and write in English.

Other character traits shown: *Generosity*

Brenner, Barbara. *The Boy Who Loved to Draw: Benjamin West.* Illus. by Olivier Dunrea. Boston: Houghton Mifflin, 1999.

The Pennsylvania artist who begins drawing as a boy eventually becomes well known on both sides of the Atlantic.

Resourcefulness: Benjamin needs paint to correctly draw a robin. The local Indians show him how to take the colored clay in the area and mix it with bear grease to make paint. His mother gives him a stick of bluing from her laundry supplies. With red, yellow, and blue he can mix them to make other colors. He needs a paintbrush to apply the paint. A traveling man informs him that he should use a camel hair brush. Lacking this professional quality tool, he snips fur from his cat, wraps it on a quill pen with yarn and tries to apply paint with his homemade brush.

Other character traits shown: *Diligence, Helpfulness, Perseverance*

Chocolate, Debbi. *The Piano Man.* Illus. by Eric Velasquez. New York: Walker & Co., 1998.

A young African American girl recalls the life story of her grandfather, who performed in vaudeville and played piano for the silent movies.

Resourcefulness: Her grandfather's versatile skills made him equally capable of thrilling moviegoers with background music, copying the styles of great musicians such as Scott Joplin and Jelly Roll Morton, amusing an audience at the Snake Doctor's medicine show with daring feats and tricks, and providing the right accompaniment for vaudeville acts. And, when the silent movies and vaudeville ends, he uses his talents to become a piano tuner.

Other character traits shown: *Empathy*

Cole, Babette. *Bad Habits (or The Taming of Lucretzia Crum).* New York: Dial Books for Young Readers (Penguin), 1999.

What can be done about a girl with such awful behavior and the kids who want to be just like her?

Resourcefulness: Facing the anger of other parents and Lucretzia's teacher, her parents are charged with controlling her behavior. First, her father invents machines to address her various bad habits. But when the machines are removed, she is wilder than ever. Next they plan a memorable birthday party for her. The children copy Lucretzia's bad habits and soon trash the house. Then some unexpected guests burst in, really big monsters. They spit, scream, kick, fart, and behave worse than the children. They eat all the party food and leave, taking Lucretzia's presents with them. Who are they? Her parents tell her, "They were children once, but they turned into monsters because they grew up doing what you do!" Suddenly Lucretzia and her friends don't want to be monsters "if that's what happens to us." A phone call from Lucretzia's happy parents to the other children's parents tell them the good news. They are removing costumes and having a party of their own, "because their monster trick had worked so well."

Other character traits shown: *Perseverance*

*Cutler, Jane. *The Cello of Mr. O.* Illus. by Greg Couch. New York: Dutton Children's Books (Penguin Putnam), 1999.

When a concert cellist plays in the square for his neighbors in a war-besieged city, his priceless instrument is destroyed by a mortar shell, but he finds the courage to return the next day to perform with a harmonica.

Resourcefulness: There is little left in the town that indicates a normal life. But Mr. O does what he can to create a semblance of culture. Every day at four in the afternoon, when the supply truck used to arrive, he presents a concert out in the street. And, when a bomb blast takes away his cello his concerts continue anyway. He plays classical music on a harmonica.

Other character traits shown: *Courage, Fortitude, Generosity, Hope, Perseverance*

Daly, Niki. *Bravo Zan Angelo! A Commedia Dell'arte Tale with Story and Pictures.* New York: Farrar, Straus & Giroux, 1998.

In Renaissance Venice, Angelo, longing to be as famous a clown as his grandfather, decides to do something special with his small part in his grandfather's act during Carnival.

Resourcefulness: To play a rooster, Angelo needs a last minute costume. Soon, his helpful friends have made him a mask, found him a neck ruffle and tied up his coat like a rooster tail, and even given him a glove for a cockscomb. With nothing but determination, Angelo struts on stage like the rooster he imitates. His efforts win him cheers.

Other character traits shown: *Courage, Courtesy, Helpfulness, Hope, Kindness, Perseverance*

*Edwards, Pamela Duncan. *Honk!* Illus. by Henry Cole. New York: Hyperion Books for Children, 1998.

A ballet-loving swan wins acclaim when she manages to join the dancers in a performance of Swan Lake.

Resourcefulness: When thrown out of the Opera House, Mimi is certain there must be some mistake. She does not accept rejection. She tries various disguises in an attempt to slip past the Opera House manager. She tries to pass through with a ticket stub she finds on the floor. She tries to hide under a gentleman's cloak, on a lady's hat, in a rubbish bin, and with a top hat over her head. Each time she is caught and told to leave. Finally, she follows a late-arriving ballerina in through a side door and onto the stage. Her efforts win her accolades during the performance.

Other character traits shown: *Hope, Perseverance, Tolerance*

Edwards, Pamela Duncan. *The Worrywarts.* Illus. by Henry Cole. New York: HarperCollins, 1999.

Wombat, Weasel, and Woodchuck won't be wimps when they wander the world using wise means of outwitting not-so-wicked rascals.

Resourcefulness: The friends imagine terrible scenarios and proceed to take what they believe to be resourceful action against them. If water is a danger, they will have water wings; if a fierce whirlwind blows, they will wear wooly underwear. But when the actual danger confronts them, it is not the planned precautions they need. It is their food snacks and book of words that enable them to get by safely.

Other character traits shown: *Courage, Prudence*

Fleischman, Paul. *Weslandia.* Illus. by Kevin Hawkes. Cambridge, MA: Candlewick Press, 1999.

Wesley's garden produces a crop of huge, strange plants, which provide him with clothing, shelter, food, and drink, thus helping him create his own civilization and changing his life.

Resourcefulness: Wesley is soon self-sufficient. He garners first the scorn, then curiosity, and finally admiration of neighbors and schoolmates. Once the object of ridicule, Wesley, who is uninterested in traditional sports, makes up his own games, "rich with strategy and complex scoring systems" using many parts of the plant. Spectators look on with envy. Wesley "tried to be patient with the other players' blunders." He allows them to help crush the plant's seeds to collect oil from which he makes suntan lotion and mosquito repellent. He charges his "former tormentors $10 a bottle" for this. Wesley's new civilization becomes a craze. "He had no shortage of friends."

Other character traits shown: *Respect*

Fleming, Candace. *A Big Cheese for the White House: The True Tale of a Tremendous Cheddar.* Illus. by S. D. Schindler. New York: DK Ink, 1999.

In 1801 in Cheshire, Massachusetts, Elder John Leland organizes his fellow townspeople to make a big cheese for President Jefferson, who up until that time had been forced to eat inferior cheeses.

Resourcefulness: There is no cheese press big enough for the cheese they are making, so they use the town's apple press. There is no cheese hoop big enough, so the blacksmith makes a special one. They take turns monitoring the aging progress. They even hitch two horses to the wagon to pull the giant cheese to the sailing ship to Washington, DC. Whatever is needed is worked out.

Other character traits shown: *Cooperation, Courtesy*

Fleming, Candace. *When Agnes Caws.* Illus. by Giselle Potter. New York: Anne Schwartz Book, Atheneum Books for Young Readers (Simon & Schuster), 1999.

When eight-year-old Agnes Peregrine, an accomplished bird caller, travels with her mother to the Himalayas in search of the elusive pink-headed duck, she encounters a dastardly foe.

Resourcefulness: Colonel Pittsnap, the collector of stuffed birds, captures not only the rare pink-headed duck, but "by chance caught the golden-throated birdcaller, too." He orders Agnes to "call some birds for my collection." She declares she won't, and "You can't make me." But "by the look on his face, Agnes knew he meant business." She must resort to her own resourcefulness to save herself and the life of the pink-headed duck. "There was only one thing to do." She proceeds to call all the birds at once. They fly in "from all corners of the world" and promptly dispatch Colonel Pittsnap, chasing him off the mountain.

Other character traits shown: *Justice*

Goodhart, Pippa. *Noah Makes a Boat.* Illus. by Bernard Lodge. Boston: Walter Lorraine Books (Houghton Mifflin), 1997.

Noah and his grandson Little Noah, build a great boat, collect the animals, and survive the great flood.

Resourcefulness: Noah tells God he doesn't know how to make a boat. God tells Noah, "Work it out." Little Noah remarks that "the birds floating on the water must be the right shape for a boat." Noah says they are all different shapes. Then Little Noah looks up at the floating birds from under the water and notes that "underneath they are all the same." So that is the shape they decide they need for the boat. But how to make it? A hollowed tree log wouldn't be big enough. At supper they cook fish and notice the fish skeleton. The boat needs bones. But what kind of material will be the bones? They will use wooden bones and planks over the bones to keep the water out. What about food? They can catch fish; the hens will lay eggs. The boat needs to be big. Better do some measuring to allow enough space for tall creatures like the giraffe and fat creatures like the hippo. They did, indeed, work it out with their resourceful thinking.

Grifalconi, Ann. *Tiny's Hat.* New York: HarperCollins, 1999.

A young girl, who misses her father, a traveling blues musician, lifts her own spirits by wearing his hat and singing his songs.

Resourcefulness: Time passes and her father does not return from his last trip. Tiny is bereft until one day, wearing the bowler hat he left her, she hears his horn in her head. She begins to sing along with the tune he plays. Soon, the sadness melts away. Wearing his hat brings back his spirit. She finds herself able to "catch the tears" and sing her blues away so well even her Mama begins to smile, too. She has found a way, as he promised her, for him to "be around no matter how."

Haley, Gail E. *A Story, A Story.* New York: Atheneum, 1970. (Caldecott–1971)

Explains how the African Spider Man, Ananse, came into possession of all the stories on earth through his clever cunning.

Resourcefulness: Though the price seems impossible, the smaller, weaker, human is able to buy, as requested, from the strong Sky God the right to the golden box of stories. By resourceful trickery Ananse ties up the leopard by telling it he can be the cat's lunch after they play the "binding binding game." By pretending to make rain, he lures hornets into a calabash "so that the rain will not tatter your wings." Making a tar-baby-like doll, he captures a fairy. These gifts Ananse takes in a spider web net to Sky God and, thus, brings back to earth all the stories of the world.

Hall, Donald. *Ox-Cart Man.* Illus. by Barbara Cooney. New York: Viking Press, 1979. (Caldecott–1980)

This story describes the day-to-day life throughout the changing seasons of an early nineteenth-century New England family.

Resourcefulness: The family loads up all the things they have made by hand throughout the year and takes them to town in the fall to sell. They pack a bag of wool, a shawl the wife wove on a loom from yarn spun from wool, pairs of mittens the daughter knit from the yarn, candles, linen, shingles that were hand split, birch brooms hand cut, a barrel of apples, honey and honeycombs, turnips and cabbages, and other goods. Resourcefully, besides these things, the family even sells the wooden box that carried the maple sugar, the barrel that carried the apples, the bag that carried the potatoes, the ox cart that carried everything, the ox, and the ox's yoke and harness. The farmer walks home with next year's supplies and leftover cash. Throughout the winter the farmer carves a new yoke for the young ox, saws planks for a new cart, and splits shingles. The wife and daughter make flax into linen and embroider the linen. The son carves Indian brooms from birch, and everyone makes candles. After collecting maple syrup and shearing sheep in the spring, a new cycle of planting and harvesting begins again in an ultimate lifestyle of resourcefulness.

*Hearne, Betsy. *Seven Brave Women.* Illus. by Bethanne Andersen. New York: Greenwillow (William Morrow), 1997.

A young girl recounts the brave exploits of her female ancestors, beginning with her great-great-great-grandmother, who came to America in a wooden sailboat. *Resourcefulness:* Among these women is a farmer who, after finishing a week of hard labor, rides a horse all day to the nearest town to take art lessons, only to ride all the way home to do chores the next evening. When growing family responsibilities mean there is no time to paint on paper or canvas, she paints on the china they eat from. Another woman loves buildings all her life. She designs a house for her husband and children, then she builds it. When she is 80 years old she writes a book about buildings. Everyone loves her book, so she writes another one about builders, which is published when she is 89.
Other character traits shown: *Fortitude, Respect*

Hong, Lily Toy. *Two of Everything: A Chinese Folktale* Morton Grove, IL: Albert Whitman, 1993.

A poor farmer finds a magic brass pot that doubles whatever is placed inside it. *Resourcefulness:* It is good to double the moneybag but a nightmare when the wife falls into the pot. The farmer says, "One wife is enough for me!" The wife doesn't want a second wife because, "I am your one and only wife!" When the farmer also falls into the pot, they realize, "It is good that the other Mrs. Haktak has her own Mr. Haktak. Perhaps we will become best friends." After all, they are so much alike they will be like brother and sister to the farmer and his wife. The farmer has dealt effectively and promptly with a potential problem.

Hopkinson, Deborah. *Sweet Clara and the Freedom Quilt.* Illus. by James Ransome. New York: Alfred A. Knopf, 1993.

A young slave stitches a quilt with a map pattern, which guides her and other slaves to freedom in the North.

Resourcefulness: The runaway slaves need a map that will show the way to freedom. The girl uses her ability to stitch and piece to work into a quilt a design that serves as a map.

Other character traits shown: *Diligence, Helpfulness*

Hughes, Monica. *A Handful of Seeds.* Illus. by Luis Garay. New York: Orchard Books, 1993.

Forced into the barrio by her grandmother's death, Concepcion takes with her a legacy of chili, corn, and bean seeds and finds that they hold the key to her survival.

Resourcefulness: Though living in squalid conditions, Concepcion abides by her grandmother's advice to always save seeds for the next planting so that you won't go hungry. Even here, she digs a garden to grow vegetables in order to eat and to have produce to sell.

Other character traits shown: *Diligence, Fortitude, Generosity, Helpfulness, Perseverance*

Hutchins, Hazel. *Believing Sophie.* Illus. by Dorothy Donohue. Morton Grove, IL: Albert Whitman, 1995.

When a little girl is unjustly accused of shoplifting, she bravely tries to prove her innocence.

Resourcefulness: Sophie manages to carry her purchases on her bicycle by tucking her receipt in her sock, her change into her wrist purse, the cough drops in her belt, and holding on to the bag of candy. Later, that receipt in her sock is her means to proving her honesty.

Other character traits shown: *Courage, Honesty*

James, J. Alison. *The Drums of Noto Hanto.* Illus. by Tsukushi. New York: DK Ink, 1999.

The people in a small village in ancient Japan manage to drive off the forces of a powerful warlord using only their ingenuity.

Resourcefulness: The villagers know they cannot win a fighting battle. They can't match the powerful samurai's weapons. So, instead, they concentrate on preventing the enemy from coming ashore. Using trickery, they instill fear through sight and sound. They make bonfires, dance in fierce costumes, and employ their famous drums that can make powerful resonating booms.

Other character traits shown: *Courage*

Jolly, Mike. *Grunter: A Pig with an Attitude.* Illus. by Deborah Allwright. Brookfield, CT: Millbrook Press, 1999.

Grunter, a pig with an obnoxious attitude, gets an explosive surprise from the other farmyard animals on his birthday.

Resourcefulness: Everyone has borne the brunt of Grunter's awful behavior. He is too big for his britches. Finally, on his birthday, they find a way to teach him a lesson. Grunter is all alone. He apparently doesn't understand why there is no celebration for him. Despite his conduct, a confused Grunter is capable of experiencing a sorrowful look of loneliness. He thinks no one has remembered. Then, he sees what looks like a sparkling candle. The animals have not forgotten him. Grunter discovers too late as he approaches the "candle" that it is really a firecracker. It explodes and sends him up high and away from the farm. But, lest the animals rejoice prematurely, there is a footnote. "What goes up must come down." Eventually, there will have to be a reckoning between Grunter and the other farm animals. This is a to-be-continued story.

Krupinski, Loretta. *Best Friends.* New York: Hyperion Books for Children, 1998.

When a settler's young daughter learns that soldiers will force the Nez Perce off the nearby land, she uses a doll to warn her Indian friend of impending danger.

Resourcefulness: It is too dangerous to go directly to the Indian village to warn them. But the medicine doctor makes regular trips to the village. No one would find it odd for him to deliver the toy to a child at the village. The soldiers would not suspect him of sabotaging their efforts. So, the white girl sacrifices her beloved doll by enclosing a message in it and asking the unsuspecting doctor to deliver a final gift to her playmate.

Other character traits shown: *Generosity, Helpfulness, Justice, Kindness, Loyalty, Respect*

Lee, Milly. *Nim and the War Effort.* Illus. by Yangsook Choi. New York: Frances Foster Books (Farrar, Straus & Giroux), 1997.

Nim and a schoolmate are rivals in a contest to collect newspapers for the war effort until the final day when it seems Nim can't possibly win.

Resourcefulness: Nim has been cheated of a pile of papers that should have gone into her collection. She has begged as many papers from Chinatown as are available. If she is to win the contest, she must go farther away to Nob Hill to seek papers. When she finds a whole garage stacked with papers her dream of winning is assured, if she can find a way to get them to the school before the end of the day. She remembers the police have said that they should be called if there is a need, and she has a need. So, though they aren't thrilled with her request, she does successfully enlist their help. The paddy wagon serves the job of transporting the garage's contents.

Other character traits shown: *Fortitude, Loyalty, Perseverance, Self-discipline*

Levitin, Sonia. *Nine for California.* Illus. by Cat Bowman Smith. New York: Orchard Books, 1996.

Amanda travels by stagecoach with her four siblings and her mother from Missouri to California to join her father.

Resourcefulness: Mother packs a sack with "everything we'll need" for the long journey west. But the bag does not contain clothing or supplies for life in their new home. It does, however, make the trip getting there much more bearable. When the children begin to quarrel restlessly in the cramped stagecoach, she provides them with sugar lumps from the bag. There are prunes to help make the daily ration of beans more palatable. And, when hungry Indians threaten attack, there is corn pone. Some licorice whips warm the bones following a cold muddy rainstorm. A jar of red pepper staves off a thundering herd of buffalo, and a whistle blown sharply frightens away would-be robbers. When they arrive in California, the bag is empty. Pa can't see why anyone would bring an empty sack from Missouri. "I'm glad you've come to me, my dear. These children need someone with good sense to take care of them." Mama doesn't dispute him. She just folds the sack and takes it to their new home where it comes in handy again when it is filled with goose feathers and lies as a pillow on the family bed.

Other character traits shown: *Helpfulness*

Lied, Kate. *Potato: A Tale from the Great Depression.* Illus. by Lisa Campbell Ernst. Washington, DC: National Geographic Society, 1997.

During the Depression, a family seeking work finds employment for two weeks digging potatoes in Idaho.

Resourcefulness: The loss of the family farm does not stop this family. Father takes a job in a coal mine until it closes. Then they go to Idaho to pick potatoes to earn cash. In the night they pick up leftover potatoes to bring back home to trade for other things they need. "They worked very hard to live on what little they had."

Other character traits shown: *Fortitude, Perseverance*

Mathers, Petra. *Lottie's New Beach Towel.* New York: Anne Schwartz Book, Atheneum Books for Young Readers (Simon & Schuster), 1998.

Lottie the chicken has a number of adventures at the beach, during which her new towel comes in handy.

Resourcefulness: Lottie finds many resourceful uses for her new gift. She first uses it to step on to avoid the hot beach sand. It becomes a sail for her friend's boat when his motor fails. It's also a picnic tablecloth and finally an emergency veil for a bride's wedding.

McCully, Emily Arnold. *Mouse Practice.* New York: Arthur A. Levine Books (Scholastic Press), 1999.

Monk needs to learn his baseball skills, but his parents aren't natural athletes, so he must rely on his own ingenuity.

Resourcefulness: Monk's father tries to demonstrate throwing a ball. His mother tries to demonstrate catching it. Because the one can't pitch a ball that the other can catch, Monk must be resourceful. The music stand makes a good target. Maybe he could hit it again. Mother says, "We'll see, dear." Monk paints a bull's-eye on the fence instead. The clock pendulum gives him an idea for creating a means for batting practice. A rope in the tree with a ball attached enables him to whack at a moving ball. Catching the ball by tossing it against the fence helps him field moving balls. Finally, he is ready to show the team he has the skills needed to play baseball.

Other character traits shown: *Perseverance*

Reiser, Lynn. *Best Friends Think Alike.* New York: Greenwillow (William Morrow), 1997.

Two best friends have a brief disagreement, but then decide that playing together is better than having your own way alone.

Resourcefulness: Because both want to be the horse rather than the rider and neither wants to play alone, they determine that their new game will involve each girl being both horse and rider "together."

Other character traits shown: *Cooperation*

Root, Phyllis. *Aunt Nancy and Cousin Lazybones.* Illus. by David Parkins. Cambridge, MA: Candlewick Press, 1998.

When Cousin Lazybones comes to visit Aunt Nancy but refuses to help with any of the work around the house, Aunt Nancy must figure out a scheme to get rid of him.

Resourcefulness: Cousin Lazybones comes up with ideas to avoid work. Feed the chickens right in the house, so that you don't have to carry food and water to them. When a plate is dirty, use the other side to cut down on the number of times it needs washing. When water is needed, set a pail outside. Sooner or later it will rain and fill it up. The only way to get rid of this moocher (who likes big meals) is to come up with a good idea of her own. Aunt Nancy fakes miseries. "I woke up this morning with a bone in my leg, so's I can hardly walk." Her chest is full of breath, and she has such a mess of brains in her head she can hardly think. And this is spring-cleaning day. "Lucky for me you're here to help, you having two good legs and a head full of good ideas." Before she's finished listing all the jobs that need to be done, Cousin Lazybones is hightailing it "out the door like a chicken at a fox convention."

*Stanley, Diane. *Rumpelstiltskin's Daughter*. New York: William Morrow, 1997.

Rumpelstiltskin's daughter may not be able to spin straw into gold, but she is more than a match for a monarch whose greed has blighted an entire kingdom. **Resourcefulness:** Instead of calling upon the help of her father, who can spin straw into gold, the girl makes a plan to improve the lives of people in the kingdom who have nothing because of the king's greed. First, she tells the monarch that gold is grown. Each farmer must be given two pieces of gold coin, one to plant and one "for his trouble." When the king returns to collect the "gold," he finds pumpkins and grain. But the people are so happy they praise the king's goodness. The king wants her to try to think again how gold is made. This time the girl seems to remember that maybe gold is knitted with golden knitting needles. Yellow yarn and golden needles and a gold coin "for her trouble" goes to each of the grandmothers in the kingdom. When he comes to collect his gold, people are wearing golden colored warm clothing. They shower the king with gifts for his kindness. Now the king doesn't need his shifty eyed mean-looking guards anymore. The girl suggests putting them to work tearing down the moat and building a zoo for the crocodiles that swam in it. The king would still like to have more gold, but she did try her best. He decides to make her his queen. She asks for the job of prime minister instead. Her resourcefulness has changed a kingdom, if not a king.

Other character traits shown: *Kindness*

Steig, William. *Pete's a Pizza*. New York: Michael di Capua Books (HarperCollins), 1998.

Pete is in a bad mood because it rains when he wants to play ball with his friends, so his father makes him into a pizza. **Resourcefulness:** Without the aid of toys, Pete's father is able to engage the boy's attention and distract him from his disappointment. To cheer him up, Pete's father lays him on a table and begins to make him into a pizza, kneading the dough, stretching it and whirling it in the air. Even Pete's mother begins to catch on and enter into the spirit of the game. Oil (water) is generously applied. Some flour (talcum powder) is sprinkled on him. Tomatoes (checkers) are placed on the "pizza," but his mother says she doesn't like tomatoes on her pizza. They are removed, and cheese (bits of paper) is added. Pretty soon the dough gets tickled and laughs like crazy. Then the pizza is baked in a nice hot oven (the couch). When it's time to slice up the pizza, it runs away. The pizza-maker chases him—and captures and hugs him. Then the sun comes out. So, the pizza decides to go look for his friends.

Other character traits shown: *Empathy*

Taback, Simms. *Joseph Had a Little Overcoat*. New York: Viking (Penguin Putnam) 1999. (Caldecott–2000)

A very old overcoat is recycled numerous times into a variety of garments.

Resourcefulness: This coat's owner is nothing if not resourceful. The coat becomes a succession of smaller fresh items. The narrator creates first a jacket, then a vest, a scarf, a necktie, and finally a button to fasten his suspenders to his pants. When he loses the button, it would appear that he has nothing. But not quite. He makes a book about his coat and its many transformations, which proves you can always make something out of nothing.

Tunnell, Michael. *Mailing May*. Illus. by Ted Rand. New York: Greenwillow (William Morrow), 1997.

In 1914, because her family cannot afford a train ticket to her grandmother's town, May gets mailed and rides the mail car on the train to see her grandmother. *Resourcefulness*: Her parents know how much May was looking forward to the visit with her grandmother. So, when they cannot afford the $1.55 for a passenger ticket, they think up another plan. With the cooperation of the postal officer and the help of Cousin Leonard, who oversees the mail car on the train, they look up the rules and regulations about package size. May is under 50 pounds. And she is not a lizard, insect, or anything smelly, so the postal code has no regulation against mailing her. After all, baby chicks can be mailed. The stamp to mail May costs 53 cents. The stamp and a label with her grandmother's address on it are attached to the back of her coat. She will ride in the mail car. May will be able to visit her grandmother after all.

Other character traits shown: *Perseverance*

Zemach, Harve. *Duffy and the Devil*. Illus. by Margot Zemach. New York: Farrar, Straus & Giroux, 1973. (Caldecott–1974)

Duffy is hired by the squire to knit his clothes, but because she can neither spin thread nor knit, she must make a deal with the devil in order to keep her job. *Resourcefulness*: Kicked out from her last place of employment, Duffy lands on her feet just at the right moment at the feet of the squire and boldly affirms that she can "spin like a saint and knit like an angel." Hired on false pretenses, she makes a hash of the spinning and knitting task. A devil agrees to do all this work for her for three years, at which time, he will take her away. Her "skills" impress her employer. He marries her. Then the three years come to an end. She can retain her freedom only if she can guess the devil's name. She can't. But her good friend the housekeeper helps her discover the devil's name. He, of course, is furious and causes every item he's knitted to turn to ash. The squire is left out on the moors when his clothes disappear off him. And all through the house are little piles of ashes. The resourceful Duffy quickly exclaims loudly: "'All my work! Gone up in smoke! I swear I'll never knit another thing ever again!' And she never did."

Other character traits shown: *Prudence*

RESPECT

Feelings of deference, regard, and honor.

Appelt, Kathi. *Someone's Come to Our House.* Illus. by Nancy Carpenter. Grand Rapids, MI: Eerdmans Books for Young Readers, 1999.

Members of a family celebrate the arrival of a new baby.

Respect: All the celebration with food, fun, and good companionship is in honor of a new life. The faces of young and old show they regard this birth with feelings of deference and great joy.

Other character traits shown: *Generosity*

Bogart, Jo Ellen. *Jeremiah Learns to Read.* Illus. by Laura Fernandez and Rick Jacobsen. New York: Orchard Books, 1997.

Elderly Jeremiah decides that it's finally time to learn to read.

Respect: Just because Jeremiah can't read doesn't mean he lacks other kinds of skills. His family respects him just the way he is. But he believes he can be better. At school, his kind of knowledge is respected. There is sharing between him and the students and teacher. They help him with his letters; he teaches them how to chirp like a chickadee and honk like a goose, how to whittle with a pocketknife, how to make applesauce, and how to whistle through their teeth.

Other character traits shown: *Diligence, Generosity*

Borden, Louise. *A. Lincoln and Me.* Illus. by Ted Lewin. New York: Scholastic Press, 1999.

A boy who is tall for his age and awkward learns about the great possibilities for his future by studying the life of the person who shares his birth date.

Respect: Kids laugh at the boy's clumsiness when he fails to see "wet paint" signs until his hands and feet are smeared. But the teacher tells them Mr. Lincoln was called names for being tall and having big feet and hands. Though poor and lacking sophisticated manners, he grew up able to pull 36 states back together. And, though nobody can be another A. Lincoln, everyone is unique. The boy thinks, "Nobody can be another me."

Other character traits shown: *Empathy*

Bruchac, Joseph. *The Great Ball Game: A Muskogee Story.* Illus. by Susan L. Roth. New York: Dial Books for Young Readers, 1994.

Bat, who has both wings and teeth, plays an important part in a game between the Birds and the Animals to decide which group is better.

Respect: Bat is eager to join the ball game, but neither side is willing to have him. Finally, after Bat begs, "Bear took pity" on him, recognizing that even though he is not very big, he might be able to help. Because Bear shows respect for another creature, his team ends up winning the game. The team learns to respect the contributions of one who did not seem to be able to offer anything useful.

Other character traits shown: *Empathy, Helpfulness, Kindness, Patience, Responsibility, Tolerance*

Bunting, Eve. *I Have an Olive Tree*. Illus. by Karen Barbour. New York: Joanna Cotler Books (HarperCollins), 1999.

After her grandfather's death, eight-year-old Sophia fulfills his last request and journeys to Greece with her mother to see the land where her roots are.
Respect: Sophia doesn't understand what an island resident meant when he asked "if we were going home." Sophia tells her mother, "But we're not." Then she sees her family tree. As she places the beads "like liquid gold" and "big bubbles of honey" that "glitter in the sunlight" up high on a branch, she comes to realize the journey "had to do with Mama and me and all of us being part of the island." She has learned respect for her heritage.
Other character traits shown: *Loyalty*

Bunting, Eve. *On Call Back Mountain*. Illus. by Barry Moser. Blue Sky Press (Scholastic), 1997.

Two brothers encounter a lone wolf on the spot where each summer night they had signaled their friend the fire watchman.
Respect: For years, the boys have looked forward to Bosco coming to the mountain. When he does not answer the nightly lantern signal, the family knows something is wrong. The parents go up the mountain to the watchtower. Then a helicopter flies up to the mountain. The parents come back down with Bosco's mules but not Bosco. The boys learn Bosco has died of a heart attack and their parents "sat beside him till the copter came. And Mr. Caruso sang for him." Bosco loves the music of Enrico Caruso. The boys ask if someone else will be sent to take his place. Their father says, "Not this year." The boys say, "Nobody could take his place." Nobody could, agrees their father. The boys notice up on a ledge the first wolf that has returned since a forest fire a few years back. This wolf, a lone wolf like Bosco, stands there reminding them of Bosco's long skinny legs. Bosco would be pleased about the wolf's return.
Other character traits shown: *Discernment*

Bunting, Eve. *A Picnic in October*. Illus. by Nancy Carpenter. New York: Harcourt Brace, 1999.

A boy finally comes to understand why his grandmother insists that the family come to Ellis Island each year to celebrate Lady Liberty's birthday.

Respect: The birthday party ritual is irritating. But when a new family to America brings a fresh perspective to the boy, he finds himself suddenly ashamed of his petty grievances. Lady Liberty's birthday really is a big deal. It means the end of a long journey and a new beginning for people like the new family and his grandparents, who still marvel at their good fortune. He has learned respect for the nation that accepts "the tired, the poor, and the huddled masses" yearning to breathe free.

Other character traits shown: *Loyalty*

Bunting, Eve. *So Far From the Sea.* Illus. by Chris K. Soentpiet. New York: Clarion Books (Houghton Mifflin), 1998.

When seven-year-old Laura and her family visit Grandfather's grave at the Manzanar War Relocation Center, the Japanese American child leaves behind a special symbol.

Respect: The family is making one last trip to the abandoned detention center before moving from California to Massachusetts. It is at this site that Grandfather died, from pneumonia the doctors said. But "Grandfather began dying the day the soldiers came for them, to put them in buses to bring them here...so far from the sea." He had been a tuna fisherman. The family now respectfully brings silk flowers that will last longer than the real flowers they used to bring. Back when people were rounded up and taken to the camp, Grandfather told his little son to put on his Cub Scout uniform so that "they will know you are a true American and they will not take you." Now, Laura brings her father's old neckerchief, "because he was a true American" and wedges it at the grave site with a tree root. She sees it "flutter free like a boat, a boat with sails skimming the wind, heading away from this unhappy place. A boat, moving on."

Other character traits shown: *Forgiveness, Justice*

Bunting, Eve. *Summer Wheels.* Illus. by Thomas B. Allen. New York: Harcourt Brace Jovanovich, 1992.

The Bicycle Man fixes up old bicycles and offers both his friendship and the use of the bikes to the neighborhood kids.

Respect: The Bicycle Man understands why a boy might create a deliberate act of vandalism if it means he gets the opportunity to work in the shop. He respects an older boy's pride in being unable to just hang around like little kids do. So, there is no judgmental scolding about a damaged bike. The tough boy shows his regard for the Man by bringing back not only the trashed bike but also a jelly donut, the Man's favorite treat.

Other character traits shown: *Courage, Empathy, Forgiveness, Generosity, Justice, Kindness, Responsibility, Tolerance*

Bunting, Eve. *Train to Somewhere*. Illus. by Ronald Himler. New York: Clarion Books (Houghton Mifflin), 1996.

In the late 1800s, Marianne travels westward on the Orphan Train with other children who hope to be placed with caring families.

Respect: Miss Randolph, who chaperones the children on their trip, respects the children's differences, their concerns about the future, and their need for the right family. Each one is somehow matched to the right couple. Nowhere is this more apparent than in her careful handling of Marianne, who is old enough to see the world's truths but young enough to fear facing them. She might not be chosen. Miss Randolph doesn't need to point this out. Instead, she outlines plans for what the future may bring. There is a nice hotel farther down the line. And Miss Randolph will be "glad of the company," and "on the journey back." She is letting Marianne know that going back to New York may be a logical eventuality, which they will take in stride. When it is time to meet the last couple, Miss Randolph asks, "Are you ready, Marianne?" She doesn't try to persuade her with promises of a wonderful life. But when Marianne agrees to go with the couple, Miss Randolph shows her understanding of the situation and its satisfactory outcome. She asks, with confidence and with denouement the same question with the addition of one more word. "Are you ready now, Marianne?" She respects Marianne's growing acceptance of her own future.

Other character traits shown: *Courage, Empathy, Hope, Kindness, Patience, Prudence*

Christelow, Eileen. *The Five-Dog Night*. New York: Clarion Books (Houghton Mifflin), 1993.

Cantankerous Ezra keeps rebuffing his nosy neighbor Old Betty when she tries to give him advice on how to survive cold winter nights, until she finally discovers that his five dogs are his private source for warmth.

Respect: Ezra refuses to acknowledge the kind courtesies of Old Betty. He calls her a nosy busybody. Not until he angrily orders her one last time not to keep checking in on him, does he begin to miss her attentions. He can't figure out why he's "feeling gloomy as a stormy sky." His dogs are good company, but they can't brew a pot of tea to go with the cookies he made. He puts on his cleanest shirt and pays Betty a visit. He has learned to respect her kind efforts and realizes he needs more than his dogs to be happy. Now it is Ezra who chastises and looks after Betty when she pronounces the night had been only "a one-dog night." He says, "You'll catch your death of pneumonia! Last night was a two-dog night!" Betty, also, has learned to respect Ezra's means of taking care of himself. She, too, has acquired a pile of dogs to keep her warm at night. These two won't be name-calling anymore.

Other character traits shown: *Courtesy, Generosity, Helpfulness, Kindness, Perseverance*

Duncan, Alice Faye. *Miss Viola and Uncle Ed Lee.* Illus. by Catherine Stock. New York: Atheneum Books for Young Readers (Simon & Schuster), 1999.

A young boy helps his two neighbors, one as neat as a pin and the other as junky as a packrat, become friends.

Respect: As a measure of their respect for each other, Uncle Ed Lee cleans up his yard and makes lemonade for his guest. Miss Viola can see his yard isn't "neat-neat," but she appreciates the efforts he has made for her.

Other character traits shown: *Courtesy, Helpfulness, Honesty, Kindness, Tolerance*

Fleischman, Paul. *Weslandia.* Illus. by Kevin Hawkes. Cambridge, MA: Candlewick Press, 1999.

Wesley's garden produces a crop of huge, strange plants, which provide him with clothing, shelter, food, and drink, thus helping him create his own civilization and changing his life.

Respect: This square peg doesn't fit into the round hole of suburban life. He is "an outcast from the civilization around him." He has no friends but plenty of tormentors. "Fleeing them was the only sport he was good at." For a summer project, he decides to grow his own staple food crop and found his own civilization. Overnight his plowed ground is mysteriously seeded with a new crop that eventually generates respect and admiration among neighbors and peers. His parents note improved morale. "It's the first time in years he's looked happy." His schoolmates "were scornful, then curious." In Tom Sawyer-like behavior, he "grudgingly allowed them ten minutes apiece at his mortar," crushing the plant's seed to collect the oil for which he charges them $10 a bottle for a suntan lotion and mosquito repellent that he makes.

Other character traits shown: *Resourcefulness*

*Frasier, Debra. *Out of the Ocean.* New York: Harcourt Brace, 1998.

A young girl and her mother walk along the beach and marvel at the treasures cast up by the sea and the wonders of the world around them.

Respect: What the mother is sharing with her daughter is more than the treasures the ocean washes up on the beach. These are good, but they are always there to take. What is most important is the remembering to look. Notice the wonders each day. There is a sun that comes up every day. There is water from the ocean every day and from the clouds. Just to be sure that they always respect these natural gifts, "every day we help each other look."

Other character traits shown: *Empathy, Discernment*

*Garland, Sherry. *I Never Knew Your Name.* Illus. by Sheldon Greenberg. New York: Ticknor & Fields (Houghton Mifflin), 1994.

A small boy laments the lonely life of a teenage suicide whose neighbors didn't even know his name.

Respect: While the rest of the world takes no notice of the teenager, one young boy observes him from his window and admires what he sees. He alone sees someone who can sure shoot the hoop, someone kind to stray dogs, someone who has a crush on his sister, despite her unkind comments to him, someone who throws pebbles at a lamppost while other teens go to the prom, someone who enjoys feeding breadcrumbs to pigeons on the roof, like he does. The young boy wishes he would have reached out as a friend to the lonely teen instead of being so wrapped up in his own problems of shyness. He fears that his lack of courage may have contributed to the older boy's feeling that no one cared if he lived or died.

Other character traits shown: *Courage, Kindness*

*Garland, Sherry. *The Lotus Seed.* Illus. by Tatsuro Kiuchi. New York: Harcourt Brace Jovanovich, 1993.

A young Vietnamese girl saves a lotus seed and carries it with her everywhere to remember a brave emperor and the homeland that she has to flee.

Respect: The girl keeps the seed for many years. When her thoughtless grandson plants it, she is devastated at her loss. This seed has been a symbol of her beloved emperor and her homeland. What she discovers once the seed grows and blooms with its own seed pod is that there are now many more seeds to pass among the relatives. They, too, can hold in respect the memory of their ancestral home. The lotus is the flower of their heritage. Every time it is planted, it will be the flower "of my country." Now the seeds will be passed on through the generations. It is the flower of life and hope, the flower of Vietnam.

Other character traits shown: *Hope, Loyalty*

George, Jean Craighead. *Snow Bear.* Illus. by Wendell Minor. New York: Hyperion Books for Children, 1999.

Bessie and a polar bear cub named Snow Bear play on the ice, while her older brother and Snow Bear's mother watch to make sure everyone is safe.

Respect: The cub's mother respects the human holding the gun, because guns can kill. The big brother respects the mother polar bear, because bears with cubs will kill. And everyone quickly realizes the danger presented by the large male bear, who suddenly enters the scene. In this arctic tale, all players are cautious and respectful of the harm that each is capable of inflicting.

Other character traits shown: *Discernment, Empathy, Patience, Prudence*

Gove, Doris. *One Rainy Night.* Illus. by Walter Lyon Krudop. New York: Atheneum, 1994.

A boy and his mother go out on a rainy night to collect animals for a nature center that releases its specimens to the wild after two weeks.

Respect: Though captured and on display for the enlightenment of those who visit the nature center, the animals are actually considered residents of their natural habitat. The center does not keep them permanently. While in the center's care, each creature is provided the kind of temporary home it prefers. Out of respect for the sanctity of life, after two weeks, each one is taken back to the site where it was found and released.

Other character traits shown: *Kindness*

*Hearne, Betsy. *Seven Brave Women.* Illus. by Bethanne Andersen. New York: Greenwillow (William Morrow), 1997.

A young girl recounts the brave exploits of her female ancestors, beginning with her great-great-great-grandmother who came to America in a wooden sailboat.

Respect: The history books mark time by the wars men fight. But the women in this story also made a kind of history. Though they lived during the Revolutionary War, the War of 1812, the Civil War, the Spanish-American War, the First World War, the Second World War, the Korean War, and the Vietnam War, they did not fight any wars. The author says they "did great things" anyway. There are "other ways to tell time."

Other character traits shown: *Fortitude, Resourcefulness*

Hendry, Diana. *Back Soon.* Illus. by Carol Thompson. New York: BridgeWater Books (Troll Associates), 1995.

A kitten does not like it when his mother goes away without him, but after enjoying some time by himself, he understands why she does it.

Respect: Mother, who rather cavalierly would leave Herbert with a babysitter, telling him she would be "back soon," learns one day how it feels to be the one worrying and waiting. Herbert learns how pleasant being off by one's self can be and now understands why mother does it. Both then agree to respect the other's need for time alone, and both will "always remember to come back."

Other character traits shown: *Empathy, Tolerance*

High, Linda Oatman. *Barn Savers.* Illus. by Ted Lewin. Honesdale, PA: Boyds Mills Press, 1999.

A young boy and his father recycle the pieces of a nineteenth-century barn.

Respect: The boy and his father consider old barns a treasure that need to be protected from the bulldozers. They will save all the venerated parts that composed the structure. The barn "will live for another hundred years in a hundred different places." Barns will be saved to enhance other living spaces. Barn savers show regard and deference and honor for these valuable pieces of architecture.

Other character traits shown: *Responsibility*

Jackson, Isaac. *Somebody's New Pajamas.* Illus. by David Soman. New York: Dial Books for Young Readers (Penguin), 1996.

When two boys from different backgrounds become friends and sleep over at each other's homes, they exchange ideas about sleepwear as well as about family life.

Respect: Jerome feels ashamed when he is offered a pair of his friend's pajamas at a sleepover. However, when his father explains why they use a stained and tattered tablecloth and how Grandma wouldn't have it any other way, he begins to respect the way his family does things its own way.

Other character traits shown: *Courtesy, Honesty, Loyalty*

Joosse, Barbara M. *I Love You the Purplest.* Illus. by Mary Whyte. San Francisco, CA: Chronicle Books, 1996.

Two boys discover their mother loves them equally but in different ways.

Respect: When the competitive boys ask their mother who has collected the most worms, who rows the boat the best, who is the best fisherman, and, finally, who she loves the best, the diplomatic mother answers by respecting their individual differences and finding something positive to say about each child. Her responses are satisfying, and her love is evident.

Jukes, Mavis. *I'll See You in My Dreams.* Illus. by Stacey Schuett. New York: Alfred A. Knopf, 1993.

A girl preparing to visit her seriously ill uncle in the hospital imagines being a skywriter and flying over his bed with a message of love.

Respect: The girl's uncle is an airline pilot. If she could, she would demonstrate her respect by an act designed especially to please him. She would use an old bi-plane like the one in the photo on her uncle's wall. It would have printed on it "Scratch with the chickens or fly with the Eagles," the motto he lived by. She'd buzz the hospital roof. Her uncle would open his eyes and look out the window. She'd draw a heart with white smoke and roar back, making an arrow through it. "She'd do a loop, then a hammerhead." She'd write "Good-bye" in the clouds. Behind her the letters "would be blown across the sunset." In the night she would come back and write one more message. Across the face of the moon in silver letters she'd write, "I love you. I'll see you in my dreams."

Other character traits shown: *Courage*

Krupinski, Loretta. *Best Friends.* New York: Hyperion Books for Children, 1998.

When a settler's young daughter learns that soldiers will force the Nez Perce off the nearby land, she uses a doll to warn her Indian friend of impending danger.

Respect: It could put her own family in danger to go against the soldiers of her country, but the white settler girl has too much respect for her new Indian friend to allow her and her village to be swept up and forced onto a reservation. They are, after all, living on their own land, which had been theirs long before the white settlers arrived. She does what is necessary to enable the Indians to escape the soldiers.

Other character traits shown: *Generosity, Helpfulness, Justice, Kindness, Loyalty, Resourcefulness*

Lester, Helen. *Hooway for Wodney Wat.* Illus. by Lynn Munsinger. Boston: Walter Lorraine Books (Houghton Mifflin), 1999.

All of his classmates make fun of Rodney because he can't pronounce his name, but it is Rodney's speech impediment that drives away the class bully.

Respect: All of the students are overwhelmed by the one who declares herself the biggest, meanest, and smartest. Not until the student they have been teasing is able to frustrate Camilla Capybara and run her off, do the class members suddenly develop respect for Rodney. His innocent leadership in a game of "Simon Says" makes her misinterpret every one of his commands. The other students gratefully observe this and, for the first time, respect his uniqueness. Suddenly, Rodney becomes their hero. "Hooway for Wodney Wat!" The rodents never tease him again.

Other character traits shown: *Justice*

Little, Mimi Otley. *Yoshiko and the Foreigner.* New York: Frances Foster Books (Farrar, Straus & Giroux), 1996.

Though well-brought-up Japanese girls didn't talk to foreigners, there are exceptions, and when a young American Air Force Officer mispronounces the language, Yoshiko's heart softens in a way that will change her life forever.

Respect: Though not welcomed in Yoshiko's home, the young man, nevertheless, pays his respect to the father by donating goldfish for his garden pond, shows his respect for their customs by providing wine and rice (the best he can afford) to contribute to the household ancestor shrine, and takes the trouble of learning to write as well as speak Japanese.

Other character traits shown: *Courtesy, Tolerance*

*Littlesugar, Amy. *Jonkonnu: A Story from the Sketchbook of Winslow Homer.* Illus. by Ian Schoenherr. New York: Philomel Books, 1997.

A young southern girl tells of the time Winslow Homer came to town to paint pictures and defied the town by portraying the lives of the poor Black people who lived down the red clay road.

Respect: Because of Homer's quiet courage facing the angry prejudice of her town, Cilla also opens her mind to begin to see the world as the painter does. At first she cannot think of anything down the red clay road except "maybe a girl or two workin' cotton, or a barefoot boy too shy to say 'Hey!'" Then she watches Homer paint the Blacks' preparations for their holiday, Jonkonnu, an old freedom holiday from slavery days. She begins to imagine how they are probably explaining to the artist that they are still lonesome for Jamaica and the music of their islands and how they aren't allowed to march in the Fourth of July parade. Probably they enjoy harking back to the one holiday that "filled them with hopin' and wishin'" for freedom. She is able to see and respect the painter's role as one who "lights up the darkness" with a fresh vision.

Other character traits shown: *Courage, Discernment*

*Look, Lenore. *Love as Strong as Ginger.* Illus. by Stephen T. Johnson. New York: Anne Schwartz Book, Atheneum Books for Young Readers (Simon & Schuster), 1999.

A Chinese American girl comes to realize how hard her grandmother works to fulfill her dreams when they spend a day together at the grandmother's job site cracking crabs.

Respect: The factory ladies ride a bus to the crab chong. They notice the child has no rubber gloves, rubber apron, or tall rubber boots. When one asks where her gloves are, her grandmother replies that no size fits her. The lady then says, "May that always be so." The work is hard and messy; they want a better life for the young. There is hot steam, deafening noise, and difficulty cracking shells. "Every minute is another penny!" At the end of a crab-smeared work day, the child asks, "How can you keep going?" Her grandmother deflects the question by saying she is really a famous actress making a movie in a crab chong. But on the bus home, "tears leaked out of the corners of her eyes; she was tired." Gratefully, the girl eats her evening meal, "made with love as strong as ginger and dreams as thick as black-bean paste." She fills herself with the flavors of her grandmother's hard work. It is with respect that she now understands the sacrifices made in her behalf.

Lorbiecki, Marybeth. *Sister Anne's Hands.* Illus. by K. Wendy Popp. New York: Dial Books for Young Readers (Penguin), 1998.

Seven-year-old Anna has her first encounter with racism in the 1960s when an African American nun comes to teach at her parochial school.

Respect: Sister Anne wins the children's respect through her frank discussion of racism following a nasty incident in which a paper airplane with a cruel poem printed on it goes sailing past her head. She gives the children a second chance. They recognize her value as both a teacher and a good-hearted person. Her unique, fresh ways of teaching prompt Anna to observe, "I'd never had so much fun at school!"

Other character traits shown: *Courage, Forgiveness, Tolerance*

Michelson, Richard. *Grandpa's Gamble.* Illus. by Barry Moser. New York: Marshall Cavendish, 1999.

When Grandpa tells a boy and his sister why he prays so much, they stop thinking that he is just a boring old man.

Respect: The boy and girl don't like to have to always be quiet while their grandfather engages in his never-ending prayers. They think this seemingly lackluster old grandfather who sits in a yarmulke is "borrrrring." He is not exciting like Esther's grandpa who owns a movie theater, or Yetta's grandpa who played for the Yankees, or Molly's grandpa who is a millionaire, or Ernie's grandpa who was a pirate king. Not until they learn the reason behind his daily praying, do they understand his story is more exciting than their friends' grandfathers.' At first they are titillated because he was once a gambler. They grow to respect him when they hear that he stopped gambling and began to pray when his daughter fell ill. No longer are they irritated by his constant praying. "Our grandpa is the best grandpa in the world." Now, they shush others "while he's saying his prayers."

Other character traits shown: *Self-discipline*

Miller, William. *The Piano.* Illus by Susan Keeter. New York: Lee & Low Books, 2000.

A young black girl's love of music leads her to a job in the house of an older white woman, who not only teaches her to play the piano, but also the rewards of intergenerational friendship.

Respect: Tia can't keep her hands off the piano in Miss Hartwell's living room. She tries to imitate the sounds she hears from the white woman's phonograph but knows she will need a teacher to really make those same sounds. Miss Hartwell recognizes Tia's desire to play. Tia asks for lessons in exchange for forfeiting her wages as maid. Miss Hartwell does not chastise her for neglecting her household duties and won't hear of not paying her. She recognizes Tia's desire to learn, and that is enough to arouse her desire to teach. But, she finds her hands are too stiff. Tia's thoughtful ministrations enable her to play once again. And, Miss Hartwell's turn-about ministrations enable Tia to practice more easily when she hurts her hands doing another employee's manual labor. These two are separated by age, race, and economic status. But, they respect one another and their mutual love for music.

Other character traits shown: *Generosity, Helpfulness, Kindness*

Mitchell, Barbara. *Red Bird.* Illus. by Todd Doney. New York: Lothrop, Lee & Shepard, 1996.

Katie, also known as Red Bird, joins her family and other Indians at the annual powwow in southern Delaware, where they celebrate their Nanticoke heritage with music, dancing, and special foods.

Respect: Though busy with modern life, once a year the various tribes and outsiders who wish to participate, celebrate the Algonquian identity and culture with stories, dance, special clothing, and fellowship. This respect keeps "the heartbeat of The People" alive all year long.

Other character traits shown: *Cooperation, Loyalty*

Moyer, Marshall M. *Rollo Bones, Canine Hypnotist.* Berkeley, CA: Tricycle Press, 1998.

Although he has won worldwide success with his ability to hypnotize human beings, Rollo, a soulful yellow dog, takes a stand for what he really wants to be and do.

Respect: It is Rollo's belief that success has gone to the head of his human, the Amazing Brain. He needs to be taught a lesson. After Rollo hypnotizes him, the Amazing Brain realizes his dog wants a break from their hectic show schedule. He acknowledges and respects the companionship they used to share as well as the dog's skills. Together they return to taking walks and playing together "just like the old days."

Other character traits shown: *Empathy*

Perkins, Lynn Rae. *Clouds for Dinner.* Greenwillow (William Morrow), 1997.

It takes a visit to her aunt's house to make Janet appreciate her parents and their unusual way of looking at everything.

Respect: Janet wants regular meals, sitting down together for dinner. What's the big deal in her household about looking at clouds? And what a nuisance are those 87 steps up to the house just because that's where the view is. Janet admires her aunt's regular family where people sit down to meals and do ordinary things like washing the dog, watching a soccer game, and planning a party. But when Janet wakes up early at Aunt's house during a visit and watches a spectacular sunrise, there is no one who understands and can share the beauty with her. Aunt only wonders why she awoke early. Was she chilly? Then she dismisses the sunrise by saying that they need to "clear the dishes and get a move on." Janet suddenly begins to value and respect the ways of her family. When her mother comes to collect her, Janet describes the sunrise. Her mom responds, "What a lucky thing to see. I wish I'd been there." Janet says, "Me too."

Other character traits shown: *Discernment*

*Rylant, Cynthia. *The Dreamer.* Illus. by Barry Moser. New York: Blue Sky Press (Scholastic), 1993.

From his dreams an artist creates the earth, sky, trees, and all the creatures that dwell on our planet.

Respect: The artist sees things in his mind and, in the fashion of artists, sets about creating what he imagines. He appreciates his efforts and wishes to share with someone else who is an artist. He makes an artist and makes more of them. Soon "the world began filling up with artists." And he calls them his children. They, in turn, call him God. This story of creation shows that things lovingly created are respected.

*Rylant, Cynthia. *Scarecrow.* Illus. by Lauren Stringer. New York: Harcourt Brace, 1998.

Although made of straw and borrowed clothes, a scarecrow appreciates his peaceful, gentle life and the privilege of watching nature at work.

Respect: The scarecrow has a sound self-image. He "understands right away that he is just borrowed parts made to look like somebody." He knows that, "he can as quickly be turned back into straw and buttons as he was turned into a man." And "he doesn't care." He is satisfied with nature that has "rained and snowed and blossomed and wilted and yellowed and greened and vined itself all around him." He understands "there is not much else a person might want." The scarecrow respects himself and the nature of his life.

Schertle, Alice. *That's What I Thought.* Illus. by John Wallner. New York: Harper & Row, 1990.

A little girl imagines different, exciting, and dangerous situations and is comforted by her parents' loving reassurance.

Respect: Her questions are relentless, but her parents answer them all with dignity and regard for the feelings expressed behind them. "What would you do if I were really naughty and wouldn't stop?" Her parents tease her with silly scenarios that even she knows are untrue. Perhaps she could be sold to someone who wanted a naughty child to scare people away from the door if they didn't want visitors. But when the child probes, "Would you really sell me?" Daddy is quick to say, "Not for a million dollars." And Mama adds, "Not for the sun and the moon and all of the stars."

Other character traits shown: *Patience*

*Schur, Maxine Rose. *The Peddler's Gift.* Illus. by Kimberly Bulcken Root. New York: Dial Books for Young Readers (Penguin), 1999.

A young boy in rural Russia at the turn of the twentieth century learns that appearances are often deceiving after he steals a dreidel.

Respect: A peddler who had once been the object of ridicule comes to be seen in an entirely different way. He knows the boy to be a thief and has, even so, forgiven him. Though the peddler returns for many years, the boy says, "I never again called him Shnook." He was "Shimon the wise, the strong, the kind."

Other character traits shown: *Courage, Forgiveness, Honesty, Kindness, Responsibility*

*Shannon, George. *This Is the Bird*. Illus. by David Soman. Boston: Houghton Mifflin, 1997.

A cumulative tale about a wooden bird carved by a little girl's maternal ancestor, and passed down lovingly from mother to daughter through the generations. **Respect:** Each girl feels the bird symbolizes a momentous event in her life. Over the generations, its history adds to its sentimental value and reminds the latest woman of her respect for the family members before her. Mother hands the carved bird to daughter at a time when she most needs personal encouragement. Each woman feels a respect for the physical item because of the background it represents.

Other character traits shown: *Hope*

Shea, Pegi Deitz. *The Whispering Cloth: A Refugee's Story*. Illus. by Anita Riggio. Stitched by You Yang. Honesdale, PA: Boyds Mills Press, 1995.

A young girl from Laos, Cambodia in a Thai refugee camp during the Vietnam war finds the story within herself to create her own Pa'ndau (story cloth). **Respect:** The Pa'ndau tells in folk-art stitchery something important to the artist. The young girl and her grandmother sell Pa'ndaus to earn enough money to leave the refugee camp and find a new home. Mai begins to tell her own story of the killing of her parents, her grandmother rescuing her in a basket on her back, fleeing through paddies to riverboats, meeting soldiers on the other side of the river, and living in a temporary camp. Her grandmother says the cloth is worth nothing, because it is not finished. Mai looks beyond the camp fence and then adds to the story. Now the story cloth shows a plane "gliding over boxes of land to a village where homes were big as mahogany trees." It shows Mai and her cousins building "men with white crystals." It shows the new life Mai and her grandmother will live. Now, the cloth is worth much money. But the respect Mai feels for her past and future makes her decide "it is not for sale."

Other character traits shown: *Fortitude, Hope*

Sisulu, Elinor Batezat. *The Day Gogo Went to Vote: South Africa, April 1994*. Illus. by Sharon Wilson. New York: Little, Brown & Co., 1997.

Thembi and her beloved great-grandmother, who has not left home for many years, go together to vote on the momentous day when black South Africans are allowed to vote for the first time. **Respect:** The township recognizes and respects their oldest resident. They make provision for her special needs when she says she will go to the voting precinct to vote. A rich man provides his car and driver to take her. Polling officials bring her inside to vote first so that she doesn't have to wait in line. After her vote, the newspaper takes her photo. There are township celebrations in honor of getting to vote for the first time for their elected leader. The old woman has lived through a lot of history.

Other character traits shown: *Helpfulness, Justice, Responsibility*

Stewart, Dianne. *Gift of the Sun: A Tale from South Africa.* Illus. by Jude Daly. New York: Farrar, Straus & Giroux, 1996.

Lazy Thulani attempts to simplify his life by selling the cow that he won't have to milk and ends up with another animal that, in turn, ends up in a series of exchanges, which finally result in something surprisingly useful.

Respect: Thulani has no self-respect. He is lazy and finds milking the cow onerous. But his wife is displeased with the goat he trades the cow for. Back he goes to the store and trades the goat for a sheep. At least, his wife Dora notes, there will be fleece to sell. Then Thulani thinks he will sell the wool and the sheep. Next he buys three geese, because they will eat anything and won't be much work. But his wife needs seed to plant because the goat ate their seed crop. He trundles the geese back to the store and returns with seed. He plants them, but they turn out to be sunflowers. What good are they? Poor Thulani only wants to please Dora. He gathers up the falling sunflower seeds and feeds them to the chickens. This signals a change in his fortunes. The hens lay more eggs. He sells the eggs and buys a sheep. The sheep has twin lambs. When they are sold he proudly brings home a cow again. Dora is delighted. Success breeds more success. Soon Thulani's confidence and respect for himself has improved so much that he is too busy trading animals to have time to sit about in the sun. "Life was too exciting!" But he always finds time to sit down and milk the cow. After all, his best thoughts come to him when he's milking.

*Thurber, James. *Many Moons.* Illus. by Louis Slobodkin. New York: Harcourt Brace, 1943. (Caldecott–1944)

Though many try, only the court jester is able to fulfill Princess Lenore's wish for the moon.

Respect: The intellectuals rely upon their own wisdom. In their superior knowledge, they dismiss the princess' request as unattainable. The modest court jester does not presume wisdom. Therefore, his careful questions and his naïve respect for the substance of the princess's answers enable him to achieve satisfaction for her.

Other character traits shown: *Prudence*

*Whitcomb, Mary E. *Odd Velvet.* Illus. by Tara Calahan King. San Francisco: Chronicle Books, 1998.

Although she dresses differently and does unusual things, Velvet eventually teaches her classmates that an outsider has something to offer.

Respect: When the students first meet her, they find her odd because instead of bringing a gift of potpourri and cinnamon tea to their teacher, Velvet brings "an egg carton filled with seven rocks, her favorite red shoelaces, and half a sparrow's egg." Her clothes the first day of school are not new. During show and tell she brings a milkweed pod. Luckily the other girls bring a talking doll, a wetting doll, and a crying doll, "and saved the day." But, gradually, things begin to change. Velvet explains how her father named her. "The sun was just rising over the mountains, and outside it looked as though the world had been covered with a blanket of smooth, soft, lavender velvet." The kids were "thinking of how beautiful that morning must have been." And, when they see a picture of the apple she draws, one child says it looked "so real I would like to eat it." It is "the most beautiful apple the children had ever seen." Soon "the things that Velvet says, and the things that Velvet does began to make sense." They conclude that, "Velvet was different. But, maybe, she wasn't so odd after all."

*Wiesniewski, David. *Golem*. New York: Clarion Books (Houghton Mifflin), 1996. (Caldecott–1997)

A saintly rabbi miraculously brings to life a clay giant who helps watch over the Jews of sixteenth-century Prague.

Respect: Though the creature is not human, the Jews have appreciated his loyalty and service to them. When they are once again out of danger from invasion, the golem must cease living. Still, in a show of respect for what he did, they save the clay that was their savior against persecution and store it reverently in the synagogue attic under tattered prayer books instead of throwing it outside. And, as a further measure of their regard, they recite the Kaddish, the prayer for the dead, for him.

Other character traits shown: *Helpfulness, Loyalty, Justice*

RESPONSIBILITY

Use for DEPENDABILITY, TRUSTWORTHINESS
Accountable and dependable.

Atwell, Debby. *River*. Boston: Houghton Mifflin, 1999.

A river gradually becomes depleted as more and more people use its resources to build cities, transport goods, and handle sewage.

Responsibility: People remember how the river used to be and begin to restore it by stopping sources of pollution at the factories and planting trees along the banks. Then, they allow the river to "rest" from human use. They had caused the destruction and now help with the healing.

Other character traits shown: *Responsibility*

Brown, Margaret Wise. *The Little Scarecrow Boy*. Illus. by David Diaz. New York: Joanna Cotler Books (HarperCollins), 1998.

Early one morning a little scarecrow whose father warns him that he is not fierce enough to frighten a crow away goes out into the cornfield alone to try his luck.

Responsibility: So determined to prove himself capable, the little scarecrow boy disobeys his father and works to make fierce faces at the crows. It proves more taxing than he imagined, but he finally succeeds in showing he can be depended on to do the job.

Other character traits shown: *Hope, Perseverance*

Bruchac, Joseph. *The Great Ball Game: A Muskogee Story.* Illus. by Susan L. Roth. New York: Dial Books for Young Readers, 1994.

Bat, who has both wings and teeth, plays an important part in a game between the Birds and the Animals to decide which group is better.

Responsibility: Small though he is, Bat is prepared, when his turn comes, to use his special abilities to help his team win the ball game. The game is long. Darkness is falling. His team is tiring. Now, it is time. He steals the ball and darts from side to side across the field, "for he did not need light to find his way." Bat takes on the responsibility of carrying the ball for his team over the goal. When they needed him, he came through.

Other character traits shown: *Empathy, Helpfulness, Kindness, Respect, Patience, Tolerance*

Bunting, Eve. *Summer Wheels.* Illus. by Thomas B. Allen. New York: Harcourt Brace Jovanovich, 1992.

The Bicycle Man fixes up old bicycles and offers both his friendship and the use of the bikes to the neighborhood kids.

Responsibility: There are shop rules. Kids know them and are expected to obey them. Bikes have to be checked out and must be returned by four o'clock that afternoon. And if anything breaks when a kid has the bike out, the kid must help repair it the next day. When the new tough boy breaks the rules, the other kids help him assume his responsibility because "The Man's our friend." The Bicycle Shop runs smoothly.

Other character traits shown: *Courage, Empathy, Forgiveness, Generosity, Justice, Kindness, Respect, Tolerance*

Burningham, John. *Whaddayamean.* New York: Crown, 1999.

When God sees what a mess has been made of the world, He gets two children to convince everyone to help make it the lovely place it was meant to be.

Responsibility: "We must change at once," said the people responsible for the earth's ailments. The businessmen planted trees and stocked fish and stopped fouling the air. The religious clerics joined forces in cooperation instead of bickering. Military persons destroyed their weapons of destruction. Ordinary people became informed about problems.

Other character traits shown: *Diligence, Justice*

Carter, Dorothy. *Wilhe'mina Miles: After the Stork Night.* New York: Frances Foster Books (Farrar, Straus & Giroux), 1999.

Because her father is out of town working, eight-year-old Wilhe'mina must go for help when the stork visits her mother to bring her a new brother.

Responsibility: Though she is afraid of the dark and the rickety bridge she must cross in order to fetch Mis' Hattie, Wilhe'mina knows she has to go. There is no one else to help Mama. Mama is depending on her to get help.

Other character traits shown: *Courage*

Davol, Marguerite W. *The Paper Dragon.* Illus. by Robert Sabuda. New York: Atheneum Books for Young Readers (Simon & Schuster), 1997.

The power of the artist's vision and the ever-sustaining nature of love are brought together when a humble artist agrees to confront the terrifying dragon that threatens to destroy his village.

Responsibility: The messenger brings the awful news of imminent destruction. "Someone must face the dragon." Mi Fei says he is no hero. He is "only a simple artist who paints the past." But the people turn to him one by one. "You know all about gods and heroes." He tries to tell them that all he knows of heroic deeds has been told to him by others. But the villagers crowd around him pleading for his help. "Looking into their worried faces, he knew he could not refuse." He takes on the daunting responsibility alone of facing the enemy.

Other character traits shown: *Courage, Discernment, Fortitude*

dePaola, Tomie. *The Legend of the Indian Paintbrush.* New York: G.P. Putnam's Sons, 1988.

Little Gopher follows his destiny, as revealed in a Dream-Vision, of becoming an artist for his people and eventually is able to bring the colors of the sunset down to earth.

Responsibility: Little Gopher would like to be one of the warriors, but he must follow another Dream-Vision. He has the responsibility of recording the deeds of the People and the dreams of the shaman. He follows his tasks faithfully.

Other character traits shown: *Diligence, Hope, Loyalty, Patience, Perseverance, Self-discipline*

Ehlert, Lois. *Top Cat.* New York: Harcourt Brace, 1998.

Top Cat is reluctant to accept the arrival of a new kitten but decides to share various survival secrets with it.

Responsibility: It is up to the experienced cat to clue in the kitten on appropriate behavior. Top Cat admonishes the kitten to "watch me" leap on the couch, leaving lots of hair, eat plant leaves bare, drink from the sink when company's there, dance on the table with the silverware, and other such vital skills important to cats living with humans.

Other character traits shown: *Tolerance*

Friedrich, Elizabeth. *Leah's Pony.* Illus. by Michael Garland. New York: Boyds Mills Press, 1996.

A young girl sells her pony and raises enough money to buy back her father's tractor, which is up for auction on this Depression-era farm.

Responsibility: Leah's family is faced with severe economic loss if their means of planting crops is sold. They will likely become bankrupt. Leah believes she can bear some of the responsibility for saving the farm. Though she loves her pony, she is willing to sell it in order to get money to buy back the tractor. Without being asked, she sacrifices her favorite possession to help save the farm. The farm neighbors recognize her gesture and soon follow suit, refusing to bid against her dollar. They go on to buy possessions for a fraction of their true value and then give them back to the family.

Other character traits shown: *Generosity, Helpfulness*

Gill, Janet. *Basket Weaver and Catches Many Mice.* Illus. by Yangsook Choi. New York: Alfred A. Knopf, 1999.

A little gray cat saves the day when Basket Weaver is ordered into a competition to make the perfect basket for the Emperor's newborn daughter.

Responsibility: Though Basket Weaver enjoys living where he is, he knows it will do no good to try to avoid his responsibility. So he proceeds to make the best basket he can. If he wins the contest, he will be living at the palace. The basket is ready on time, and he presents himself at the palace on time. If he loses the contest, he will be working in the underground mines. "For seven years he would not see the bright birds, not hear the rippling stream." He goes through the basket review, knowing that there is a good possibility he will lose the contest.

Other character traits shown: *Diligence, Generosity, Honesty, Loyalty*

Harshman, Marc. *The Storm.* Illus. by Mark Mohr. New York: Cobblehill Books (Dutton), 1995.

Though Jonathan lives with the aid of a wheelchair, he faces the terror of a tornado all by himself and saves the lives of the horses on the family farm.

Responsibility: Jonathan's mother has given him the responsibility of getting the horses into the barn if she is late returning home. Jonathan tells her he will take care of them. He has adjusted to life in a wheelchair even though some of the school kids consider him to have a "condition." When the storm comes, he must use all his skills and strength to lure the horses back to safety in the barn and to keep them calm.

The tasks aren't easy, but he shows his sense of responsibility and earns the praise of his parents and pride in his own accomplishments.

High, Linda Oatman. *Barn Savers.* Illus. by Ted Lewin. Honesdale, PA: Boyds Mills Press, 1999.

A young boy and his father recycle a nineteenth-century barn.
Responsibility: A boy and his father are conscientious about their task of saving the pieces of an old barn. They will carefully take apart and keep "everything, boards and beams, joists and rafters, and lightening rods, flooring and siding and roofing, windows and doors and the date stone that says 1893, even this old pig trough." They will not leave anything for the bulldozer to destroy.
Other character traits shown: *Respect*

Joosse, Barbara. *Lewis & Papa: Adventure on the Santa Fe Trail.* Illus. by Jon Van Zyle. San Francisco: Chronicle Books, 1998.

While accompanying his father on the wagon train along the Santa Fe Trail, Lewis discovers what it is to be a man.
Responsibility: When his father explains how things on the wagon should be stacked, Lewis follows directions and earns from Papa the praise that, "You're as nimble as a cat." Later during the journey Lewis behaves with practical common sense when he gathers branches and shrubs to throw them down the riverbanks to keep the oxen from sliding in the sand. One of the men remarks, "Lewis had a fine idea, and he does a grown man's work." Throughout the trip, Lewis takes seriously his responsibility to help his father, even when it's a matter of emotional comfort. His father needs a loving hug when he has to shoot his faithful ox after they run out of water in the desert.
Other character traits shown: *Courage, Fortitude, Honesty*

Kay, Verla. *Gold Fever.* Illus. by S.D. Schindler. New York: G.P. Putnam's Sons, 1999.

Jasper leaves his family during the gold rush to pursue his dream.
Responsibility: Soon enough Jasper realizes his mistake. There is no wealth to be realized in panning stream bed gold. He quickly leaves behind this fool's pursuit and comes back to the world he knows best. His farming responsibilities, momentarily forgotten, are picked up again, happily.
Other character traits shown: *Hope*

Ketteman, Helen. *I Remember Papa.* Illus. by Greg Shed. New York: Dial Books for Young Readers (Penguin), 1998.

After saving to buy a baseball glove, a young farm boy takes a memorable trip to town with his father.

Responsibility: Audie loses the money intended to buy his baseball glove. When his father uses his money to buy the boy a glove instead of buying badly needed work shoes for himself, the boy determines he will pay his father back. He writes the price of the glove on a piece of paper. "For many Saturdays afterward, instead of taking a quarter, I had Papa help me subtract it from my balance, until I had repaid him." He is demonstrating responsibility for his debts.

Other character traits shown: *Generosity*

Martin, Jacqueline Briggs. *Snowflake Bentley.* Illus. by Mary Azarian. Boston: Houghton Mifflin, 1998. (Caldecott–1999)

A self-taught scientist photographs thousands of individual snowflakes in order to provide the world with a view of their unique formations.

Responsibility: It is a hardship to go out time after time in snowstorms to collect snowflakes. But "others can provide daily quarts of milk;" this farmer/scientist will give something equally important to the world. He develops the microphotographic technique to reveal the grandeur and mystery of the snowflake.

Other character traits shown: *Diligence, Fortitude, Perseverance*

Nolen, Jerdine. *Raising Dragons.* Illus. by Elise Primavera. New York: Silver Whistle (Harcourt Brace), 1998.

A farmer's young daughter shares numerous adventures with the dragon that she raises from infancy.

Responsibility: Her parents want no part of the huge egg she finds. When it hatches into a dragon they refuse to acknowledge it. So the girl assumes all responsibility for its care and feeding. She even finds the perfect place for him to live when the public begins to intrude. Though hard to give him up, she "knew he had found the perfect place to be."

Other character traits shown: *Cooperation, Diligence, Kindness, Loyalty*

Pilkey, Dav. *The Paperboy.* New York: Orchard Books, 1996.

The paperboy and his dog enjoy the quiet of the early morning as they go about their rounds.

Responsibility: While others are still sleeping, the paperboy must crawl out of bed each chilly morning and tend to his task of getting the paper delivered in a timely fashion.

Other character traits shown: *Diligence*

Rael, Elsa Okon. *What Zeesie Saw on Delancey Street.* Illus. by Marjorie Priceman. New York: Simon & Schuster, 1996.

A young Jewish girl living on Manhattan's Lower East Side attends her first "package party" where she learns about the traditions of community giving among Jewish immigrants in the early 1900s.

Responsibility: When Zeesie slips into the room where she is not allowed to go, she sees something that she should not have observed. Her father explains that when the men go one by one into the "money room" they either put money into the box or take out what they need. No one knows which it is and no one ever talks about it. When Zeesie sees Max take money from the box, it puts Zeesie in an uncomfortable position. She feels guilty for her knowledge of Max's need, but she knows she must not confess what she has done. She feels the need to take responsibility for her action. Her grandparents have given her a dollar to spend on her birthday. She places that dollar in the money box and escapes the room. Now, she won't ever have to talk about her disobedience.

Other character traits shown: *Generosity, Justice*

Rylant, Cynthia. *Mr. Griggs' Work.* Illus. by Julie Downing. New York: Orchard Books (Franklin Watts), 1989.

Mr. Griggs so loves his work at the post office that he thinks of it all the time, and everything reminds him of it.

Responsibility: Here is a worker who takes very seriously his job responsibilities. He still thinks about the missing fruitcake Mrs. McTacket had sent her sister 15 Christmases ago! He gets to thinking about the cost of mailing a one-pound package to New Zealand or a three ounce letter to Taiwan and can hardly keep himself from going in the middle of the night to the post office just to find out. On the day he is sick and can't go to work, he worries about someone else doing a poor job. Thank goodness he is better the next morning. He greets his lined-up customers such as Emma Bradshaw (Box 98) and Frank Shrewsberry and his son Junior (Box 171) with wild enthusiasm. He lines up the tools of his trade (his meters and punchers and letter scale) and "in all the world that day there was nothing finer than Mr. Griggs' work."

Other character traits shown: *Diligence*

Schertle, Alice. *Down the Road.* Illus. by E.B. Lewis. New York: Browndeer Press (Harcourt Brace), 1995.

Hetty is very careful with the eggs she has bought on her first trip to the store, but she runs into trouble when she stops to pick apples.

Responsibility: Hetty is aware of the responsibility her parents have given her and is determined to be trustworthy. She avoids walking on rocks across a steam so that she won't slip with the egg basket. She keeps a sharp eye out for obstacles in the road after a near miss. All goes well until she sees an apple tree full of "sweet, juicy, crackly-crisp apples." They are Papa's favorites. Mama's too. And Hetty is very fond of apples herself. The eggs break when the basket tips while she reaches for apples. She climbs right up into the tree as high as she could go "just thinking, and feeling sad, and not wanting to go home." But when Papa comes, she does tell him what happened. And, when Mama comes, she tells her, too. Hetty may not have wanted to tell them why there would be no eggs for breakfast, but she faced her responsibility.

Other character traits shown: *Empathy, Forgiveness, Honesty, Kindness*

*Schur, Maxine Rose. *The Peddler's Gift.* Illus. by Kimberly Bulcken Root. New York: Dial Books for Young Readers (Penguin), 1999.

A young boy in rural Russia at the turn of the twentieth century learns that appearances are often deceiving after he steals a dreidel.

Responsibility: It would be easy to keep the toy. The peddler probably would not even miss it. But the boy knows he is a thief and, regardless of the consequences, must take responsibility for his behavior. He goes out during a bad storm to hunt for the peddler, finds him in the synagogue, and admits what he has done.

Other character traits shown: *Courage, Forgiveness, Honesty, Kindness, Respect, Responsibility*

Sisulu, Elinor Batezat. *The Day Gogo Went to Vote: South Africa, April 1994.* Illus. by Sharon Wilson. New York: Little, Brown & Co., 1997.

Thembi and her beloved great-grandmother, who has not left home for many years, go together to vote on the momentous day when black South Africans are allowed to vote for the first time.

Responsibility: The old woman's great age places an equally great responsibility upon her. Because she has lived through so much history, it is appropriate for her to lead the way, when the right to vote finally occurs. Not age, not frail health, not big crowds, not long lines, will keep her from doing her duty and setting the example for others to follow.

Other character traits shown: *Helpfulness, Justice, Respect*

Van Allsburg, Chris. *Jumanji.* Boston: Houghton Mifflin, 1981. (Caldecott–1982)

Left on their own for an afternoon, two bored and restless children find more excitement than they bargained for in a mysterious and mystical jungle adventure board game.

Responsibility: This game requires players to be responsible and follow directions. By reading the directions, the children learn that the game will not end until one player has completed the board path to its conclusion. Having taken on the challenge, they soon discover they are no longer bored, and this is not an ordinary board game. They fervently hope that they can conclude quickly. By the time they manage to reach the end, they are more than happy to return the game to the spot in the park where they found it. And they put away all the toys they had earlier strewn about. Their mother's guest later comments on the hard puzzle they are quietly putting together and adds that her two boys never finish anything they start and don't read directions either. "I guess they'll learn." The children say, "I hope so." They look out their window and see the boys pick up the same game that had brought them a flood, a stampede, a volcano, and sleeping sickness right in their home.

Ward, Lynd. *The Biggest Bear.* Boston: Houghton Mifflin, 1952. (Caldecott–1953)

Johnny wanted a bearskin on his barn like the other farms had, but what he got was a bear cub that ate huge quantities of food wherever it could be found.
Responsibility: The bear belongs to Johnny. When its appetite grows beyond the ability of the family to feed him and when the neighbors complain about raids on their food supply it is Johnny's responsibility to take the bear back to the woods. Unfortunately, the bear keeps coming back. Johnny knows what the last course of action is. He does not back away from his responsibility. He takes the bear and his gun into the woods for the last time. Fate saves Johnny from having to shoot his nuisance bear, but he was prepared to do his duty.
Other character traits shown: *Courage*

Zagwyn, Deborah Turney. *Turtle Spring.* Berkeley, CA: Tricycle Press, 1998.

The changing seasons bring surprises to Clee, including a new baby brother and a turtle.
Responsibility: When winter arrives, Clee forgets to bring inside the southern breed of turtle that her Uncle had given her. When she remembers, she finds the turtle beneath a layer of grass clippings and rotting leaves "stone still, stone cold." She is sorry for her failure to protect her pet and buries him deep in the compost heap, "deep so the coyotes wouldn't dig it up." In the northern seasons, her mother tells her, "weather can bring both good and bad surprises." Clee is reminded of her forgetfulness every time she looks out at the snow-topped garden compost, imagining her turtle "curled up and frozen beneath it." She makes trails for her brother out in the snow, but "never in that direction." When spring arrives, so does the turtle "inching its way down the compost slope." Clee is delighted to discover her assistance burying the turtle deep has enabled him, after all, to thrive in hibernation, alive and safe.
Other character traits shown: *Empathy*

SELF-DISCIPLINE

Use for INTEGRITY, TEMPERANCE
Controlling one's conduct and desires.

Aardema, Verna. *The Lonely Lioness and the Ostrich Chicks.* Illus. by Yumi Heo. New York: Alfred A. Knopf, 1996.

In this Masai tale, a mongoose helps an ostrich get her chicks back from the lonely lioness, who has stolen them.

Self-discipline: Though lonely, the lioness fails to control her desires, showing her lack of self-discipline. She relies on her superior fierceness to avert retribution and takes another mother's children, apparently convincing herself that they are her own. When another animal politely points out, "If those little creatures are your children, shouldn't they have four feet?" The lioness snaps that, "Their front feet are just beginning to grow," as she points to "a little wing on the nearest chick."

Other character traits shown: *Courage, Helpfulness, Honesty, Justice, Perseverance, Prudence*

Bang, Molly. *When Sophie Gets Angry—Really, Really Angry.* New York: Blue Sky Press (Scholastic), 1999.

When Sophie gets angry, she runs out and climbs her favorite tree.

Self-discipline: Though she is mad enough to explode like a volcano, Sophie runs outside until the trees, ferns, birds, and the wide view of nature make her feel calm again. She can go back home happy and be received by her loving family.

Other character traits shown: *Forgiveness*

Daly, Niki. *Jamela's Dress.* New York: Farrar, Straus & Giroux, 1999.

Jamela gets in trouble when she takes the material intended for a new dress for Mama, parades it in the street, and allows it to become dirty and torn.

Self-discipline: Jamela has been given the task of guarding the newly washed material as it dries on the line. Instead of making sure Taxi, the dog, "doesn't jump up and dirty" it, she forgets her responsibility and soon is wearing the beautiful fabric "proud as a peacock." Her self-discipline has failed her. When she realizes what she has done, it is too late. The dress material is ruined, and everyone is cross with her. Even "Jamela is cross with Jamela" because "she hadn't meant to ruin Mama's material. It just happened."

Other character traits shown: *Forgiveness, Generosity*

dePaola, Tomie. *The Legend of the Indian Paintbrush.* New York: G.P. Putnam's Sons, 1988.

Little Gopher follows his destiny, as revealed in a Dream-Vision, of becoming an artist for his people and eventually is able to bring the colors of the sunset down to earth.

Self-discipline: Though Little Gopher tries to keep up with the other boys who were always riding, running, shooting their bows, and wrestling to prove their strength, he is too small. He wants to be one of them, but the wise shaman tells him not to struggle against the special gift he has. The others will grow up to be warriors. Little Gopher will "be remembered for a different reason." Even as he pursues his destiny of painting the life of the People, he "sometimes longed to put aside his brushes and ride out with the warriors." But he remembers his Dream-Vision and "did not go with them." He puts aside his desires for the sake of his life's work.

Other character traits shown: *Diligence, Hope, Loyalty, Patience, Perseverance, Responsibility*

Feiffer, Jules. *I Lost My Bear.* New York: Morrow Junior Books, 1998.

When she cannot find her favorite stuffed toy, a young girl asks her mother, father, and older sister for help.

Self-discipline: The child frets that no one will help her find her bear. So, she cries. But nobody stops her, so she stops herself. She carefully follows their suggestions about hunting for the missing bear, but it remains lost until she climbs into bed and finds it there under the covers, at which time she pronounces herself just the "best detective" for finding Bearsy.

Other character traits shown: *Diligence, Prudence*

Henkes, Kevin. *Lilly's Purple Plastic Purse.* New York: Greenwillow (William Morrow), 1996.

Lilly loves everything about school, especially her teacher, but when he asks her to wait a while before showing her new purse, she does something for which she is very sorry later.

Self-discipline: It is a difficult lesson for Lilly to learn. And it is hard to hold back, but she learns to wait before showing her special purse. She peeks at it in her desk, but she doesn't disturb anyone.

Other character traits shown: *Patience*

Lee, Milly. *Nim and the War Effort.* Illus. by Yangsook Choi. New York: Frances Foster Books (Farrar, Straus & Giroux), 1997.

Nim and a schoolmate are rivals in a contest to collect newspapers for the war effort until the final day when it seems Nim can't possibly win.

Self-discipline: Nim passes "two large bundles of morning newspapers waiting for Mr. Wong, the newspaper vendor. She looked at them longingly." She would like to add them to her collection, but, unlike her competitor, she does not steal them.

Other character traits shown: *Fortitude, Loyalty, Perseverance, Resourcefulness*

Markoe, Merrill. *The Day My Dogs Became Guys.* Illus. by Eric Brace. New York: Viking (Penguin Putnam), 1999.

When an eclipse of the sun turns Carey's three dogs into people, they cause enormous problems continuing to behave like dogs.

Self-discipline: Carey has trouble controlling his dogs, but it's nothing compared to the grief they cause him as people. He wishes he could explain things to them. When he can, they don't listen very well. The dogs, now people, have no self-control. They beg for snacks, but now they can open the refrigerator and help themselves. They don't have to wait for Carey to take them for a walk. They can open the door or window and let themselves out. They rid the neighborhood of squirrels. They chase cars that are getting away. When they are dirty, Carey doesn't feel right about just hosing them down, like he used to when they were dogs, so he tries to take them to the bathroom. They try to wedge themselves under the bed and hide in the closet. Carey decides they make better dogs than they do people.

Marshall, James. *Swine Lake*. Illus. by Maurice Sendak. New York: HarperCollins, 1999.

A wolf becomes entranced watching a ballet and forgets his intention to eat the performers.

Self-discipline: When the show begins, in spite of himself, the "mangy wolf found himself absorbed in the story." And, suddenly, "without knowing why, the wolf sprang out of his seat, leapt over the railing, sailed right over the orchestra pit and onto the stage." He becomes carried away with the music as he whirls around with the confused pig bride. And, though he carries her offstage amid tremendous applause, he does not take the opportunity to eat the pig ballerina, but, rather, rushes past a startled stage manager and does not stop running until he is home. When his landlady interprets his disheveled appearance to "leading a life of crime, no doubt," he can only reply, "You wouldn't understand." The wolf has controlled his desires in favor of a nobler art as "he executed a couple of flashy dance steps" after reading a review of his performance.

Other character traits shown: *Tolerance*

Michelson, Richard. *Grandpa's Gamble*. Illus. by Barry Moser. New York: Marshall Cavendish, 1999.

When Grandpa tells a boy and his sister why he prays so much, they stop thinking that he is just a boring old man.

Self-discipline: As the old man tells his story, he reveals that as a young man he was an unprincipled gambler. When his daughter becomes ill, he realizes with shame that, "My parents had not sent me to a new land to learn to cheat and steal." He gave away the fine hat that was a reflection of his ego, and replaced it with "the plainest black yarmulke." He begins, then, a habit of praying every day for his parents' forgiveness and every evening for the young daughter's health. His wife chastises him for being "not so important that God's plans depend on your prayers." But he "was as stubborn as Moses." The "Angel of Death" did pass over his daughter. She recovered, but he has maintained his prayers over the years with the self-discipline of one reformed and thankful.

Other character traits shown: *Respect*

Naylor, Phyllis Reynolds. *Sweet Strawberries.* Illus. by Rosalind Charney Kaye. New York: Atheneum Books for Young Readers (Simon & Schuster), 1999.

A wife and her grumpy husband go to market.

Self-discipline: Because his wife seemed to react so badly the last time they met all the "unpleasant people" on the way to market, this time the husband carefully does not scold any "lasses in a hurry, any lazy lads, any selfish oafs, or stingy tradesmen." He meets the girl with the geese and "slowed his horse," calling out, "Fine day to you, Miss!" His courteous behavior all day long has a marked improvement on his wife's disposition as well as on all those with whom he had contact. He seems unaware that improved relations are directly the result of his own self-discipline. "Isn't it remarkable how everyone has changed so in only a week?"

Other character traits shown: *Courtesy, Forgiveness, Tolerance*

Potter, Beatrix. *The Tale of Peter Rabbit.* London: Frederick Warne & Co., 1992.

Mrs. Rabbit goes out on errands after admonishing her children to stay away from Mr. McGregor's garden.

Self-discipline: Apparently, the lure of forbidden fresh vegetables causes Peter to risk the fate his father met in the McGregors' garden. He lacks the self-discipline to reject possible disaster. He squeezes under the gate and begins happily nibbling lettuces, French beans, and radishes. He doesn't stop until he feels "rather sick." Once spotted by the farmer, his indulgence no longer seems worth the risk, but it is too late. He barely escapes with his life. His clothes are lost, he has caught a cold, and he goes to bed without supper.

Other character traits shown: *Justice*

Snape, Juliet, and Charles Snape. *The Boy with Square Eyes* New York: Prentice-Hall Books for Young Readers (Simon & Schuster), 1987.

When Charlie's eyes turn square from watching television and everything else starts looking square too, he cures himself by reading books and stimulating his mind.

Self-discipline: When his only cure for televisionitis is to exercise his eyes, Charlie begins his therapy with reluctance. His mother takes him first to an art gallery, then to the library and the park. At home they unplug the TV set. Charlie doesn't know what to do. But his mother suggests reading a book, doing a puzzle, drawing a picture, and looking at the sky. Charlie follows directions. By sticking to the task of self-recovery, Charlie's mind soon fills with questions about the world around him. And his eyes are back to normal. But "he never saw things quite the same way again." His old life of idle television watching is finished.

Soto, Gary. *Too Many Tamales.* Illus. by Ed Martinez. New York: G.P. Putnam's Sons, 1993.

Maria tries on her mother's wedding ring while helping make tamales for a Christmas family get-together. Panic ensues when, hours later, she realizes the ring is missing.

Self-discipline: Maria sees her mother's ring on the table and, feeling grownup, she proceeds to try it on without seeking permission. Then, she forgets about the ring and begins kneading the tamale dough. She never gives the ring another thought until evening when she is thinking about Christmas gifts. Her lack of self-discipline earlier causes her to try to rectify the problem by hunting for the ring in the baked tamales. She asks her three cousins to help by eating the tamales in hopes of recovering the missing ring.

Other character traits shown: *Honesty*

Yolen, Jane. *Owl Moon.* Illus. by John Schoenherr. New York: Philomel Books, 1987. (Caldecott–1988)

On a winter's night under a full moon, a father and daughter trek into the woods to see the Great Horned Owl.

Self-discipline: This is her first time owling, and she has waited a long time to go. Her legs are short and she must run to keep up, but she doesn't call out. You have to be quiet when you go owling. She is patient when the first calls bring no results. Sometimes there is an owl and sometimes not, her brothers have told her. She is cold but says nothing. You make your own heat when you go owling. The night has black shadows and things that could be hiding behind trees, but when you go owling you have to be brave. She listens so hard her ears hurt and her eyes get cloudy with the cold. She remains quiet. When the owl arrives, they look at each other maybe a minute or a hundred minutes. The owl departs silently. Afterward, she could talk or laugh out loud, but she is a shadow walking home. When you go owling you don't need words or warm or anything but hope. She has proven herself a worthy owl-calling participant.

Other character traits shown: *Empathy, Hope*

Yorinks, Arthur. *The Flying Latke.* Illus. by William Steig. Photos by Paul Colin and Arthur Yorinks. New York: Simon & Schuster, 1999.

A family argument on the first night of Chanukah results in a food fight and a flying latke that is mistaken for a flying saucer.

Self-discipline: There is little self-control among these family members. They ruin a dinner event over a petty quarrel, which soon degenerates into food throwing. When a flying potato pancake sails out a window and is mistaken for a flying saucer, the family holes up at the house for eight days to escape reporters. Fighting finally ends only after the latke returns through the window as a miracle.

Other character traits shown: *Courtesy, Forgiveness, Tolerance*

SHARING. *SEE* GENEROSITY

TEMPERANCE. *SEE* SELF-DISCIPLINE

THOUGHTFULNESS. *SEE* COURTESY, HELPFULNESS, KINDNESS

TOLERANCE

Use for INTEGRITY
Accepting that which one may not especially like.

Bruchac, Joseph. *The Great Ball Game: A Muskogee Story.* Illus. by Susan L. Roth. New York: Dial Books for Young Readers, 1994.

Bat, who has both wings and teeth, plays an important part in a game between the Birds and the Animals to decide which group is better.

Tolerance: Bat has characteristics of both the Birds and the Animals. He seeks to join one side or the other in their ball game. He is rejected first by the Animals, who use the excuse that even though he has teeth, he can fly like a bird. It would not be fair for him to play on the side of the Animals. But he is also rejected by the Birds, who foolishly dismiss him because, "You are too little to help us. We don't want you," they jeer. When he returns to the Animals, he begs to be allowed to join their team because, "The Birds laughed at me and would not accept me." Bear, the Animals' leader, recognizes that "sometimes even the small ones can help." His tolerance of Bat pays off. It is Bat, who, after the others tire and can no longer see the goalpost well at the end of the day when darkness falls, enters the game and wins it for the Animals. They were willing to be tolerant of one who was different.

Other character traits shown: *Empathy, Helpfulness, Kindness, Patience, Respect, Responsibility*

Bunting, Eve. *Summer Wheels.* Illus. by Thomas B. Allen. New York: Harcourt Brace Jovanovich, 1992.

The Bicycle Man fixes up old bicycles and offers both his friendship and the use of the bikes to the neighborhood kids.

Tolerance: Lawrence likes to check out a favorite bike. When one day another boy selects "his" bike, he wants to object. Then he realizes, "The bike's not mine. I only think it is." He doesn't like it, but he has to accept the right of another to also enjoy the bike.

Other character traits shown: *Courage, Empathy, Forgiveness, Generosity, Justice, Kindness, Respect, Responsibility*

Duncan, Alice Faye. *Miss Viola and Uncle Ed Lee.* Illus. by Catherine Stock. New York: Atheneum Books for Young Readers (Simon & Schuster), 1999.

A young boy helps his two neighbors, one as neat as a pin and the other as junky as a packrat, become friends.

Tolerance: Bradley pronounces that the two would be a "kooky combination" for friendship because "Y'all are totally different." It's clear Uncle Ed Lee's yard, even after a quick clean-up, isn't "neat-neat, but it was much better than before." And Miss Viola finds it good enough for her visit. She enjoys making friends. His efforts to clean up for her are tolerable for an afternoon of lemonade and a game of hearts.

Other character traits shown: *Courtesy, Helpfulness, Honesty, Kindness, Respect*

*Edwards, Pamela Duncan. *Honk!* Illus. by Henry Cole. New York: Hyperion Books for Children, 1998.

A ballet-loving swan wins acclaim when she manages to join the dancers in a performance of Swan Lake.

Tolerance: The opera theater manager does not want Mimi in the building. She is a bird. It's not tolerated. But Mimi will not accept her limitations. She manages to get on stage and proves to be a hit with the audience. Now, the stage manager must accept and tolerate her presence, because the audience wants her back. He finds himself in the uncomfortable position of having to say, "Hey you, Bird, can you come again tomorrow?" She has taught him the necessity of tolerance.

Other character traits shown: *Hope, Perseverance, Resourcefulness*

Egan, Tim. *Distant Feathers.* Boston: Houghton Mifflin, 1998.

Sedrick is visited by an enormous, annoying bird that wreaks havoc on the town, but when the bird is presumed dead after a violent hurricane, Sedrick finds he misses it.

Tolerance: Feathers has been a nuisance in town. He breaks things he sits on, is rather clumsy, and isn't very brave when the town could have used his help, but, "he had become a wonderful, if somewhat destructive, part of their lives, and they missed him very much." When he miraculously returns, Sedrick doesn't mind that Feathers "was ruining his roof." Everyone accepts him back "though they insisted he stay in Sedrick's yard from then on." The bird "entertains with stories of his life back on Earth, the planet he's from." So, everyone tolerates a situation that is not of their own choosing.

Ehlert, Lois. *Top Cat.* New York: Harcourt Brace, 1998.

Top Cat is reluctant to accept the arrival of a new kitten but decides to share various survival secrets with it.

Tolerance: Top Cat does not want another cat in the household, preferring to remain the only cat. But, after trying to discourage it by fighting with it and biting it, he determines it is there to stay. He will tolerate it. "Guess I'm stuck with you, striped cat." A sign of his acceptance of a situation he does not especially like is his decision to teach the youngster how to behave in the house according to cat standards. There is "more to do than eat and sleep." There is jumping on the couch, nibbling plants, drinking from the sink faucet when company is present, and similar activities.

Other character traits shown: *Responsibility*

Fowler, Susi Gregg. *Beautiful*. Illus. by Jim Fowler. New York: Greenwillow (William Morrow), 1998.

A young gardener and Uncle George collaborate on a garden, so that when a very sick Uncle George comes home from the doctor he is greeted with beautiful flowers.

Tolerance: The boy does not like the way things are. "I miss Uncle George the way he used to be." He, nevertheless, accepts what is reality. Uncle George can't go to look at the boy's new thriving garden. He can't even come to the table to eat with the family. He can barely whisper. So, the boy brings blooms from his garden in to Uncle George's room. The boy knows by looking in his eyes that Uncle George would say "Beautiful," if he could speak.

Other character traits shown: *Courage, Helpfulness, Honesty*

Gretz, Susanna. *Rabbit Food*. Cambridge, MA: Candlewick Press, 1999.

Uncle Bunny, who has been summoned to make sure that John joins his fellow rabbits, is trying to set a good example for the picky eater.

Tolerance: How can Uncle Bunny get John to try his peas and mushrooms when he, himself, dislikes carrots and celery? He manages to hide his problem for awhile. But John is observant, and asks him directly. They have just returned from a mountain climb and are very hungry. They eat everything. By the time he finishes watching the news, there is nothing left but carrots for Uncle Bunny. The young rabbits jump on him and, tit for tat, admonish him to just try a little, one teeny tiny bite, so you'll grow big and strong like us. And, in a spirit of tolerance, Uncle Bunny does bite off a very tiny piece of carrot and chew it very slowly. He discovers, like John, that "they're not bad."

Hendry, Diana. *Back Soon*. Illus. by Carol Thompson. New York: BridgeWater Books (Troll Associates), 1995.

A kitten does not like it when his mother goes away without him, but after enjoying some time by himself, he understands why she does it.

Tolerance: Herbert wishes his mother would not leave him with babysitters. One day he enjoys some playtime by himself in the garden and finds out how pleasant being alone can be. So, now when mother goes out, he accepts her outings. He will still miss her, "but it's very nice having some time to yourself." Mother, too, must accept those times when Herbert is out by himself. Each agrees such times are ok "as long as you always remember to come back."

Other character traits shown: *Empathy, Respect*

Hest, Amy. *The Purple Coat.* Illus. by Amy Schwartz. New York: Four Winds Press, 1986.

Despite her mother's reminder that "navy blue is what you always get," Gabby begs her tailor grandfather to make her a beautiful purple fall coat.

Tolerance: It is not what she wants for her daughter, but mother gives in gracefully and is able to say, "I have a sneaky suspicion this is going to be the best purple coat ever." Grandfather is uncertain about the wisdom of Gabby's choice, but he will combine his knowledge with her wishes. She will get purple, a kick pleat in back to make it easy when she runs, and even a hood if there is enough fabric. But it will not go quite down to her ankles and it will not have purple lining as she asks. "Don't push your luck," he warns. Gabrielle knows how much she has gained. She is satisfied with navy blue lining and is even able to tell her mother that there may be days when she doesn't feel like purple. Having the coat reversible will be just fine.

Other character traits shown: *Courage, Empathy, Prudence*

Little, Mimi Otley. *Yoshiko and the Foreigner.* New York: Frances Foster Books (Farrar, Straus & Giroux), 1996.

Though well-brought-up Japanese girls didn't talk to foreigners, there are exceptions, and when a young American Air Force Officer mispronounces the language, Yoshiko's heart softens in a way that will change her life forever.

Tolerance: Yoshiko's family can't imagine allowing in a foreigner. But Yoshiko counters every argument successfully. "He will not understand the ways of our people. Americans only laugh and scoff at our customs." Yet he provides the rice and plum wine for the ancestral altar even though he does not expect to be invited inside the house. "Americans are fast people. They are complicated; they think highly of their own advancement." Yet he raises goldfish and donates two of them for an empty garden pond in their house compound. "America is full of proud people. This American could not understand what it means to honor our family and our people." Yet he honors them by learning to speak Japanese and then how to write in perfect Japanese characters. Finally, there is nothing more to argue. Yoshiko's mother tells her days later that, "Perhaps one day you will come back, and this time you will bring your American with you." Her family has given her their blessing. They may not wish her to marry a foreigner, but they will tolerate what they cannot find fault with.

Other character traits shown: *Courtesy, Respect*

Lorbiecki, Marybeth. *Sister Anne's Hands.* Illus. by K. Wendy Popp. New York: Dial Books for Young Readers (Penguin), 1998.

Seven-year-old Anna has her first encounter with racism in the 1960s when an African-American nun comes to teach at her parochial school.

Tolerance: Following an initial incident in which a paper airplane with a racist poem on it goes sailing past the teacher's desk, students are quickly taught awareness of racial bias. Sister Anne brings pictures showing black people experiencing cruelty from fearful and prejudiced whites. She tells the class, "One thing you're going to learn is that some folks have their hearts wide open, and others are tight as a fist. The tighter they are, the more dangerous." The class has a wonderful year, because their sensitive teacher is also a very good teacher with interesting, fun ways of helping children learn. And, in the process, they learn tolerance for human diversity.

Other character traits shown: *Courage, Forgiveness, Respect*

Loredo, Elizabeth. *Boogie Bones.* Illus. by Kevin Aawkes. New York: G.P. Putnam's Sons, 1997.

Boogie Bones, a skeleton that loves to dance, disguises himself as a living person and leaves his graveyard home to enter a dance contest.

Tolerance: The dancers are at first horrified when Boogie Bones' costume comes off during a fast dance. The cheering and clapping stop. They discover that the contest's best dancer is a skeleton. His dance partner slinks away from him. The band stops playing. Suddenly, a little girl, who is "not afraid of any old bones," offers to be his dancing partner. The audience quakes in their boots. Their knees knock. Their teeth rattle. This sounds like music to Boogie Bones. He spins his partner, and the dancing continues. After a while the band starts up; people begin to clap. They feel a little silly about being afraid when a child is dancing the lindy hop, "not the least bit scared." The crowd has been shown tolerance by the child.

Lyon, George. *A Traveling Cat.* Illus. by Paul Brett Johnson. New York: Orchard Books, 1998.

When discovered on a playground in front of the drive-in movie screen, Boulevard, a stray cat, stays in her new home a short while before taking to the road.

Tolerance: After staying long enough to produce kittens, the cat leaves the family. "Dad says Boulevard stayed a long time for such a traveling cat." The little girl replies, "Maybe, but not long enough." She accepts what she can't change, and she hopes the new family doesn't expect to keep Boulevard, because, "She's a traveling cat."

Manson, Christopher. *Two Travelers.* New York: Henry Holt, 1990.

The emperor's messenger Isaac must accompany a gift elephant from Baghdad to France, and during the difficult journey, an unexpected friendship develops between man and beast.

Tolerance: The messenger and the elephant aren't sure they like each other. The man has a funny hat and smells strange. The elephant is built like a monster and could hurt the messenger. But they will make the best of their situation and try to get along through the journey ahead. To ease the elephant's concern, Isaac shows how safe is the raft upon which they must cross the river. He covers the elephant's ears during the cold part of the journey. The elephant shows his growing regard for Isaac by shading him with his big ears during the hot part of the journey and lifting him with his trunk to save him from going overboard during a storm at sea.

Other character traits shown: *Cooperation, Helpfulness, Kindness*

Marshall, James. *Swine Lake.* Illus. by Maurice Sendak. New York: HarperCollins, 1999.

A wolf becomes entranced in a ballet and forgets his intention to eat the performers.

Tolerance: It takes a tremendous effort of will, but the wolf exchanges his desire to eat pork for a moment of impromptu glory as he thrusts himself on stage and enters the ballet performance. He doesn't like the circumstances, but he curbs his appetite and tolerates the pigs in order to play in the drama. It wouldn't be fair to eat a fellow performer.

Other character traits shown: *Self-discipline*

*Meddaugh, Susan. *Cinderella's Rat.* Boston: Walter Lorraine Books (Houghton Mifflin), 1997.

One of the rats that was turned into a coachman by Cinderella's fairy godmother tells his story.

Tolerance: Turned into a coachman first and then back into a rat, the rat pronounces that "life is full of surprises, so you may as well get used to it." His sister rat is turned into a girl at the hands of a wizard who doesn't quite get it right. She "woofs." But that's better than being the cat he first turned her into. Now, she has access to food, a cottage, and can scare away cats from the rat family. So, you learn to accept what you get.

Other character traits shown: *Justice*

Naylor, Phyllis Reynolds. *Sweet Strawberries.* Illus. by Rosalind Charney Kaye. New York: Atheneum Books for Young Readers (Simon & Schuster), 1999.

A wife and her grumpy husband go to market.

Tolerance: Each of her husband's unjustified attacks on the people they see going to market are tolerated with forbearance. His behavior mirrors the flaws he accuses others of displaying. But the wife is at her wits' end when he stubbornly refuses to buy her strawberries, when he knows how much she has been looking forward to them. She lashes out, "You are the most stingy, selfish, lazy, impatient, complaining man I have ever seen!" Her tolerance for his meanness has reached its limit. She refuses to talk to him all the way home from the market. He is dumbfounded, never suspecting that he is the reason she is upset. It must have been all the "unpleasant" people they met along the way. Therefore, the next time they go to market, he hopes they don't meet "any of those lasses in a hurry, any lazy lads, any selfish oafs, or stingy tradesmen." He makes sure his wife is not upset again. During this trip he carefully makes no unkind remarks to anyone he meets. He tolerates them all. And, remarkably, he notes "how everyone has changed so in only a week."

Other character traits shown: *Courtesy, Forgiveness, Self-discipline*

Say, Allen. *Allison.* Boston: Walter Lorraine Books (Houghton Mifflin), 1997.

When Allison realizes that she looks more like her favorite doll than like her parents, she comes to terms with this unwelcome discovery with the help of a stray cat.

Tolerance: Allison does not like to think that her real parents gave her away to strangers. But then she meets a cat without a home. It's good that others are ready to step in when circumstances might sometimes separate loved ones. Just as her parents have lovingly taken her for their own, Allison takes in the cat that also needs a family. There are times when one must tolerate what can't be changed.

Other character traits shown: *Discernment, Empathy, Generosity*

Scheffler, Ursel. *Stop Your Crowing, Kasimir!* Illus. by Silke Brix-Henker. Minneapolis: Carolrhoda, 1988.

Katy's neighbors appeal to the authorities to silence her extremely loud rooster, but the final result is very different from what they had in mind.

Tolerance: If the neighbors had learned to be tolerant of the simple farm woman and her animals, they would not have discovered themselves living next to a disco instead, which they soon realize is much worse.

Other character traits shown: *Cooperation, Justice*

Uchida, Yoshiko. *The Bracelet.* Illus. by Joanna Yardley. New York: Philomel Books (Putnam & Grosset), 1976.

Emi, a Japanese American in the second grade is sent with her family to an internment camp during World War II, but the loss of the bracelet her best friend has given her proves that she doesn't need a physical reminder of that friendship.

Tolerance: Emi is not even a day at the temporary camp when the new bracelet is lost. She believes she now has nothing by which to remember her best friend. Then she discovers that memories of her friend are in her head. She can remember whenever she chooses. Meanwhile, she accepts their time apart in the internment camps. She doesn't like the separation, but she is at peace, knowing that the government cannot take away her memories. "Laurie would always be her friend, no matter where she was sent."

Other character traits shown: *Kindness, Patience*

Yorinks, Arthur. *The Flying Latke*. Illus. by William Steig. Photos by Paul Colin and Arthur Yorinks. New York: Simon & Schuster, 1999.

A family argument on the first night of Chanukah results in a food fight and a flying latke that is mistaken for a flying saucer.

Tolerance: The adults in this tale behave without self-control. They do not acknowledge the right of one another to possess differing views and soon fall to quarreling and throwing food. A bit more tolerance would have prevented their self-imposed isolation.

Other character traits shown: *Courtesy, Forgiveness, Self-discipline*

TRUSTWORTHINESS. *SEE* RESPONSIBILITY

TRUTHFULNESS. *SEE* HONESTY

APPENDIX A
Friendship Resources

This appendix lists books that especially exhibit a particular focus on some aspect of friendship.

Beautiful by Susi Gregg Fowler, 1998. A boy learns gardening skills in order to please his dying uncle with a presentation of beautiful flowers.

Best Friends by Loretta Krupinski, 1998. A white girl helps her Native American friend to escape impending danger from soldiers as she sacrifices her favorite doll in order to send a message of warning.

Best Friends Think Alike by Lynn Reiser, 1997. Two friends decide playing together is better than having their own way alone.

Biggest Bear (The) by Lynd Ward, 1952. (Caldecott–1953) A boy finds he prefers the companionship of a live bear cub to a bearskin tacked on his barn like other farms had.

Brave Horace by Holly Keller, 1998. When a mean older brother frightens birthday party guests, a child steps forth first to accept a dare when he notices his friend is near tears at the prospect of facing the challenge.

Chicken Salad Club (The) by Marsha Diane Arnold, 1998. A boy persis-

tently and gently works to seek a companion for his great-grandfather when he realizes the old man needs the right kind of fresh audience for his stories.

Degas and the Little Dancer by Laurence Anholt, 1996. A young dancer who faces the loss of her budding career begins to understand she has something in common with the grumpy artist for whom she must pose each day.

Distant Feathers by Tim Egan, 1998. Though a terrible nuisance, a giant bird becomes companion to a townsman who finds he misses it when a hurricane appears to have swept it away.

Don't Need Friends by Carolyn Crimi, 1999. Two formerly rival junkyard creatures discover a mutual need.

Five-Dog Night (The) by Eileen Christelow, 1993. One neighbor tries valiantly to help another cantankerous neighbor to take care of himself during cold winter nights until the tables are turned and the stubborn one suddenly becomes the caregiver.

Hey, Al by Arthur Yorinks, 1986. (Caldecott–1987) A low-income janitor is nagged by his dog to seek a better life, until their dream comes true and they find themselves desperate to return to things the way they used to be.

Honest to Goodness Truth (The) by Patricia McKissack. Illus. by Giselle Potter. New York: Atheneum Books for Young Readers (Simon & Schuster), 2000. After promising never to lie, Libby learns that truth without kindness can hurt feelings.

Marven of the Great North Woods by Kathryn Lasky, 1997. A boy would have had a lonely time away from his parents in a Minnesota logging camp were it not for one of the lumberjacks, who befriends him.

Mirette on the High Wire by Emily Arnold McCully, 1992. (Caldecott–1993) A grateful young tightrope walker repays her master for teaching her the skills of highwire performing when she helps him overcome his fear of heights.

Miss Viola and Uncle Ed Lee by Alice Faye Duncan, 1999. A boy, who likes both his neighbors, helps them overcome some issues that have prevented them from becoming acquainted.

No Such Thing by Jackie French Koller, 1997. A boy afraid there might be a monster under his bed and a monster afraid there might be a boy on top of the bed discover they have something in common, not least of which is a surprise for their mothers.

Officer Buckle and Gloria by Peggy Rathmann, 1995. (Caldecott–1996) Though jealous at first of the dog's attention, a policeman finds his safety talks go better when his dog is with him and do not succeed as well when either he performs alone or his dog performs alone.

On Call Back Mountain by Eve Bunting, 1997. Two brothers find they look forward keenly each summer night to signaling their fire watchman friend up at his tower and miss this interaction when he dies.

Piano (The) by William Miller. Illus. by Susan Keeter. New York: Lee & Low Books, 2000. A young black girl's love for music leads her to companionship with an older white woman, who teaches her how to play the piano and the rewards of intergenerational friendship.

Pumpkin Soup by Helen Cooper, 1998. It takes cooperation to make their special soup, and when they forget, three friends come to realize it's more important to make allowances for failings than to adhere to strict routine.

Rabbit Pirates by Judy Cox, 1999. Though two restaurateurs disagree about many things, they loyally work together when an outside force threatens their business and their lives.

Raising Dragons by Jerdine Nolen, 1998. A farmer's young daughter cares responsibly for a grateful dragon from infancy, and the two bond together on the farm until she can be assured the dragon will have a good life on its own.

Somebody's New Pajamas by Isaac Jackson, 1996. Two boys from different backgrounds sleep over at each other's homes and sensitively exchange ideas about sleepwear as well as family life.

Star of Fear, Star of Hope by Jo Hoestlandt, 1995. A child is haunted for years by an act of cruelty against a friend who disappeared forever on the night of their quarrel.

Starry Night(The) by Neil Waldman, 1999. A boy receives an unexpected boost of support from a special fellow artist.

Summer Wheels by Eve Bunting, 1992. A bicycle repairman fixes bikes and offers them and his friendship to neighborhood kids.

Two Travelers by Christopher Manson, 1990. A conscientious messenger develops a mutual companionable respect and closeness to the huge animal he is accompanying to its new home.

Wally, the Worry-Warthog by Barbara Shook Hazen, 1990. When the two finally speak of their respective fears, two new friends discover each had been needlessly fearing the other.

You're Not My Best Friend Anymore by Charlotte Pomerantz, 1998. After harsh words are spoken, two longtime friends part, but the habit of thoughtfulness makes them buy each other a last birthday present that serves to reunite them.

APPENDIX B
All-Ages Resources

This appendix lists picture books suitable for all ages. They exhibit a depth of content appreciated, particularly, by older students. These books are starred in the main section.

Cello of Mr. O (The) 1999. Cutler, Jane.
  Courage, Fortitude, Generosity,
    Hope, Perseverance,
    Resourcefulness
Cinderella's Rat 1997. Meddaugh, Susan.
  Justice, Tolerance
Don't Need Friends 1999. Crimi, Carolyn.
  Courtesy, Generosity, Helpfulness
Dreamer (The) 1993. Rylant, Cynthia.
  Respect
Gardener (The) 1997. Stewart, Sarah.
  Diligence, Discernment, Generosity,
    Patience
Golem 1996. Wiesniewski, David.
  Helpfulness, Justice, Loyalty, Respect
Grandfather's Journey 1993. Say, Allen.
  Discernment, Empathy
Hip Cat 1993. London, Jonathan.
  Diligence, Perseverance
Honk! 1998. Edwards, Pamela Duncan.
  Hope, Perseverance,
    Resourcefulness, Tolerance

I Never Knew Your Name 1994. Garland, Sherry.
  Courage, Kindness, Respect
Jonkonnu 1997. Littlesugar, Amy.
  Courage, Discernment, Respect
Katie's Trunk 1992. Turner, Ann.
  Justice, Kindness
Lotus Seed (The) 1993. Garland, Sherry.
  Hope, Loyalty, Respect
Love as Strong as Ginger 1999. Look, Lenore.
  Respect
Many Moons 1943. (Caldecott–1944) Thurber, James.
  Prudence, Respect
Odd Velvet 1998. Whitcomb, Mary E.
  Respect
Out of the Ocean 1998. Frasier, Debra.
  Empathy, Respect
Peddler's Gift (The) 1999. Schur, Maxine Rose.
  Courage, Forgiveness, Honesty,
    Kindness, Respect, Responsibility

Raising Sweetness 1999. Stanley, Diane.
  Kindness, Loyalty

Rumpelstiltskin's Daughter 1997. Stanley, Diane.
  Kindness, Resourcefulness

Scarecrow 1998. Rylant, Cynthia.
  Respect

Seven Brave Women 1997. Hearne, Betsy.
  Fortitude, Resourcefulness, Respect

Small Miracle (A) 1997. Collington, Peter.
  Generosity, Kindness

Star of Fear, Star of Hope 1995. Hoestlandt, Jo.
  Courtesy, Discernment, Forgiveness, Hope

Starry Night (The) 1999. Waldman, Neil.
  Generosity, Helpfulness, Hope

Swan in Love. Bunting, Eve. 2000
  Loyalty, Patience

Sweetest Fig (The) 1993. Van Allsburg, Chris.
  Justice

Tea with Milk 1999. Say, Allen.
  Empathy, Fortitude, Perseverance

This Is the Bird 1997. Shannon, George.
  Hope, Respect

Through the Mickle Woods 1992. Gregory, Valiska.
  Discernment, Empathy, Forgiveness, Generosity, Helpfulness, Hope, Kindness, Perseverance

Victor and Christabel 1993. Mathers, Petra.
  Justice, Kindness

APPENDIX C
Curriculum Tie-Ins

CURRICULUM TIE-INS

This appendix lists books that can be used to teach other aspects of the curriculum. The first list is by subject, the second, by author. Starred books are appropriate for readers of all ages.

BY SUBJECT

Arts

Ballet
*Honk! Edwards, Duncan. Hyperion Books for Children, 1998.
Swine Lake. Marshall, James. HarperCollins, 1999.

Biography
Boy Named Giotto (A). Guarnieri, Paolo. Farrar, Straus & Giroux, 1998.
Boy Who Loved to Draw (The): Benjamin West. Brenner, Barbara. Houghton Mifflin, 1999.
Degas and the Little Dancer: A Story abaout Edgar Degas. Anholt, Laurence. Barron's Educational Series, 1996.
*Jonkonnu: A Story from the Sketchbook of Winslow Homer. Littlesugar, Amy. Philomel Books, 1997.
*Starry Night (The). Waldman, Neil. Boyds Mills Press, 1999.

Health and Safety

Autism
Ian's Walk: A Story about Autism. Lears, Laurie. Albert Whitman, 1998.

Physical Disabilities
Storm (The). Harshman, Marc. Dutton, 1995.

Speech Disorders
Hooway for Wodney Wat. Lester, Helen. Houghton Mifflin, 1999.

History

Aviation
Glorious Flight (The). Provensen, Alice, and Martin Provensen. Viking Press, 1983. (Caldecott–1984)

Biography
A. Lincoln and Me. Borden, Louise. Scholastic Press, 1999.

Civil War—United States
Promise Quilt (The). Ransom, Candice F. Walker & Co., 1999.

Eighteenth-Century America—Declaration of Independence
Hatmaker's Sign (The). Fleming, Candace. Orchard Books, 1998.

Ethnicity—African American
Virgie Goes to School with Us Boys. Howard, Elizabeth Fitzgerald. Simon and Schuster Books for Young Readers, 2000.

Ethnicity—Jews
*Golem. Wiesniewski, David. Clarion, 1996. (Caldecott–1997)

Ethnicity—Native American
Red Bird. Mitchell, Barbara. Lothrop, Lee & Shepard, 1996.

Frontier Life—United States
Biggest Bear (The). Ward, Lynd. Houghton Mifflin, 1952. (Caldecott–1953)

Great Depression—United States
Leah's Pony. Friedrich, Elizabeth. Boyds Mills Press, 1996.
Potato: A Tale from the Great Depression. Lied, Kate. National Geographic Society, 1997.

Immigration—Japanese
*Grandfather's Journey. Say, Allen. Houghton Mifflin, 1993.
*Tea with Milk. Say, Allen. Houghton Mifflin, 1999.

Nineteenth-Century America
Big Cheese for the White House (A): The True Tale of a Tremendous Cheddar. Fleming, Candance. Dorling Kindersley Inc., 1999.
Ox-Cart Man. Hall, Donald. Viking Press, 1979. (Caldecott–1980)

Nineteenth-Century America—Gold Rush
Gold Fever. Kay, Verla. G.P. Putnam's Sons, 1999.

Nineteenth-Century America—Orphan Trains
Train to Somewhere. Bunting, Eve. Houghton Mifflin, 1996.

Nineteenth-Century America—Santa Fe Trail
Lewis & Papa: Adventure on the Santa Fe Trail. Joosse, Barbara. Chronicle Books, 1998.

Nineteenth-Century America—Textile Mill Unions
Bobbin Girl (The). McCully, Emily Arnold. Dial Books for Young Readers, 1996.

Nineteenth-Century America—Women's Suffrage
Ballot Box Battle (The). McCully, Emily Arnold. Alfred A. Knopf, 1996.

Nineteenth-Century Russia
*Peddler's Gift (The). Schur, Maxine Rose. Dial Books for Young Readers, 1999.

Paleontology—Biography
Mary Anning and the Sea Dragon. Atkins, Jeannine. Farrar, Straus & Giroux, 1999.

Race Relations
Best Friends. Krupinski, Loretta. Hyperion Books for Children, 1998.

Railroads—Women Engineers
True Heart. Moss, Marissa. Harcourt Brace, 1999.

Renaissance—Street Performance
Bravo Zan Angelo! A Comedia Dell'arte Tale with Story and Pictures. Daly, Niki. Farrar, Straus & Giroux, 1998.

Revolutionary War—United States
*Katie's Trunk. Turner, Ann. Macmillan, 1992.

Rome
Roman Twins (The). Gerrard, Roy. Farrar, Straus & Giroux, 1998.

Slavery—United States
Sweet Clara and the Freedom Quilt. Hopkinson, Deborah. Alfred A. Knopf, 1993.

South Africa
Day Gogo Went to Vote (The). Sisulu, Elinor Batezat. Little, Brown, 1997.

Statue of Liberty—Ellis Island
Picnic in October (A). Bunting, Eve. Harcourt Brace, 1999.

Twentieth Century—Ethnic Conflict
*Cello of Mr. O (The). Cutler, Jane. Penguin Putnam Books for Young Readers, 1999.

Twentieth Century—Influenza
Marven of the Great North Woods. Lasky, Kathryn. Harcourt Brace, 1997.

Twentieth-Century America—Vaudeville
Piano Man (The). Chocolate, Debbi. Walker & Co., 1998.
Song and Dance Man. Ackerman, Karen. Alfred A. Knopf, 1988.

Vietnam War—Cambodian Refugees
Whispering Cloth (The). Shea, Pegi Deitz. Boyds Mills, 1995.

Vietnam War—Vietnamese Refugees
*Lotus Seed (The). Garland, Sherry. Harcourt Brace Jovanovich, 1993.

Westward Expansion—United States
Nine for California. Levitin, Sonia. Orchard Books, 1996.

Women
*Seven Brave Women. Hearne, Betsy. William Morrow, 1997.
*This Is the Bird. Shannon, George. Houghton Mifflin, 1997.

World War II—American Home Front
Nim and the War Effort. Lee, Milly. Farrar, Straus & Giroux, 1997.

World War II—Japanese American Internment
Bracelet (The). Uchida, Yoshiko. Philomel Books, 1976.
So Far From the Sea. Bunting, Eve. Houghton Mifflin, 1998.

World War II—Jewish Holocaust
*Star of Fear, Star of Hope. Hoestlandt, Jo. Walker & Co., 1995.

Literature

Fables—Russia
Duck, Duck, Goose? Arnold, Katya. Holiday House, 1997.

Folktales—Africa
Koi and the Kola Nuts. Aardema, Verna. Atheneum Books for Young Readers, 1999.
Lonely Lioness and the Ostrich Chicks (The). Aardema, Verna. Alfred A. Knopf, 1996.
Story, A Story (A). Haley, Gail E. Atheneum, 1970. (Caldecott–1971)

Folktales—China
Painted Fan (The). Singer, Marilyn. Morrow Junior Books, 1994.
Paper Dragon (The). Davol, Marguerite W. Atheneum Books for Young Readers, 1997.
Two of Everything. Hong, Lily Toy. Albert Whitman, 1993.

Folktales—Ireland
Duffy and the Devil. Zemach, Harve.
  Farrar, Straus & Giroux, 1973.
  (Caldecott–1974)

Folktales—Native American
Love Flute. Goble, Paul. Macmillan,
  1992.

Folktales—Peru
Chancay and the Secret of Fire. Charles,
  Donald. G.P. Putnam's Sons, 1992.

Folktales—Russia
Baboushka and the Three Kings. Robbins,
  Ruth. Houghton Mifflin, 1960.
  (Caldecott–1961)

Folktales—South Africa
Gift of the Sun. Stewart, Dianne. Farrar,
  Straus & Giroux, 1996.

Legends—Japan
Drums of Noto Hanto (The). James, J.
  Alison. Dorling Kindersley Inc., 1999.

Legends—Native American
Legend of the Indian Paintbrush (The).
  dePaola, Tomie. G.P. Putnam's Sons,
  1988.

Parody
*Cinderella's Rat. Meddaugh, Susan.
  Houghton Mifflin, 1997.
*Rumplestiltskin's Daughter. Stanley,
  Diane. William Morrow, 1997.

Music
Jazz
*Hip Cat. London, Jonathan. Chronicle
  Books, 1993.

Opera
Bantam of the Opera. Auch, Mary Jane.
  Holiday House, 1997.

Science

Animal Behavior
Owl Moon. Yolen, Jane. Philomel Books,
  1987. (Caldecott–1988)
Snow Bear. George, Jean Craighead.
  Hyperion Books for Young Readers,
  1999.
Turtle Spring. Zagwyn, Deborah Turney.
  Tricycle Press, 1998.

Animal Habitat
One Rainy Night. Gove, Doris.
  Macmillan, 1994.

Coal Mining
Boy of the Deeps. Wallace, Ian. Dorling
  Kindersley Inc., 1999.

Ecology
River. Atwell, Debby. Houghton Mifflin,
  1999.

Photography
Snowflake Bentley. Martin, Jacqueline
  Briggs. Houghton Mifflin, 1998.

Recycling
Barn Savers. High, Linda Oatman. Boyds
  Mills Press, 1999.

Social Science

Adoption
Allison. Say, Allen. Houghton Mifflin,
  1997.

Anger
*When Sophie Gets Angry—Really, Really
  Angry.* Scholastic Press, 1999.

Behavior
*Bad Habits (or The Taming of Lucretzia
  Crum).* Cole, Babette. Dial Books for
  Young Readers, 1999.

Bullies
Grunter: A Pig with an Attitude. Jolley, Mike. Millbrook Press, 1999.
Rabbit Pirates: A Tale of the Spinach Main. Cox, Judy. Harcourt Brace, 1999.

Death
Beautiful. Fowler, Susi Gregg. Greenwillow, 1998.
I'll See You in My Dreams. Jukes, Mavis. Alfred A. Knopf, 1993.
On Call Back Mountain. Bunting, Eve. Scholastic Press, 1997.

Diversity
Great Ball Game (The): A Muskogee Story. Bruchac, Joseph. Dial Books for Young Readers, 1994.
*Odd Velvet. Whitcomb, Mary E. Chronicle Books, 1998.

Ethnicity—Chinese
*Love as Strong as Ginger. Look, Lenore. Simon & Schuster, 1999.

Ethnicity—Greece
I Have an Olive Tree. Bunting, Eve. HarperCollins, 1999.

Ethnicity—Japanese American
Yoshiko and the Foreigner. Little, Mimi Otley. Farrar, Straus & Giroux, 1996.

Ethnicity—Jews
Flying Latke (The). Yorinks, Arthur. Simon & Schuster, 1999.
What Zeesie Saw on Delancey Street. Rael, Elsa Okon. Simon & Schuster Books for Young Readers, 1996.

Family Relationships
Aunt Nancy and Cousin Lazybones. Root, Phyllis. Candlewick Press, 1998.
Back Soon. Hendry, Diana. Troll Associates, 1995.
Carousel. Cummings, Pat. Macmillan, 1994.

Chicken Salad Club (The). Arnold, Marsha Diane. Dial Books for Young Readers, 1998.
Clouds for Dinner. Perkins, Lynn Rae. William Morrow, 1997.
Down the Road. Schertle, Alice. Harcourt Brace, 1995.
Goose. Bang, Molly. Scholastic, 1996.
Grandpa's Gamble. Michelson, Richard. Marshall Cavendish, 1999.
Gullible's Troubles. Shannon, Margaret. Houghton Mifflin, 1998.
I Lost My Bear. Feiffer, Jules. Morrow Junior Books, 1998.
I Love You the Purplest. Joosse, Barbara M. Chronicle Books, 1996.
I Remember Papa. Ketteman, Helen. Dial Books for Young Readers, 1998.
Island Magic. Stiles, Martha Bennett. Atheneum Books for Young Readers, 1999.
Jamela's Dress. Daly, Niki. Farrar, Straus & Giroux, 1999.
Little Scarecrow Boy (The). Brown, Margaret Wise. HarperCollins, 1998.
Mabel Dancing. Hest, Amy. Candlewick Press, 2000.
Mickey's Class Play. Caseley, Judith. Greenwillow, 1998.
Mountain Wedding. Gibbons, Faye. Morrow Junior Books, 1996.
Mouse Practice. McCully, Emily Arnold. Scholastic Press, 1999.
Our Snowman. Goffstein, M.B. Harper & Row, 1986.
Pete's a Pizza. Steig, William. HarperCollins, 1998.
Purple Coat (The). Hest, Amy. Four Winds Press, 1986.
*Raising Sweetness. Stanley, Diane. G.P. Putnam's Sons, 1999.
Somebody's New Pajamas. Jackson, Isaac. Dial Books for Young Readers, 1996.
Someone's Come to Our House. Appelt, Kathi. Eerdmans Books for Young Readers, 1999.
Sweet Strawberries. Naylor, Phyllis Reynolds. Atheneum Books for Young Readers, 1999.

Sylvester and the Magic Pebble. Steig, William. Simon & Schuster, 1969. (Caldecott–1970)

Tale of Peter Rabbit (The). Potter, Beatrix. Frederick Warne, 1902.

That's What I Thought. Schertle, Alice. Harper & Row, 1990.

Three Cheers for Catherine the Great. Best, Cari. Dorling Kindersley Inc., 1999.

Tiny's Hat. Grifalconi, Ann. HarperCollins, 1999.

Too Many Tamales. Soto, Gary. G.P. Putnam's Sons, 1993.

Where the Wild Things Are. Sendak, Maurice. HarperCollins, 1963. (Caldecott–1964)

Wilhe'mina Miles: After the Stork Night. Carter, Dorothy. Farrar, Straus & Giroux, 1999.

Greed

Princess Penelope's Parrot. Lester, Helen. Houghton Mifflin, 1996.

*Sweetest Fig (The). Van Allsburg, Chris. Houghton Mifflin, 1993.

Grief

*Through the Mickle Woods. Gregory, Valiska. Little, Brown, 1992.

Poverty—Mexico

Handful of Seeds (A). Hughes, Monica. Orchard Books, 1993.

Prejudice

Sam Johnson and the Blue Ribbon Quilt. Lothrop, Lee & Shepard, 1983.

Sister Anne's Hands. Lorbiecki, Marybeth. Dial Books for Young Readers, 1998.

Race Relations

Smokey Night. Bunting, Eve. Harcourt Brace, 1994. (Caldecott–1995)

Self-Esteem

Emma's Rug. Say, Allen. Houghton Mifflin, 1996.

Summer Wheels. Bunting, Eve. Harcourt Brace Jovanovich, 1992.

Suicide

*I Never Knew Your Name. Garland, Sherry. Houghton Mifflin, 1994.

BY AUTHOR

Aardema. Verna. *Koi and the Kola Nuts.* Atheneum Books for Young Readers, 1999. *Literature (Folktales—Africa)*

Aardema, Verna. *The Lonely Lioness and the Ostrich Chicks.* Alfred A. Knopf, 1996. *Literature (Folktales—Africa)*

Ackerman, Karen. *Song and Dance Man.* Alfred A. Knopf, 1988. (Caldecott– 1989) *History (Twentieth Century— Vaudeville)*

Anholt, Lurence. *Degas and the Little Dancer: A Story about Edgar Degas.* Barron's Educational Series, 1996. *Art (Biography)*

Appelt, Kathi. *Someone's Come to Our House.* Eerdmans Books for Young Readers, 1999. *Social Science (Family Relationships)*

Arnold, Katya. *Duck, Duck, Goose?* Holiday House, 1997. *Literature (Fables—Russia)*

Arnold, Marsha Diane. *The Chicken Salad Club.* Dial Books for Young Readers (Penguin Putnam), 1998. *Social Science (Family Relationships)*

Atkins, Jeannine. *Mary Anning and the Sea Dragon.* Farrar, Straus & Giroux, 1999. *History (Paleontology—Biography)*

Atwell, Debby. *River.* Houghton Mifflin, 1999. *Science (Ecology)*

Auch, Mary Jane. *Bantam of the Opera.* Holiday House, 1997. *Music (Opera)*

Bang, Molly. *Goose.* Scholastic, 1996. *Social Science (Family Relationships)*

Bang, Molly. *When Sophie Gets Angry— Really, Really Angry.* Scholastic, 1999. *Social Science (Anger)*

Best, Cari. *Three Cheers for Catherine the Great.* DK Ink, 1999. *Social Science (Family Relationships)*

Borden, Louise. *A. Lincoln and Me.* Scholastic Press, 1999. *History (Biography)*

Brenner, Barbara. *The Boy Who Loved to Draw: Benjamin West.* Houghton Mifflin, 1999. *Arts (Biography)*

Brown, Margaret Wise. *The Little Scarecrow Boy.* HarperCollins, 1998. *Social Science (Family Relationships)*

Bruchac, Joseph. *The Great Ball Game: A Muskogee Story.* Dial Books for Young Readers, 1994. *Social Science (Diversity)*

Bunting, Eve. *I Have an Olive Tree.* HarperCollins, 1999. *Social Science (Ethnicity—Greece)*

Bunting, Eve. *On Call Back Mountain.* Scholastic, 1997. *Social Science (Death)*

Bunting, Eve. *A Picnic in October.* Harcourt Brace, 1999. *History (Statue of Liberty—Ellis Island)*

Bunting, Eve. *Smoky Night.* Harcourt Brace, 1994. (Caldecott–1995) *Social Science (Race Relations)*

Bunting, Eve. *So Far From the Sea.* Houghton Mifflin, 1998. *History (World War II—Japanese American Internment)*

Bunting, Eve. *Summer Wheels.* Harcourt Brace Jovanovich, 1992. *Social Science (Self-Esteem)*

Bunting, Eve. *Train to Somewhere.* Houghton Mifflin, 1996. *History (Nineteenth-Century America—Orphan Trains)*

Carter, Dorothy. *Wilhe'mina Miles: After the Stork Night.* Farrar, Straus & Giroux, 1999. *Social Science (Family Relationships)*

Caseley, Judith. *Mickey's Class Play.* Greenwillow, 1998. *Social Science (Family Relationships)*

Charles, Donald. *Chancay and the Secret of Fire.* G.P. Putnam's Sons, 1992. *Literature (Folktales—Peru)*

Chocolate, Debbi. *The Piano Man.* Walker & Co., 1998. *History (Twenti- eth-Century America—Vaudeville— Piano)*

Cole, Babette. *Bad Habits (or The Taming of Lucretzia Crum).* Dial Books for young Readers, 1999. *Social Science (Behavior)*

Cox, Judy. *Rabbit Pirates: A Tale of the Spinach Main*. Harcourt Brace, 1999. Social Science *(Bullies)*

Cummings, Pat. *Carousel*. Macmillan, 1994. Social Science *(Family Relationships)*

*Cutler, Jane. *The Cello of Mr. O*. Penguin Putnam Books for Young Readers, 1999. History *(Twentieth Century—Ethnic Conflict)*

Daly, Niki. *Bravo Zan Angelo! A Comedia Dell'arte Tale with Story and Pictures*. Farrar, Straus & Giroux, 1998. History *(Renaissance—Street Performance)*

Daly, Niki. *Jamela's Dress*. Farrar, Straus & Giroux, 1999. Social Science *(Family Relationships)*

Davol, Marguerite W. *The Paper Dragon*. Atheneum Books for Young Readers (Simon & Schuster), 1997. Literature *(Folktales—China)*

dePaola, Tomie. *The Legend of the Indian Paintbrush*. G.P. Putnam's Sons, 1998. Literature *(Legends—Native American)*

*Edwards, Duncan. *Honk!* Hyperion Books for Children, 1998. Arts *(Ballet)*

Ernst, Lisa Campbell. *Sam Johnson and the Blue Ribbon Quilt*. Lothrop Lee & Shepard, 1983. Social Science *(Prejudice)*

Feiffer, Jules. *I Lost My Bear*. Morrow Junior Books, 1998. Social Science *(Family Relationships)*

Fleming, Candace. *A Big Cheese for the White House: The True Tale of a Tremendous Cheddar*. DK Ink, 1999. History *(Nineteenth-Century America)*

Fleming, Candace. *The Hatmaker's Sign: A Story Told by Benjamin Franklin*. Orchard Books, 1998. History *(Eighteenth-Century America—Declaration of Independence)*

Fowler, Susi Gregg. *Beautiful*. Greenwillow, 1998. Social Science *(Death)*

Friedrich, Elizabeth. *Leah's Pony*. Boyds Mills Press, 1996. History *(Great Depression—United States)*

*Garland, Sherry. *I Never Knew Your Name*. Houghton Mifflin, 1994. Social Science *(Suicide)*

*Garland, Sherry. *The Lotus Seed*. Harcourt Brace Jovanovich, 1993. History *(Vietnam War—Refugees)*

George, Jean Craighead. *Snow Bear*. Hyperion Books for Children, 1999. Science *(Animal Behavior)*

Gerrard, Roy. *The Roman Twins*. Farrar, Straus & Giroux, 1998. History *(Rome)*

Gibbons, Faye. *Mountain Wedding*. Morrow Junior Books, 1996. Social Science *(Family Relationships)*

Goble, Paul. *Love Flute*. Macmillan, 1992. Literature *(Folktales—Native American)*

Goffstein, M.B. *Our Snowman*. Harper & Row, 1986. Social Science *(Family Relationships)*

Gove, Doris. *One Rainy Night*. Atheneum, 1994. Science *(Animal Habitat)*

*Gregory, Valiska. *Through the Mickle Woods*. Little, Brown & Co., 1992. Social Science *(Grief)*

Grifalconi, Ann. *Tiny's Hat*. HarperCollins, 1999. Social Science *(Family Relationships)*

Guarnieri, Paolo. *A Boy Named Giotto*. Farrar, Straus & Giroux, 1998. Arts *(Biography)*

Haley, Gail E. *A Story, A Story*. Atheneum, 1970. (Caldecott–1971) Literature *(Folktales—Africa)*

Hall, Donald. *Ox-Cart Man*. Viking Press, 1979. (Caldecott–1980) History *(Nineteenth-Century America)*

Harshman, Marc. *The Storm*. Dutton, 1995. Health & Safety *(Physical Disabilities)*

*Hearne, Betsy. *Seven Brave Women*. Greenwillow, 1997. History *(Women)*

Hendry, Diana. *Back Soon*. Troll Associates, 1995. Social Science *(Family Relationships)*

Hest, Amy. *Mabel Dancing*. Illus. by Christine Davenier. Cambridge, MA: Candlewick Press, 2000. Social Science *(Family Relationships)*

Hest, Amy. *The Purple Coat*. Four Winds Press, 1986. *Social Science (Family Relationships)*

High, Linda Oatman. *Barn Savers*. Boyds Mills Press, 1999. *Science (Recycling)*

*Hoestlandt, Jo. *Star of Fear, Star of Hope*. Walker & Co., 1995. *History (World War II—Jewish Holocaust)*

Hong, Lily Toy. *Two of Everything*. Albert Whitman, 1993. *Literature (Folktales—China)*

Hopkinson, Deborah. *Sweet Clara and the Freedom Quilt*. Alfred A. Knopf, 1993. *History (Slavery—United States)*

Howard, Elizabeth Fitzgerald. *Virgie Goes to School with Us Boys*. Simon & Schuster Books for Young Readers, 2000. *History (Ethnicity—African American)*

Hughes, Monica. *A Handful of Seeds*. Orchard Books, 1993. *Social Science (Poverty—Mexico)*

Jackson, Isaac. *Somebody's New Pajamas*. Dial Books for Young Readers, 1996. *Social Science (Family Relationships)*

James, J. Alison. *The Drums of Noto Hanto*. DK Ink, 1999. *Literature (Legends—Japan)*

Jolley, Mike. *Grunter: A Pig with an Attitude*. Milbrook Press, 1999. *Social Science (Bullies)*

Joosse, Barbara M. *I Love You the Purplest*. Chronicle Books, 1996. *Social Science (Family Relationships)*

Joosse, Barbara. *Lewis & Papa*. Chronicle Books, 1998. *History (Nineteenth-Century America—Santa Fe Trail)*

Jukes, Mavis. *I'll See You in My Dreams*. Alfred A. Knopf, 1993. *Social Science (Death)*

Ketteman, Helen. *I Remember Papa*. Dial Books for Young Readers, 1998. *Social Science (Family Relationships)*

Kay, Verla. *Gold Fever*. G.P. Putnam's Sons, 1999. *History (Nineteenth-Century America–Gold Rush)*

Krupinski, Loretta. *Best Friends*. Hyperion Books for Children, 1998. *History (Race Relations)*

Lasky, Kathryn. *Marven of the Great North Woods*. Harcourt Brace, 1997. *History (Twentieth Century—Influenza)*

Lears, Laurie. *Ian's Walk: A Story about Autism*. Albert Whitman, 1998. *Health & Safety (Autism)*

Lee, Milly. *Nim and the War Effort*. Farrar, Straus & Giroux, 1997. *History (World War II—American Home Front)*

Little, Mimi Otley. *Yoshiko and the Foreigner*. Farrar, Straus & Giroux, 1996. *Social Science (Ethnicity—Japanese American)*

Lorbiecki, Marybeth. *Sister Anne's Hands*. Dial Books for Young Readers, 1998. *Social Science (Prejudice)*

Lester, Helen. *Hooway for Wodney Wat*. Houghton Mifflin, 1999. *Health & Safety (Speech Disorders)*

Lester, Helen. *Princess Penelope's Parrot*. Houghton Miffflin, 1996. *Social Science (Greed)*

Levitin, Sonia. *Nine for California*. Orchard Books, 1996. *History (Westward Expansion—United States)*

Lied, Kate. *Potato: A Tale from the Great Depression*. National Geographic Society, 1997. *History (Great Depression—United States)*

*Littlesugar, Amy. *Jonkonnu: A Story from the Sketchbook of Winslow Homer*. Philomel Books, 1997. *Arts (Biography)*

*London, Jonathan. *Hip Cat*. Chronicle Books, 1993. *Music (Jazz)*

*Look, Lenore. *Love as Strong as Ginger*. Atheneum Books for Young Readers, 1999. *Social Science (Ethnicity—Chinese)*

McCully, Emily Arnold. *The Ballot Box Battle*. Alfred A. Knopf, 1996. *History (Nineteenth-Century America—Women's Suffrage)*

McCully, Emily Arnold. *The Bobbin Girl*. Dial Books for Young Readers, 1996. *History (Nineteenth-Century America—Textile Mill Unions)*

McCully, Emily Arnold. *Mouse Practice*. Scholastic Press, 1999. *Social Science (Family Relationships)*

Marshall, James. *Swine Lake.* HarperCollins, 1999. *Arts (Ballet)*

Martin, Jacqueline Briggs. *Snowflake Bentley.* Houghton Mifflin, 1998. *Science (Photography)*

*Meddaugh, Susan. *Cinderella's Rat.* Houghton Mifflin, 1997. *Literature (Parody)*

Michelson, Richard. *Grandpa's Gamble.* Marshall Cavendish, 1999. *Social Science (Family Relationships)*

Miller, William. The Piano. Lee & Low Books, 2000. *Social Science (Race Relations)*

Mitchell, Barbara. *Red Bird.* Lothrop, Lee & Shepard, 1996. *History (Ethnicity—Native American)*

Moss, Marissa. *True Heart.* Harcourt Brace, 1999. *History (Railroads—Women Engineers)*

Naylor, Phyllis Reynolds. *Sweet Strawberries.* Atheneum Books for Young Readers, 1999. *Social Science (Family Relationships)*

Perkins, Lynn Rae. *Clouds for Dinner.* William Morrow, 1997. *Social Science (Family Relationships)*

Potter, Beatrix. *The Tale of Peter Rabbit.* Frederick Warne, 1902. *Social Science (Family Relationships)*

Provensen, Alice, and Martin Provenson. *The Glorious Flight: Across the Channel with Louis Bléroit, July 25, 1909.* Viking Press, 1983. (Caldecott–1984) *History (Aviation)*

Rael, Elsa Okon. *What Zeesie Saw on Delancey Street.* Simon & Schuster Books for Young Readers, 1996. *Social Science (Ethnicity—Jews)*

Ransom, Candice F. *The Promise Quilt.* Walker & Co., 1999. *History (Civil War—United States)*

Robbins, Ruth. *Baboushka and the Three Kings.* Houghton Mifflin, 1960. (Caldecott—1961) *Literature (Folktales—Russia)*

Root, Phyllis. *Aunt Nancy and Cousin Lazybones.* Candlewick Press, 1998. *Social Science (Family Relationships)*

Say, Allen. *Allison.* Houghton Mifflin, 1997. *Social Science (Adoption)*

Say, Allen. *Emma's Rug.* Houghton Mifflin, 1996. *Social Science (Self-Esteem)*

*Say, Allen. *Grandfather's Journey.* Houghton Mifflin, 1993. *History (Immigration—Japanese)*

*Say, Allen. *Tea with Milk.* Houghton Mifflin, 1999. *History (Immigration—Japanese)*

Sendak, Maurice. *Where the Wild Things Are.* HarperCollins, 1963. (Caldecott–1964) *Social Science (Family Relationships)*

Schertle, Alice. *Down the Road.* Harcourt Brace, 1995. *Social Science (Family Relationships)*

Schertle, Alice. *That's What I Thought.* Harper & Row, 1990. *Social Science (Family Relationships)*

*Schur, Maxine Rose. *The Peddler's Gift.* Dial Books for Young Readers, 1999. *History (Nineteenth-Century Russia)*

*Shannon, George. *This Is the Bird.* Houghton Mifflin, 1997. *History (Women)*

Shannon, Margaret. *Gullible's Troubles.* Houghton Mifflin, 1998. *Social Science (Family Relationships)*

Shea, Pegi Deitz. *The Whispering Cloth: A Refugee's Story.* Boyds Mills, 1995. *History (Vietnam War—Cambodian Refugees)*

Singer, Marilyn. *The Painted Fan.* Morrow Junior Books, 1994. *Literature (Folktales—China)*

Sisulu, Elinor Batezat. *The Day Gogo Went to Vote, South Africa, April 1994.* Little, Brown, 1997. *History (South Africa)*

Soto, Gary. *Too Many Tamales.* G.P. Putnam's Sons, 1993. *Social Science (Family Relationships)*

*Stanley, Diane. *Raising Sweetness.* G.P. Putnam's Sons, 1999. *Social Science (Family Relationships)*

*Stanley, Diane. *Rumplestiltskin's Daughter.* William Morrow, 1997. *Literature (Parody)*

Steig, William. *Pete's a Pizza.* HarperCollins, 1998. *Social Science (Family Relationships)*

Steig, William. *Sylvester and the Magic Pebble.* Simon & Schuster, 1969. (Caldecott–1970) *Social Science (Family Relationships)*

Stewart, Dianne. *Gift of the Sun: A Tale from South Africa.* Farrar, Straus & Giroux, 1996. *Literature (Folktales— South Africa)*

Stiles, Martha Bennett. *Island Magic.* Atheneum Books for Young Readers, 1999. *Social Science (Family Relationships)*

*Turner, Ann. *Katie's Trunk.* Macmillan, 1992. *History (Revolutionary War— United States)*

Uchida, Yoshiko. *The Bracelet.* Philomel, 1976. *History (World War II—Japanese American Internment)*

*Van Allsburg, Chris. *The Sweetest Fig.* Houghton Mifflin, 1993. *Social Science (Greed)*

*Waldman, Neil. *The Starry Night.* Boyds Mills Press, 1999. *Arts (Biography)*

Wallace, Ian. *Boy of the Deeps.* DK Ink, 1999. *Science (Coal Mining)*

Ward, Lynd. *The Biggest Bear.* Houghton Mifflin, 1952. (Caldecott–1953) *History (Frontier Life—United States)*

*Whitcomb, Mary E. *Odd Velvet.* Chronicle Books, 1998. *Social Science (Diversity)*

*Wiesniewski, David. *Golem.* Clarion, 1996. (Caldecott–1997) *History (Ethnicity—Jews)*

Yolen, Jane. *Owl Moon.* Philomel Books, 1987. (Caldecott–1988) *Science (Animal Behavior)*

Yorinks, Arthur. *The Flying Latke.* Simon & Schuster, 1999. *Social Science (Ethnicity—Jews)*

Zagwyn, Deborah Turney. *Turtle Spring.* Tricycle Press, 1998. *Science (Animal Behavior)*

Zemach, Harve. *Duffy and the Devil.* Farrar, Straus & Giroux, 1973 (Caldecott–1974) *Literature (Folktales—Ireland)*

BIBLIOGRAPHY

"How Teachers Feel About Character Education: a Descriptive Study. *Action in Teacher Education* (Character Education Issue), v. 20, n. 4, (Winter 1998-99) *Journal of the Association of Teacher Educators.* pp 29-38.

Amundson, Kristen J. *Teaching Values and Ethics, Problems and Solutions.* Arlington, VA: American Association of School Administrators, 1991.

Beach, Waldo. *Ethical Education in American Public Schools.* Washington, DC: National Education Association of the United States, 1992.

DeRoche, Edward F., and Mary M. Williams, *Educating Hearts and Minds: A Comprehensive Character Education Framework.* Thousand Oaks, CA: Corwin Press, 1998.

Domenici, Senator Pete V. Letter to the Editor. *Time* 153, no. 23, 14 June 1999, 21.

Downey, Meriel, and A.V. Kelly. *Moral Education Theory and Practice.* London: Harper & Row, 1978.

Etzioni, Amitai. "How Not to Discuss Character Education." *Phi Delta Kappan* 79 (February 1998): 446–448.

Ferguson, Andrew. "Character Goes Back to School." *Time* 153, no. 20, 24 May 1999, 68–69.

"Fulfilling the Promise of Character Education in the Classroom, Part I." *Journal of Education*, vol. 179, no. 2, 1997. Contributions by Leslie E. Laud, James S. Leming, Charles S. White, Joseph M. O'Keefe, Thomas Lickona, and Kevin Ryan.

Gabrels, Sara Terry. "Private Ethics: The Age of Casting No Stones." *Christian Science Monitor*, 18 February 1998.

Gibbs, L.J., and E.J. Earley. "Using Children's Literature to Develop Core Values." *Phi Delta Kappa Fastbacks 362* (1994): 7–40.

Gilder, George. "Breaking the Box." *National Review,* 15 August 1994, 37–38.

Godderham, David. "Still Catching Them Young? The Moral Dimension in Young Children's Books." *Children's Literature in Education* 24, no. 2 (June 1993): 115–122.

Grant, Gerald. "Bringing the 'Moral' Back In." *NEA Today,* January 1989, 54–59.

Griffith, Kathlyn. "Young Children, the Stories They Hear, and·the Acculturation Process." *Early Child Development and Care* 90 (May, 1993): 15–22.

Harmin, Merrill. "What I've Learned about Values Education." *Fastback 91,* Bloomington, IN: Phi Delta Kappa Education Foundation, 1977.

Heischman, Daniel K. "Beyond the Bandwagon: The Place of Ethics in a School Community." *Baylor* (Spring, 1996): 2–7.

Hoff Sommers, Christina. "Are We Living in a Moral Stone Age?" *Current Directions in Psychological Science* (June 1998): 31–34.

———. "Teaching the Virtues." *Public Interest 111* (Spring 1993): 3–13.

"How Teachers Feel About Character Education: A Descriptive Study." Action in Teacher Education (Character Education Issue), Journal of the Association of Teacher Educators 20, 4 (Winter 1998–99): 23–38.

Huckabee, Mike. "Character Does Count." *World & I* (June 1998): 62–65.

Kazemek, Frances E. "Literature and Moral Development from a Feminine Perspective." *Language Arts* 63, no. 3 (March, 1986): 264–272.

Kidder, Rushworth M. "Ethics is Not a Luxury; It's Essential to Our Survival." *Education Week,* 3 April 1991, 30.

———. "Universal Human Values, Finding an Ethical Common Ground." *Futurist* (July/August, 1994): 8–13.

Kilpatrick, William, Gregory Wolfe, and Suzanne M. Wolfe. *Bonds That Build Character: A Guide to Teaching Your Child Moral Values through Stories.* New York: Touchstone Rockefeller Center, 1994.

Kohn, Alfie. "How Not to Teach Values: A Critical Look at Character Education." *Phi Delta Kappan* 78 (February 1997): 429–439.

Kuh, George D. "Shaping Student Character." *Liberal Education* (Summer 1998): 18–25.

Lamme, Linda, and others. *Literature Based Moral Education: Children's Books and Activities for Teaching Values, Responsibility, and Good Judgement in the Elementary School.* Phoenix: Oryx Press, 1992.

Larkins, A.G. "Should We Teach Values? Which Ones? How?" *Social Studies and the Young Learner* (September/October 1997): 30–32.

Leming, James. "Whither Goes Character Education? Objectives, Pedagogy, and Research in Education Programs." *Journal of Education* 179, no. 2 (1997): 26–31.

Lickona, Thomas. *Character Education in Schools and Beyond.* Washington, DC: Council in Values & Philosophy, 1993.

————. *Educating for Character: How Our Schools Can Teach Respect and Responsibility.* New York: Bantam, 1991.

————. *What is Good Character? And How Can We Develop It in Our Children?* Bloomington, IN: Poyner Center for the Study of Ethics & American Institutions, Indiana University Foundation (May 1991).

Logan, Claudia. "Character Education by the Book." *Instructor* 105 (July/August 1995): 74–79.

Murchison, William. *Reclaiming Morality in America.* Nashville: Thomas Nelson, 1994.

Palmer, George Herbert. *Ethical and Moral Instruction in Schools.* New York: Houghton Mifflin, 1908.

Rosenblatt, Roger. "Teaching Johnny to Be Good." *New York Times Magazine,* 30 April 1995): 36.

Rusnak, Tomothy, ed. *An Integrated Approach to Character Education.* Thousand Oaks, CA: Corwin Press, 1998.

Ryan, Kevin. *Questions and Answers on Moral Education.* Bloomington, IN: Phi Delta Kappa Educational Foundation, 1981.

Ryan, Kevin, and Karen Bohlin. *Building Character in Schools: Practical Ways to Bring Moral Instruction to Life.* San Francisco: Jossey-Bass, 1999.

Schaeffer, Esther. "Character Education Makes a Difference." *Principal* 78, no. 2 (November 1998): 30–32.

————. Letter to the Editor. *Time* 155, no. 23, 14 June 1999, 21.

Schluter, Otto. "Quail Trap School." *The Cedar County Historical Review* Tipton, IA: Cedar County Historical Society (July 1967): 88.

Siderius, Barbara. "Goody Twoshoes: Morality through Amusement." *Language Arts* 53, no. 1 (January 1976): 37–40.

Simon, Sidney B., and others. *Values Clarification: A Practical, Action-Directed Workbook*. New York: Warner Books, 1995.

Stein, Benjamin. "Reviving Ethics." *Commercial Appeal*, 10 March 1991, 34.

Tester, Keith. *Moral Culture*. Thousand Oaks, CA: Sage Publications, 1997.

Townsend, Kathleen Kennedy. "Why Johnny Can't Tell Right from Wrong: The Important Lesson Our Schools Don't Teach." *Washington Monthly*, December 1992, 29–32.

Woodward, Kenneth L. "What is Virtue?" *Newsweek*, 13 June 1994, 30.

Wray, Herbert. "The Moral Child." *U.S. News & World Report*, 3 June 1996, 52.

Wynne, E.A., and Kevin Ryan. *Reclaiming Our Schools*. New York: Merrill, 1993.

Yankelovich, D. "Three Destructive Trends." *Kettering Review* Dayton, OH: Charles Kettering Foundation (Fall 1995): 6–15.

AUTHOR INDEX

Lied, Kate. *Potato: A Tale from the Great Depression*. Illus. by Lisa Campbell Ernst. Washington, DC: National Geographic Society, 1997.
Fortitude, Perseverance, Resourcefulness

Little, Mimi Otley. *Yoshiko and the Foreigner*. New York: Farrar, Straus & Giroux, 1996.
Courtesy, Respect, Tolerance

Littlesugar, Amy. *Jonkonnu: A Story from the Sketchbook of Winslow Homer*. Illus. by Ian Schoenherr. New York: Philomel Books, 1997.
Courage, Discernment, Respect

London, Jonathan. *Hip Cat*. Illus. by Woodleigh Hubbard. San Francisco: Chronicle Books, 1993.
Diligence, Perseverance

Look, Lenore. *Love as Strong as Ginger*. Illus. by Stephen T. Johnson. New York: Atheneum Books for Young Readers (Simon & Schuster), 1999.
Respect

Lorbiecki, Marybeth. *Sister Anne's Hands*. Illus. by K. Wendy Popp. New York: Dial Books for Young Readers (Penguin), 1998.
Courage, Forgiveness, Respect, Tolerance

Loredo, Elizabeth. *Boogie Bones*. Illus. by Kevin Hawkes. New York: G.P. Putnam's Sons, 1997.
Tolerance

Lyon, George. *A Traveling Cat*. Illus. by Paul Brett Johnson. New York: Orchard Books, 1998.
Tolerance

McCully, Emily Arnold. *The Ballot Box Battle*. New York: Alfred A. Knopf, 1996.
Courage, Diligence, Discernment, Fortitude, Hope

McCully, Emily Arnold. *The Bobbin Girl*. New York: Dial Books for Young Readers (Penguin) 1996.
Cooperation, Courage, Justice, Perseverance, Prudence

McCully, Emily Arnold. *Mirette on the High Wire*. New York: G.P. Putnam's Sons, 1992. (Caldecott–1993)
Courage, Helpfulness, Perseverance

McCully, Emily Arnold. *Mouse Practice*. New York: Scholastic Press, 1999.
Perseverance, Resourcefulness

Manson, Christopher. *Two Travelers*. New York: Henry Holt, 1990.
Cooperation, Helpfulness, Kindness, Tolerance

Markoe, Merrill. *The Day My Dogs Became Guys*. Illus. by Eric Brace. New York: Viking (Penguin Putnam), 1999.
Self-discipline

Marshall, James. *Swine Lake*. Illus. by Maurice Sendak. New York: HarperCollins, 1999.
Self-discipline, Tolerance

Mathers, Petra. *Lottie's New Beach Towel*. Atheneum Books for Young Readers (Simon & Schuster), 1998.
Resourcefulness

Mathers, Petra. *Victor and Christabel*. New York: Alfred A. Knopf, 1993.
Justice, Kindness

Martin, Jacqueline Briggs. *Snowflake Bentley*. Illus. by Mary Azarian. Boston: Houghton Mifflin, 1998.
Diligence, Fortitude, Perseverance, Responsibility

McKissack, Patricia. *The Honest to Goodness Truth*. Illus. by Giselle Potter. New York: Atheneum Books for Young Readers (Simon & Schuster), 2000.
Honesty

1995.
Fortitude, Hope, Respect

Shulevitz, Uri. *Snow*. New York: Farrar, Straus & Giroux, 1998.
Hope

Siekkinen, Raija. *Mister King*. Illus. by Hannu Taina. Trans. by Tim Steffa. Minneapolis: Carolrhoda, 1987.
Cooperation, Generosity

Singer, Marilyn. *The Painted Fan*. Illus. by Wenhai Ma. New York: Morrow Junior Books, 1994.
Courage

Sisulu, Elinor Batezat. *The Day Gogo Went to Vote: South Africa, April 1994*. Illus. by Sharon Wilson. New York: Little, Brown & Co., 1997.
Helpfulness, Justice, Respect, Responsibility

Snape, Juliet, and Charles Snape. *The Boy with Square Eyes*. New York: Prentice-Hall Books for Young Readers (Simon & Schuster), 1987.
Self-discipline

Soto, Gary. *Too Many Tamales*. Illus. by Ed Martinez. New York: G.P. Putnam's Sons, 1993.
Honesty, Self-discipline

Stanley, Diane. *The Gentleman and the Kitchen Maid*. Illus. by Dennis Nolan. New York: Dial Books for Young Readers, 1994.
Empathy, Helpfulness

Stanley, Diane. *Raising Sweetness*. Illus. by G. Brian Karas. New York: G.P. Putnam's Sons, 1999.
Kindness, Loyalty

Stanley, Diane. *Rumpelstiltskin's Daughter*. New York: William Morrow, 1997.
Kindness, Resourcefulness

Steig, William. *Pete's a Pizza*. New York: HarperCollins, 1998.
Empathy, Resourcefulness

Steig, William. *Sylvester and the Magic Pebble*. New York: Simon & Schuster, 1969. (Caldecott–1970)
Fortitude, Hope

Stewart, Dianne. *Gift of the Sun: A Tale from South Africa*. Illus. by Jude Daly. New York: Farrar, Straus & Giroux, 1996.
Respect

Stewart, Sarah. *The Gardener*. Illus. by David Small. New York: Farrar, Straus & Giroux, 1997.
Diligence, Discernment, Generosity, Patience

Stiles, Martha Bennett. *Island Magic*. Illus. by Daniel San Souci. New York: Atheneum Books for Young Readers (Simon & Schuster), 1999.
Empathy

Taback, Simms. *Joseph Had a Little Overcoat*. New York: Viking (Penguin), 1999. (Caldecott–2000)
Resourcefulness

Thurber, James. *Many Moons*. Illus. by Louis Slobodkin. New York: Harcourt Brace, 1943. (Caldecott–1944)
Prudence, Respect ⵏ

Tunnell, Michael. *Mailing May*. Illus. by Ted Rand. New York: Greenwillow (William Morrow), 1997.
Perseverance, Resourcefulness

Turner, Ann. *Katie's Trunk*. Illus. by Ron Himler. New York: Macmillan, 1992.
Justice, Kindness

Uchida, Yoshiko. *The Bracelet*. Illus. by Joanna Yardley. New York: Philomel Books (Putnam & Grosset), 1976.
Kindness, Patience, Tolerance

Van Allsburg, Chris. *Jumanji*. Boston: Houghton Mifflin, 1981. (Caldecott–1982)
Responsibility

TITLE INDEX

Jovanovich, 1993.
Helpfulness

I'll See You in My Dreams by Mavis Jukes. Alfred A. Knopf, 1993.
Courage, Respect

Island Magic by Martha Bennett Stiles. Atheneum Books for Young Readers (Simon & Schuster), 1999.
Empathy

Jamela's Dress by Niki Daly. Farrar, Straus & Giroux, 1999.
Forgiveness, Generosity, Self-discipline

Jeremiah Learns to Read by Jo Ellen Bogart. Orchard Books, 1997.
Diligence, Generosity, Respect

Jody's Beans by Malachy Doyle. Candlewick Press, 1999.
Cooperation, Diligence, Patience

Jonkonnu: A Story from the Sketchbook of Winslow Homer by Amy Littlesugar. Philomel Books, 1997.
Courage, Discernment, Respect

Joseph Had a Little Overcoat by Simms Taback. Viking (Penguin Putnam), 1999. (Caldecott–2000)
Resourcefulness

Jumanji by Chris Van Allsburg. Houghton Mifflin, 1981. (Caldecott–1982)
Responsibility

Katie's Trunk by Ann Turner. Macmillan, 1992.
Justice, Kindness

Koi and the Kola Nuts by Verna Aardema. Atheneum Books for Young Readers (Simon & Schuster), 1999.
Generosity, Helpfulness, Kindness

Laura Charlotte by Kathryn O. Galbraith. Philomel Books, 1990.
Courage

Leah's Pony by Elizabeth Friedrich. Boyds Mills Press, 1996.
Generosity, Helpfulness, Responsibility

Legend of the Indian Paintbrush (The) by Tomie dePaola. G.P. Putnam's Sons, 1988.
Diligence, Hope, Loyalty, Patience, Perseverance, Responsibility, Self-discipline

Leon and Bob by Simon James. Candlewick Press, 1997.
Courage, Kindness

Lewis & Papa: Adventure on the Santa Fe Trail by Barbara Joosse. Chronicle Books, 1998.
Courage, Fortitude, Honesty, Responsibility

Lilly's Purple Plastic Purse by Kevin Henkes. Greenwillow (William Morrow), 1996.
Patience, Self-discipline

Little Scarecrow Boy (The) by Margaret Wise Brown. HarperCollins, 1998.
Hope, Perseverance, Responsibility

Lonely Lioness and the Ostrich Chicks (The) by Verna Aardema. Alfred A. Knopf, 1996.
Courage, Helpfulness, Honesty, Justice, Perseverance, Prudence

Lottie's New Beach Towel by Petra Mathers. Atheneum Books for Young Readers (Simon & Schuster), 1998.
Resourcefulness

Lotus Seed (The) by Sherry Garland. Harcourt Brace Jovanovich, 1993.
Hope, Loyalty, Respect

Love as Strong as Ginger by Lenore Look. Atheneum Books for Young Readers (Simon & Schuster), 1999.
Respect

Love Flute by Paul Goble. Bradbury Press, 1992.
Empathy, Helpfulness

Mabel Dancing by Amy Hest. Candlewick Press, 2000.
Empathy

Susan Hall is a journalist and government reporter in Tipton, Iowa. Previously, she was a school and public librarian working for 12 years primarily with grades K-8. Ms. Hall is now writing picture books, building from her experience with reference and resource works. She is also the author of volumes one and two of *Using Picture Storybooks to Teach Literary Devices*.